to their families. DrugFam was born out of the courage of Elizabeth, who was prepared to share her story and is now a lifeline for those affected by drugs and addiction. Her work has now been recognised with DrugFam receiving The Queen's Award for Voluntary Service and Elizabeth receiving the MBE. Both are richly deserved.

Isobel Morrow MBE

Elizabeth writes with an honesty and unflinching insight about a subject that is a living reality for far too many families. Elizabeth's story demonstrates the battle between love and the brutal selfishness of addiction. The journey and the struggle of her family created the inspiration for DrugFAM as well as a personal dedication to ensure that no family would need to suffer alone and in isolation again - it is a must-read book not just for those dealing with a loved one's addiction, but is a book everyone should read to truly understand the dangerous web of addiction in society and its ability to impact everyday families.

Sacha Cooper, mother of three children

This book and Elizabeth helped transform my attitude and outlook on life. Being in recovery for some years, I never actually took on board the catastrophic consequences that my actions had on my family and friends. After meeting Elizabeth several times I felt that I needed to step up and take responsibility to help other families; the result is that I have been a Trustee of The Nicholas Mills Foundation (DrugFAM) for several years and long may I continue to serve'.

Paul Rubin

In my work as a police officer over many years I have met many people whose lives have been deeply affected by drug addiction. Elizabeth stands out as someone who had the courage to tell her family's story and to challenge attitudes. Elizabeth has already made a difference and I am sure that all those who read this book will be both challenged and inspired.

Chief Constable Sara Thornton, National Police Chiefs' Council

The work, dedication and passion given by the DrugFam team in the pursuit of providing support to clients is incredible. Their work has filled a void and gives families a voice where there was none before. From the first time I met Elizabeth and heard the story of her sons, Nick and Simon, I was struck by her strength and resilience in striving to ensure families would be supported through their journey with their loved ones, helping to reduce stigma and improve the understanding of addiction and its impact.

Grant Geddes, Pharmaceutical Executive

Mum, can you lend me twenty quid?

What drugs did to my family

ELIZABETH BURTON-PHILLIPS, MBE

piatkus

PIATKUS

First published in Great Britain in 2007 by Piatkus
This edition published in 2017 by Piatkus

1 3 5 7 9 10 8 6 4 2

Copyright © Elizabeth Burton-Phillips, 2007, 2017

The moral right of the author has been asserted.

A CIP catalogue record for this book
is available from the British Library.

ISBN: 978-0-34941-874-2

Data manipulation by Phoenix Photosetting, Chatham, Kent
Printed and bound in Great Britain by Clays Ltd, St Ives plc

Papers used by Robinson are from well-managed forests
and other responsible sources.

Piatkus
An imprint of
Little, Brown Book Group
Carmelite House
50 Victoria Embankment
London EC4Y 0DZ

An Hachette UK Company
www.hachette.co.uk

www.littlebrown.co.uk

Dedication

Nicholas Stephen Mills
19 November 1976–19 February 2004
'Nick'

This book is dedicated to the memory of my son
Nicholas Stephen, known to all of us affectionately as Nick,
who lost his life on 19 February 2004,
a victim of drug addiction.

In the true depths of despair and mourning,
my mother found the strength and courage to turn our
tragedy into a positive. This book was the start of a new chapter
in all our lives. It is a painfully true account of how easy it is to
get involved with the wrong people and what drugs can do to a family.
Since the book was first published in 2007, Mum has founded
a charity called DrugFAM which provides support and help to
the many thousands of families affected and bereaved
by addiction. Our story will take you on a journey of
emotion, despair, love and, most of all, hope.
It really is a must-read for all parents, teachers and pupils.
Simon Mills, Elizabeth's son, Nick's twin brother

Contents

Letter from Theresa May

HOUSE OF COMMONS
LONDON SW1A 0AA
The Rt. Hon. Theresa May MP

TESTIMONIAL FOR ELIZABETH BURTON-PHILLIPS
From The Rt Hon Theresa May MP

When my constituent Elizabeth Burton-Phillips first contacted me to discuss drugs policy, I little guessed what emotional turmoil and family tragedy lay behind her request. I arranged to visit her at home and was simply not prepared for the anguish I would feel at hearing of the story of her twin sons' drug addiction, apparent rehabilitation and then the tragic death of one of them at the hand of drink and drugs. It was difficult to keep the tears from flowing such was the emotional strength of her story.

Letter from Theresa May

Her book *Mum, Can You Lend Me Twenty Quid? What Drugs Did To My Family* is a story which must be heard if others are not to go through the anguish felt by Elizabeth, Tony and her family. It is a tribute to Elizabeth's strength of character and to the deep bonds that unite her family that she has sought not to hide what happened but to use it as a means of helping others. She is the founder of the national charity DrugFAM www.drugfam.co.uk which supports the families of addicts and families bereaved by addiction.

I have heard her story and I have seen the impact it has on others. Above all else this is the story of an ordinary family caught up in a world they never thought would affect them. It shows that parental instincts to help are not always the right thing to do and it aims to provide others with the knowledge and understanding they need to meet the challenge of drugs within their family.

Elizabeth now speaks around the country on her experience and I know from seeing it at first hand that her speeches move her audience and capture their imagination in ways which can never be done by 'experts'.

Elizabeth's courage in speaking out is moving. Her ability to move others is impressive. Her commitment to helping other families avoid the tragedy that touched her family is inspirational.

Thank you Elizabeth for having the courage to channel the pain you felt for the good of others.

The Rt Hon Theresa May MP

Author's Note

The death of a child at any age makes life a wilderness of pain. As you feel your way out of the resulting darkness, your life changes for ever. I lost one of my identical twin sons at the age of twenty-seven from addiction to heroin, having kept the secret of the addiction of both of them hidden from friends and work colleagues for many years. But after my son's tragic death, I resolved to tell my story in the hope and belief that others would benefit from it. Six months later, I made the decision to speak publicly, and this, to my amazement, has brought a new dimension to my life.

Mum, Can You Lend Me Twenty Quid? is my personal testimony as a mother. It describes the impact of heroin addiction on an ordinary family. Unaware that both my sons had begun using drugs at the age of thirteen, I follow the events of their lives, which culminated in the death of one of my sons. My story highlights how my family and I became involved in my sons' attempt to try and beat their habit. It illustrates the destructive impact of addiction and emphasises the need for mechanisms to be put in place to ensure that the painful lessons we learnt can be communicated to others.

Addicts rarely realise the immense emotional and financial strain they place upon their families, particularly their mothers. By speaking both publicly and now through my book, I have been able to point out to parents and other family members and friends the reality and dangers of drug addiction within the family. Let this, my story – a mother's story – serve as a warning to all parents, to all children and to all families who read it, from every social and cultural background, religious or non-religious, that drugs can and do kill. I hope my personal experience will give all those who care for addicts, whether trained or as volunteers, greater insight into how families suffer and become the real, often forgotten victims of addiction.

This story may be a wake-up call for you, your children, your family or someone you know. I make no apologies for my stark portrayal of the truth. I want to stress that I am just an ordinary mother and wife who would never have believed, all those years ago when my twin sons were born, that my life – our lives – would be devastated by drugs. I should like to see the needs of families struggling to cope with addiction recognised alongside the needs of the addict. If you can benefit from my experiences and errors of judgement, then so much the better. My intimate relationship with drugs ultimately led to the anguish of the death of my child. I don't want that to happen to you.

If lives can be touched and turned around by my story, then Nick's death will not have been in vain. His brother Simon, now a lone twin, lives on to bear witness to his brother's life and death. Hopefully I may be able to bring dignity to that life and death. Nick would never have wanted anyone to go down the path he trod. Yet his story will not be a waste of a life if it can save other lives and avoid family heartbreak.

Passion is the bridge that took me from pain to change following the publication of the first edition of this book in 2007. By going public as an ordinary mum, I realised I was not alone.

I now know that my story is certainly not unique as many thousands of you have written to me and shared your experiences and sorrows in your own families. All of you are desperate for freedom from the isolation and shame caused by the stigma of addiction.

And so it is that this story was the driving factor behind the founding of a charity dedicated to my son's memory, because during the difficult years which you will read about in the pages ahead, I could not find anywhere to turn to for emotional help or just to talk to about how desperate I felt as his mother.

Today and every day, I am humbled and inspired by the courage and bravery of the families and friends who turn to us for support. Addiction is a family illness and DrugFAM is here for you if you are affected.

I could never have imagined that out of our family pain and loss that all these years later I would have the privilege to work with such a dedicated team of trustees, staff and volunteers. I now have a new family: the DrugFAM family of support workers and volunteers led by a truly dedicated professional lady who came to us in need and now is our Chief Executive.

In 2012 when the book was adapted as a Theatre in Education play, Carmel Baines, the Community Arts Manager who directed the play 125 times, said to me:

'To bring your tragic story to the stage was a once in a lifetime opportunity that I grasped, albeit fearfully, with both hands. When I met you for the first time after reading your book, I was in awe of your dogged determination to raise awareness and remove stigma. To walk alongside you if only for a few steps on your journey has been an honour and I am proud to call you my friend. Your tireless commitment to ensuring your story helps others knows no bounds.'

Never, ever could I have imagined that on 9 May 2017 I would give the main address at the first ever service for families affected by addiction in Westminster Abbey. I was thrilled DrugFAM was able to bring this Special Service of Celebration and Hope, called 'Lives Worth Talking About,' to national and international attention with 2000 guests from all over the world. A few days later I received this letter from Sir Stephen Lamport KCVO DL Receiver General at Westminster Abbey:

'All of us here, Elizabeth, share your views about the service for DrugFAM last week. We thought it went very well and do hope that it was a source of comfort to the many people in the congregation who have suffered, and continue to suffer, so much from the problems which DrugFAM exists to address. I hope you will regard the service as a personal triumph!'

Today DrugFAM is helping so many families, and we continue to seek ways to spread awareness and help more and more people affected by addiction.

Nick's death has been a driving force of positive change and I feel grateful and honoured that his memory has helped me and thousands of others see an opportunity to help others.

Elizabeth Burton-Phillips MBE

Prologue

The Knock at the Door

Thursday 18 February 2004 was a freezing cold day. It was the school half-term and the chill in the air was fierce. I remember the day clearly as I had organised a visit by some of the pupils, parents and staff of my school to Dukes Hall at the Royal Academy of Music in London, where some of the young musicians from Cheethams School of Music in Manchester were to perform that evening. My husband, Tony, had taken a couple of days off work as it was his birthday. The event was going to be a treat for both of us.

My desire to attend stemmed from my growing friendship with the Czech-born author Vera Gissing, whom I had met the previous summer when she came to give a talk at the school. Before the concert began we had a glass of wine with Vera and some of her friends, raising our glasses to Tony in celebration of his birthday. We took our places in the concert hall, looking forward to hearing the talented young musicians demonstrate their skills as they played the music of Stravinsky, Dvorak and Mozart. It was a marvellous evening, which ended with the

Prologue

musicians receiving rapturous applause as they played their final encore.

After we had said our goodbyes, Tony and I set off for home chatting happily about the vibrant musical talent we had witnessed. Driving home down the motorway we agreed that we should have an early night as we had a busy few days ahead of us. We went to bed in a happy mood, looking forward to the wedding we were due to attend at the weekend. There was nothing to prepare us for what we were about to face.

In the middle of the night there was a knock at the door. I didn't hear it, but I became aware of movement in the bedroom as Tony asked me to get up. He was serious, yet there was a gentle anxiety in his tone.

Still half asleep, I put on my dressing gown, my heart pounding as if it would burst. I had already guessed what I was about to face. This was it – the dreaded knock on the door for which I had so long braced myself.

As I walked into the lounge I glanced at the clock. It was 3 am. Two police officers stood there, some distance from one another. Their very stance told me that they were about to deliver devastating news. There was no easy way to tell me: 'I am sorry, but your son Nick is dead,' said the female officer. She was kind, compassionate and professional. Not a job I would like to do, delivering wretched news to families. Those nine words brought a pain that will remain with me for ever.

I sat down with total, calm resignation. Straight away, I said quietly to myself: 'He knew that I loved him, right up to the end, he knew he was loved.'

Devastated as I was and despite everything that the past seven years had done to us both, my love for my son and his for me somehow soothed the dreadful shock. I turned and asked after his identical twin, Simon. Thank God, he was alive. In the midst of my turmoil, it was a relief to learn that there had not been two deaths. At least one of my sons had survived, one life had been spared. I felt as if I was operating in two emotional dimensions, with relief and grief intertwined.

What had happened? How had it happened? An accident, perhaps? Never had I imagined what I was about to hear. As I remained seated, I was aware of the muffled conversation in the background between the police officers and my husband. In the midst of this terrible shock, the question I asked myself was, 'Dear God, where have I gone so terribly wrong?'

And my memory drifted back twenty-seven years . . .

1

Memories

IN SPRING 1976 the bump appeared, and it grew and grew. My first husband Lawrence and I were delighted that Marie, our two-year-old daughter, would soon have a playmate. We were convinced it would be a little girl. It was quite a shock both to us and the doctors when I produced not just one but two, identical, baby boys.

When Nick and Simon came home after a short stay in the special baby unit, Marie took her big sister responsibilities very seriously. I won't forget the day when she 'fed' both her hungry six-month-old brothers from a bottle with a picture of a baby on the outside. Unfortunately it was the Fairy Liquid bottle and before long the boys were foaming at the mouth. A mad dash by ambulance was followed by several anxious nights in hospital. Having three small children under the age of three was exhausting, and at times an overwhelming responsibility. I was grateful for any help I could get, particularly from their two grannies.

Eighteen months later, the boys joined their sister at a nearby nursery. Beverley, who became their favourite nursery nurse, spoke of them fondly:

Simon and Nick looked like angels, because they were beautiful boys with their blond hair, but I soon found that looks can be deceptive. They had the spirit of imps. I spent that first day trying to tell them apart and there was never a dull moment. They came in like whirlwinds; if they were ever quiet, I knew it was not a good sign. But they would soon own up to their naughtiness and express wide-eyed regret.

When I came to collect them from nursery at the end of that first day, I found myself kept waiting outside the door. What I didn't know was that Nick had managed to get his head stuck between two rungs of a chair and the staff were still trying to saw him free . . .

Mornings were always a rush. On one memorable occasion Nick arrived at nursery wearing my knickers and dared to complain that his underwear was slipping! The boys loved their food, loved to tease – especially the girls. They were inseparable and were known to all as 'The Twins'. Whenever anyone was looking for them, they had a special trick – they would rush off and hide under the nearest table, shouting excitedly, 'We're not here, we're not here!' In spite of all their antics, everyone loved them. And Marie was always their protector, even though they frequently embarrassed her too.

When Beverley announced that she wanted the three-year-old twins to be pageboys at her wedding and their sister to be a bridesmaid, everyone thought she was asking for trouble. But Marie and the twins rose to the occasion. As soon as Nick and Simon entered the church they stood on the bride's veil, nearly tearing it off. And as the service was about to begin, Simon's little voice was clearly heard by all: 'Remember, we've got to be good. Bev said.' Later, to the embarrassment of one guest at the reception, Nick's voice exclaimed from under a table: 'Look, she's got green knickers on!'

Time flew by and soon it was time to move from the nursery to school. Sister Joseph, their first infant school teacher, adored them. With their very blond hair and identical faces, she says that to her they were 'just gorgeous – and also lovable rascals'. She found it impossible to tell them apart so she decided to put name badges on their jumpers to identify them. Nick knew Sister Joseph got confused and he soon learnt to swap his badge with Simon's. Poor Sister Joseph would become very angry, often reducing Simon to tears for being naughty when it was Nick who was the culprit. What a show of loyalty at that early stage of life! Years later, Sister Joseph wrote to me about her teaching experiences with 'her twins':

> I will never forget you and the twins – you will be in my daily prayers as long as I live. Over twenty years ago your sons were my special identical boys. I often recall the days when my two boys were in trouble! It is lovely to see the close bond between you and your sons.

I remember Nick setting off to school one day wearing a pristine blue shirt and shiny new shoes. He emerged at the end of the day with a grubby shirt, its collar detached, and one shoe missing. Obviously he was learning how to defend himself. Both boys, to our delight, joined the Cubs and carefully learnt their Cub Scout promise for their official enrolment. They practised and practised, even writing it down to secure their confidence for the big day when they would recite it in front of the Chief Scout. Unfortunately, I didn't check Nick's handwriting. When he eventually recited his promise, I wanted the ground to open and swallow me up. I was embarrassed and at the same time unable to stop giggling as Nick said: 'I promise that I will do my best to do my duty to God and the Queer and to help other people and to keep the Cub Scout law.'

Family shopping trips produced their own brand of rough and tumble. One day as we were unloading at the checkout, Nick dropped a full bottle of lemonade. It split, spun round and round and managed to completely soak a well-dressed gentleman. Everybody around us was speechless. On another occasion, in the same shop, he aimed his suction gun at the deli counter, scoring a bull's-eye on the assistant's forehead. I eventually placated her with a box of chocolates. Safely on our way home in the car the boys would sing like little angels.'When a knight won his spurs in the stories of old' was their favourite hymn. At times they were a liability, but I adored them.

In 1988, as the boys approached their teens, they were invited to participate in a children's television programme called *Docurama: All About Twins*. The local newspaper took an interest in the story, featuring their picture on the front page underneath a headline which read 'Identical TV Twins Set to Steal the Show!'. The accompanying article described how a new 'identical double act' would be hitting TV screens nationwide at the end of April 1988. I am quoted as saying:

> Having identical twins is very exciting but can also be frustrating. To see them in a film is very exciting, but as often I cannot tell one from the other, it is very frustrating. But one thing is certain. They are absolutely no different from other children in their ability to make mischief; not too long ago they decided to have a camp fire with all their friends in the shed and nearly burnt it down!

There was great excitement on the day of filming. We were accompanied by a TV crew for most of the day; I had the day off work and all three children had the day off too. The boys were filmed at home and rowing on the river Thames. My heart was in my mouth as I envisaged the cameraman and the sound engineer falling in the water as the four of them squeezed into the rowing boat.

It seems that the following interview took place only yesterday. Whenever I watch the video I smile and shed a few tears at my sons' comments:

Nick: I didn't really know what a twin meant until I was twelve years old, though my mum told us many times, 'Look, you are a twin. That means you have the same GERMS!' [The television commentator explained that he meant genes.]

One day I was around my ex-girlfriend's house and Simon was coming down the road from the chip shop. A car pulled out and hit him and grazed all his arms and legs. At exactly the same time my leg hurt really badly. I couldn't walk on it. Somehow I managed to limp home. Simon had been asking for me. I knew I was with him because when I got home the pain in my leg stopped.

Simon: Well, I wouldn't like to grow up 'cos I like my life as it is now and I don't know what it is going to be like when I am growing up. If I do grow up I would like to live in the same house as my brother, with our wives, if we have any.

Nick: I don't want to do that because we would argue too much. He [Simon] gets too possessive of me. I am not that possessive . . .

Teenage years and secondary school led to the development of many friendships and the twins had great fun going skiing, skateboarding and meeting girls. By the age of thirteen, the boys also seemed to have developed a serious affliction. The headmaster diagnosed it as 'severe giggling' and deemed it so serious that he recommended we should seek medical advice. So a leading expert on twins duly saw them at the Maudsley Hospital in London. She delivered her verdict with a broad smile: 'Nicholas is fully aware that the giggling is a deliberate part of his impish character.'

We were reassured by another highly respected doctor with a more serious demeanour, who said later in a written report:

> Your sons are developing normally but they are under-standably very enmeshed with each other, which is often the case with identical twins. They are now starting to show the signs of individuation by selecting different groups of friends and expressing different interests for the future.

Both the boys were growing into handsome, popular teenagers, much sought after by girls. Once Nick opted out of a date, preferring to go fishing, so the unsuspecting girl dated Simon instead. Did she ever know? Simon and Nick would do anything for one another.

When we moved to Bath in 1991, the mischief continued. Nick's first love, Ruth, fondly remembers the time he asked her to cut his hair. Unfortunately she could only find a pair of blunt scissors, and the result was a very short haircut with several bald patches. Ruth tried to cover them up by 'colouring' the bald areas with brown felt-tip pen. After they had been going out for two years, she remembers, Nick became very romantic and cooked her a highly creative meal of beans on toast, placed on a small table with candles on it and presented to her in a candlelit room. On another occasion when Nick was in Ruth's car, he lit a cigarette for her and put it in her mouth the wrong way round. There nearly followed a nasty accident.

Their friend Tomsie tells of the time when, after a few beers at the pub, the three of them returned to his home where he fell asleep. The twins seized the moment to shave off one of Tomsie's eyebrows before they too fell asleep. On waking, Tomsie didn't disturb his friends (who would surely have confessed to their prank) but set off to an interview, without glancing in a mirror to find himself one eyebrow short. Douggie, another friend, recalls the time when Nick fell on to the nearest seat in his flat with the words: 'I'm so tired,' then threw his head back so hard that the fish tank behind shattered. Fish and water went everywhere. Ruth made Nick pick up all the fish and pay for a new fish tank.

Mark, also known as 'Teggie', vividly remembers one summer afternoon in the holidays when he and the twins were messing about in our back garden. The three of them decided to play golf with their father's clubs. All three stood outside our patio door trying to drive golf balls into the park behind our house, managing in the process to break several panes of glass in the greenhouse. Going to retrieve some golf balls, Mark looked up, only to be hit straight between the eyes by a drive from Nick. Mark says the twins were more concerned about the broken glass than the fact he was knocked out. Kai, Nick's skateboarding friend from junior school, recalls how he and Nick loved to play snooker in the playroom at our house. They thought they were really 'cool' as they played snooker and drank cherryade made from the soda siphon in our backroom. Kai said that he and Nick thought that they were the best skateboarders and snooker players in their school.

Janet, a close friend from my college days, always reminds me how kind and considerate both my boys and my daughter were towards her own children, who were younger than the twins. She often recalls how Nick, Simon and Marie always went out of their way to be warm and friendly to her own sons.

We were an ordinary, happy family – mum, dad and three children. I often experience flashbacks to the special times at Christmas or birthdays, particularly when the three children were young. Together, as a family, we had a lot of fun and laughter – at home, on holiday, just doing the ordinary things which ordinary families do. All three children made us very proud. However, it would be wrong to promote an image that my family was perfect – far from it. Just like other families there were ups and downs, fall-outs and quarrels. I did not realise that my sons were aware of our strains and stresses until Simon, then aged eight, gave me a typed note which touched my heart. I still have the original, and it captures perfectly a child's awareness of the tensions within his family:

Dear Mum

I love you most in the hole world, I hope you love me to? . . .
You give treats much too often and I love you for that, you treats us better than any other mother would
I do not understand it when you and dad don't get on but you know you really love each other
I will try not to upset my sister in any way and I will try and set Nick a good example
When you and dad are happy I like that, it fills me with joy and happiness
I hope you have enjoyed this little letter
I love you

Simon Mills
xxxxxxxxxxxxxxxxxx

Some ten or twelve years later, when he was almost twenty, Simon sent his father a note, which we found on the kitchen table, following a heavy night at the pub. This time it wasn't typed, but hastily scribbled in such a manner that it could have been written when he was ten years old. It said:

Dad, can you wake me up at 9 o'clock am?
I have work tomorrow so I have to go to work.
Please wake me up and if you can, give me a lift,
That would be good

Simon

After teaching for nearly twenty years in the same school, I became restless and wanted to change my job. In the spring of 1991 I applied for a new post which appeared to open up many opportunities for Nick, Simon and Marie. I was offered the job and, after talking it through, we decided as a family that I would accept, even though we all knew it would bring a major change in our lives. Just like most mums, all I ever wanted was to do the right thing for my children. I loved them with such intensity I would have moved heaven and earth for them. Most mothers blame themselves for things that go wrong in their children's lives, and I am no exception. But I could never have imagined the personal and family heartbreak that lay ahead.

2
It All Began with a Cigarette, Mum

FOR MANY YEARS I was ignorant of the fact, but my sons' drug lives had already begun by the age of thirteen, shortly after they moved to their senior school. After they came home, when they had completed their homework and had their tea, they were always eager to go to the park at the back of our house. Their friends would often call for them through the garden gate, which was never locked. I never realised that already they were experimenting with cigarettes. And, as Simon recalls, things quickly developed from there:

It all began with a cigarette; we were really foolish but that was our entertainment. We used to sit in the park where we lived in Berkshire and, through peer pressure, soon moved on from cigarettes to cannabis. We carried on smoking cannabis until we were twenty-seven years old. At thirteen we would go to the park in the evening and there was always one of our mates who would have enough to sell; it was very easily available. Smoking pot was accompanied with lots of drinking – mainly cider or cans of beer; groups of twenty or thirty of us would sit in the park and get drunk. We hid it from our parents – well, you just did, you tried to act normally. It wasn't like binge drinking nowadays. At that age you don't need a lot to drink to feel the effects. A bottle or two of cider between a handful of people meant you would start feeling it – because we were so young it went straight to our heads.

In fact their tolerance for cannabis was steadily building up; they ended up being able to smoke pot all day, given the opportunity. But I didn't suspect that this was happening so close to our house, and I'm sure none of the other parents suspected it either. Years seven to nine at senior school are the foundation stages of secondary education. How could they possibly make the best of those years when they were regularly smoking cannabis and drinking? Although I didn't realise it at the time, this may well have accounted for my sons' lack of motivation and interest in learning and academic achievement.

As an experienced teacher, I was certainly aware that my sons' academic progress wasn't in the same league as their sister's. Although their school had an excellent reputation, it was very large and I felt that it might be in their best interests to move them to a more intimate environment. After considerable thought, I talked to my husband about the possibility of finding a smaller school. Coupled with my own desire for a change after so many years in the same job, I believed that it was an appropriate time to make a move. I wasn't a mum with unrealistic expectations for my children, neither did I want to map out their lives for them, but I did want them to have the best educational opportunities.

I began to search the advertisements in the *Times Educational Supplement*. Marie was in the final year of her GCSE course and she indicated that she would welcome a change of school for her sixth-form studies. Nick and Simon were due to start their two-year GCSE course later in the year, so the time seemed right to find a new post for myself and, at the same time, to provide the very best for my children.

After a couple of job interviews at boarding schools, it struck me that the children could enjoy the best of both worlds if we kept the family house in Reading while they lived with me in school accommodation during term time. In the spring of 1991 I applied for a teaching position in a girls' boarding school in Bath. It was a residential post that combined part-time teaching with the pastoral care of sixty-five girls between the ages of fourteen and sixteen. Although there would be a significant change in our lifestyle, we wouldn't have to sell our home, as suitable family accommodation was offered on site. I was thrilled that the children would have the stability of the family home to return to during school holidays. Before I accepted, I explained to the headmistress that I must first make sure that it would be in the best interests of the whole family.

The school naturally wanted to meet my husband and children and we were all invited for a second 'interview'. As we were shown around, I kept thinking how such a move might benefit the children, might give them the best chance for a good education. It was an enormous relief that the rest of the family had been so keen for me to accept the post. The only downside was that Lawrence would not be able to commute daily to his job in London from Bath, as it would entail too much travelling. So it was agreed that he would stay in the family home in Reading during the week and join us at weekends.

We moved into our new accommodation in late August 1991 and I began my job on 1 September. My daughter and my sons had been accepted as day pupils in another boarding school nearby. Marie had been awarded a sixth-form scholarship following well-earned success in her GCSE results. I was proud of all my children as they set off for their first day looking so smart. I believed that this was a fantastic opportunity for them and hoped they would take advantage of studying in a smaller school which offered first-class education.

Nick, Simon and Marie settled in well and soon made new friends. Marie quickly slotted into sixth-form life, working with her usual commitment on her A levels, and was happily involved in a wide range of activities, especially music. She had a great first term. The discipline at the new school was tighter than the boys were used to and homework had to be done. Nevertheless, at the end of the first term, Simon's report confirmed my belief that the decision to move had been right for him. Father Matt, his house-master, wrote in December 1991:

> I am very pleased with the way Simon has fitted into the house. He is smart, unfailingly polite, helpful, good-humoured and popular. He has combined all of this with a very good academic performance. Without any major reservations his teachers consider him attentive, hard-working and able . . . I think that both yourselves and Simon should feel very proud of what he has achieved. It is not easy to start a new school at his age and I think what he has done is testimony to his character. I hope that he can sustain this level of achievement. If he can he has a bright future ahead of him.

Imagine my joy when I opened Nick's report and read what his
housemaster, Mr Hutchinson, had to say:

> I am pleased to report that Nicholas has risen to the chal-
> lenge and made an increasingly positive response to the
> disciplines of a new environment. After a bout of initial
> lethargy he has found greater method and energy. He has
> gained some respectable marks for routine work and
> cemented such advance with creditable end of term exam
> results . . . The polite and communicative manner is
> admirable whilst appearance and behaviour are very
> good. He has settled to a very good first term and
> warrants praise, well done!

Knowing that my children were happy was all that mattered to
me. However, I had not fully appreciated, when moving from a
day school to a boarding school, how tiring my job would be and
the demands it would place upon my free time. I was allowed just
one free day per week. Because I was teaching throughout the
day and on boarding duty in the evenings, it became very difficult
to juggle the roles of teacher and senior housemistress and to
keep an eye on my sons as well. I was on my own during the
week, and I soon began to understand how it feels to be a single
parent. Even at the weekend, when Lawrence came down, I had
to teach on Saturday morning and be on duty for the rest of the
day. But, as my three children were halfway through their GCSE
and A level courses, I gritted my teeth and soldiered on.

By the end of our first year, alarm bells were beginning to ring.
Simon's and Nick's housemasters expressed concern about their
discipline, about their peer group, which was providing them
with a less than positive influence, and, more worryingly, about
the boys smoking cigarettes. Their housemaster even suspended

them one weekend after he had caught them smoking behind the altar of the school chapel. I was really angry with them and embarrassed as well. The school caught them red-handed so we were alerted to the smoking at this point. The housemaster brought them home, and the school was very supportive – they just wanted them to comply with the rules. But it still seemed that an excess of mischief was the worst of their faults. Later that term the housemaster wrote in his report: 'Nick has many personal qualities. I think there is so much good in him.' He added as an afterthought: 'But I think he could do with a haircut as he has adopted rather a holiday mode recently.'

Despite their concerns, the masters were confident that both my sons would do well if only they would concentrate on their studies. But it was felt that there was a real danger their lives would take a downward spiral if they lost the discipline that had so far helped them to do well at school. Perhaps what gave the greatest cause for alarm were the people the boys were mixing with outside of school. After some straight talking between me and the boys, they admitted that now and then they had 'bunked off' and spent the day playing on the fruit machines in the local arcade. They confessed that they had occasionally visited a local travellers' site to get some 'wacky baccy' to share between a group of them and their mates at school.

Although we thought this was just a one-off dare, I began to feel anxious about how I was going to keep an eye on the boys. I spent so much time looking after other people's teenagers; yet, because of the job, I was able to spend little time with my own children. I often thought of our lifestyle in Reading, when we were home by 4.30 pm – how we were able to sit down for a meal together and watch TV as a family, how important it was for teenage children to have regular contact with their father. I began to believe that the move had been unwise.

I must admit that I was very lonely. I missed my old friends and had no time to make new ones. But I stuck with it because the external exams were close and despite their errant behaviour the boys were expected to do well. When the GCSE results finally came through the post in August 1993, I saw the relief on the twins' faces and briefly put my reservations to one side. They passed eight GCSEs – and with exactly the same grades. Was the examiner in a muddle, I wondered, or did their closeness as twins mean this kind of thing was inevitable? I was delighted for them both. Similarly, their sister got excellent A level results, deciding to take a gap year before going to university. I was still very unhappy living at the school, but I decided to do a third year there as Nick and Simon wanted to take A levels. I felt I had to put my personal feelings to one side for the sake of my teenage children. It didn't seem right to ask them to return to Reading because their mother was unhappy.

How I regret that decision. It was the beginning of the end of my marriage and our family life as we knew it. I had no idea what was going on – indeed, in the light of their success with their GSCEs, I couldn't believe that anything was seriously wrong – but my sons were again regularly smoking cannabis. In later years, Nick and Simon told me that when they moved to their new school they had stopped smoking altogether, but had begun again when they got involved with other pupils who secretly smoked. By then, Simon had a girlfriend who also smoked. So, under the influence of peer pressure and trying to look cool, they started smoking pot again. It gradually got much worse. The boys began to experiment with other drugs, as Simon explains:

> By the time we were in the sixth form and doing A levels, we were smoking pot in bongs or big water pipes rather than in spliffs or cigarettes. Sometimes we would smoke

£100 worth of cannabis a day between us all. We got the money from working in McDonald's on Saturdays; everyone would put in £15 and five or six of us would smoke it. You would simply mix it with a bit of tobacco to make it go further, put it in a pipe and smoke it. We would sometimes go to a friend's house if their parents were away and smoke some really heavy bongs and do acid and things like that. As youngsters, this was our life; we couldn't go to the pub so that was our entertainment.

On several occasions in the sixth form, just for a laugh, we smoked a spliff outside the back of the chapel or anywhere where we could get away with it, where we wouldn't be seen. The teachers knew what was happening when we weren't attending lessons. Eventually we were caught red-handed and taken to the head's office. He said to us: 'Your behaviour is a bad influence on this school, so make your choice – leave now or make sure that such behaviour is never repeated.' As a result we were both suspended for a week.

I know in my profession what is involved in making a decision to suspend or expel pupils. In fact I had been involved in doing exactly the same thing with pupils in my care who had been drinking at weekends. I therefore knew that a decision to suspend a pupil isn't taken lightly, or without due concern for the pupil and the family. The school did their best to deal with the situation. At the end of the boys' suspension, Lawrence and I were invited to the school to meet the headmaster and other teachers involved with their pastoral care. After some long, frank discussions, it was agreed that they could return after the Christmas vacation to make a new start.

It was now, for the first time, that I was officially told that my sons and some of their peers were using drugs. It came as a huge shock to their father and me. I remember saying to the head and his staff that we knew our sons so well. Surely we would know if they were taking drugs? But I simply hadn't been able to spot it.

One piece of advice that I would offer any parent is not to assume that because you love your children, you know their behaviour patterns well enough to be sure that they aren't using drugs. I made a huge error of judgement in thinking that I knew my sons better than the school did. When I reflected privately about what was said at the meeting, I remembered that I had noticed a change in their sleeping patterns, which I had put down to laziness and the teenage desire to sleep in all day. They were sleeping for very long periods during the day and then sneaking out late at night to return in the early hours of the morning, particularly at weekends. But it was very difficult to control them; I had so little time because of my job and their father wasn't there to discipline them because of his job in London. Simon recalls:

> With no father figure around most of the time to guide us and Mum's job keeping her away from the flat, we began to slip further and further into the world of so-called 'recreational' drugs. Nick and I had realised that things weren't right, as our parents weren't spending a lot of time together. When Dad came down there were arguments between the two of them. I don't think Dad realised when he came down that what he needed to do was 'pick up the family' like a loving husband should have done. So Nick and I lost interest in family life; there weren't any family values any more. Nick and I, as twins, just stuck with each other. But we never really thought divorce was on the cards at this stage.

With our drug use at this particular time, we had adopted a behaviour pattern that unless you try something you can't 'slate' it. Throughout this period of time we chose to progress one step further and use ecstasy, then LSD. Ultimately we ended up combining these drugs. We were regularly out of our heads. Neither Mum nor Dad had any idea what we were doing.

By Christmas 1993, I felt that everything I had hoped for was melting away. I was locked into the routine of boarding school residential life, and it had taken a severe toll. We were no longer a family. Even though I enjoyed his visits, it felt as if Lawrence and I had got used to leading separate lives. By now, it had become too demanding to combine a full-time resident pastoral position with being a teacher, a mother and a wife. I wanted my husband to lead, guide and support his children at what was clearly a crucial time in their lives, but it was a difficult role for him to fulfil part-time. Our marriage was failing; I felt that my life and my family were spiralling out of control but it was very difficult to share my feelings with other members of the family. During the school winter holiday, following a disastrous family skiing trip, Lawrence and I separated at my instigation. The distance between him and me had become enormous.

Simon recalls:

With all this going on between my parents, and my mother's job, we were left to our own devices. There was nowhere to look for guidance and because of the drugs we developed an attitude of 'whatever – who cares?'. We chose the wrong company to associate with, not that you would call them bad people today, but back then everything was a game.

I was very depressed when we returned from the skiing trip. Our sons came in one day wanting to talk to their father and me. Looking very serious, they told us they didn't want to return to school. As Simon explains, there were a number of factors that led him and Nick to want to leave:

> Academically we had found it very difficult, Nick perhaps more than me, as he struggled with his schoolwork. I'd opted for A levels in Philosophy, Politics and Economics and I found it really challenging. Nick and I thought that, given the circumstances, we could do just as well if we both got jobs rather than going the university route. So we were inclined not to want to go back after being suspended rather than to return; we didn't think it was the right thing for us any more. Also we were smoking so much cannabis that part of us just didn't care. We weren't as driven as we used to be because of the drugs.

> Then there were the finances of paying our school fees and the thought of Mum and Dad splitting up – we wondered where they were going to get the fees. Nick and I talked about it a lot and we decided that, with divorce on the cards, we should cut our losses, leave the school and get jobs.

Looking back, this was an unwise decision. Neither Lawrence nor I should have allowed it to happen. But because I was stressed and depressed, I lacked my usual strength of character to insist that the boys knuckle down and carry on with school. I felt that I was a single mother fighting the iron will of two teenage rebels.

One of the most difficult issues for me was that I felt that I had no one to talk to. I was hesitant about sharing my worries and my fears, particularly with anyone from my place of employment. It seemed too much of a risk. I hated what had happened; I believed I had let my children down and had been an inadequate mother. Friends today are quick to remind me that at that time my teenage boys had rejected parental control and took advantage of the fact that my job required such all-consuming commitment. But privately, I blamed myself for taking the job. I felt that had I not done so, none of this would have happened.

I didn't have any close friends on the school staff to whom I felt I could speak in confidence, but I decided I must try to talk to someone outside the family. When the children were small Lawrence and I had joined a local squash club, and it was here that we met Tony. Both of us had got to know him well and I had always found him extraordinarily easy to talk to. I realised that he was now the one person in whom I might be able to confide. Several years had gone by since I had last seen him and I was nervous about contacting him. But one morning I took a gamble and phoned him.

When I began to explain my troubles to him it soon became evident that he was quite ill with flu. I felt it was unfair to dump all my emotional baggage on him. But he was kind and understanding: despite his illness, he took the trouble to drive down to Bath, so concerned was he. He stayed the whole afternoon, listening to what had been going on. The opportunity to talk to him was a glimmer of light at the end of a dark tunnel. Tony laughed and said he felt so ill that the only way he could describe himself that afternoon was as an ageing knight in very rusty armour! He added that he would like to meet my sons and, indeed, my daughter, but he needed to get over his flu first.

I felt uplifted now I had someone to talk to and I began to hope that things might improve. Over the next few months, Tony and I kept in touch and I began to feel stronger. In fact Tony became my tower of strength, especially as we began to get closer. Life was beginning to look brighter.

Unbeknown to their father or me, Nick and Simon were now smoking cannabis on a daily basis. They had left school and all their friends were smoking it, so they did too. Some years later they admitted that they hadn't wanted to upset me by owning up to it. They said they were just kids who didn't want to grow up; they had given up on school and just wanted to get stoned every day.

Several months later Simon decided that he wanted to go and work in Tenerife, while Nick was spending all his time with his new girlfriend, Ruth. It seemed the right moment for me to introduce Tony to them. Simon recalls this meeting:

> When we met Tony for the first time, he explained to us that he didn't want to come between a mother and her children. He told us that he loved our mum, but he would take a step back and not go ahead if we didn't feel it was right. Whether he would have done so if we had said 'No, we don't want you to be involved with our mum' is another story; we will never know. Love is a very powerful thing and the way he approached us was admirable. I am sure a lot was to do with us all 'sussing' one another out, but Nick and I thought that he was a nice chap; as long as our mum was happy, we were happy for her. Nick had a cheeky grin on his face when he turned to Tony and said, 'Oh, by the way, if you hurt our mum, we'll come after you.'

Tony and I married in the summer of 1995. I left my job in Bath, took up a teaching post in High Wycombe and we moved into a new house together in Twyford. Marie was preparing to start her second year at Cambridge University and the boys were offered the opportunity to move back to Berkshire to live either with their father or with Tony and me. They refused. Now they were eighteen, they said, they would get their own flat and find work. I tried to explain to them that, given all the circumstances, that wasn't a sensible idea and that, if they returned, they would be able to get jobs and to contact their former Reading school friends. Nick and Simon obstinately stood their ground. They both found jobs at a chain of sports shops in the Bath area, and moved into a flat. Simon recalls:

At the time none of us, including Mum and Dad, knew that the flat we'd rented was next to one of the worst estates in the area. We moved in, innocently thinking we would be OK. But we learnt our lesson the hard way.

With too much freedom and lack of parental guidance, we became friends with unsuitable people who were substantially older than we were. These so-called friends ranged in age from twenty-two to twenty-eight. It soon came to light that all these people were involved in drugs and criminality. They were in and out of prison and young offenders' institutions. We would go out with them thinking it was a laugh, sometimes against our better judgement. But we were muppets for being so easily led.

We didn't really understand the consequences of our actions until after six months we ended up getting caught by the police. Throughout this whole period of time in our own flat we were smoking lots of cannabis; we had already done acid at school and we started using ecstasy.

If you're smoking pot then you're prepared to do ecstasy and acid, and then coke, although coke is one step further up the ladder of drug use. It isn't like you see yourself as a drug addict at that age; you say to yourself: 'Well, I haven't tried it so I can't slate it.' So we ended up combining the lot. Once again, we were regularly out of our heads.

On several occasions, Tony drove me down to visit my sons to see if they were all right. He recalls that he observed two young men who talked the talk but didn't walk the walk. One day he said to me: 'When you first introduced your sons to me, they said: "If you ever hurt our mum we'll come after you!" Yet they're the ones doing all the hurting. They've become arrogant and self-opinionated and they need strong leadership from their real father. It's really hard for me as their stepfather as I don't feel it's my responsibility to take on two wayward teenagers. I don't think it's right to take away from their father the responsibility for bringing up his children, especially now they're eighteen and are young men in their own right.'

Tony was frustrated with the situation and I was very anxious about Nick and Simon. We noticed on our visits to Bath that they appeared to have no interest in trying to make a career for themselves. They kept telling us that they were young and there was plenty of time to worry about the future. They just wanted to earn or borrow as much money as possible and do whatever they wanted. But we were still unaware that they were mixing drugs and alcohol, and that this had reinforced their blasé attitude. Simon explains:

At that time, because we were on drugs we really didn't care; the drugs had made us feel that we were still young and, selfishly, we could do whatever we liked. I got the sack because of our lifestyle, I fell asleep on the bus going to work too many times. One day they said, 'Simon, just don't come back any more.'

The drug use led to several serious incidents. Once I was out of my head on acid and ecstasy and hadn't slept for two or three days; I'd done several acid and ecstasy tablets as well as coke. I came out of a friend's house and, according to the people I was with, it was blue skies and sunny. Yet I could see snow because of the acid and the hallucinations.

There were two groups of friends and we had two cars. I was driving one of them and we decided to have a race. I remember driving no more than a mile, it may seem bizarre, but suddenly I saw a lamp post jump up in the air, shoot towards my windscreen and blow up into tiny little orange balls. Everyone told me to stop driving, but I said I would be OK. Inside two minutes we were upside down and locked in. We had to try and break out, with petrol pouring all over the place. I remember very clearly that one of my friends had thrown his cigarette out of the car literally ten seconds earlier; if he hadn't, I don't think any of us would have lived.

A number of serious incidents like that happened when we were on alcohol and drugs or both. We drove into fences, caused serious damage and had several crashes. Goodness knows how many cars we went through. One of my friends – she was head over heels in love with me – had two of her cars written off by my friends and myself and she didn't know anything about it. We had to keep it all from her.

Years later, I learnt from my sons that the school friends with whom they had experimented with drugs had recognised that Nick and Simon were getting in too deep and had warned them about it. But Nick and Simon couldn't see the danger signs. According to Simon:

> We were just stoneheads. Stupidly, we believed we were streetwise, but we weren't. We knew in a way we were being used. At first it was all very friendly but our so-called friends were taking advantage of us. We were naïve and we had a reckless attitude. Drugs made us laugh about everything because we were so stoned most of the time. Then the atmosphere in our flat became uncomfortable and unfriendly and our school friends stopped coming round.

The boys later told me that part of them cared massively; both of them knew that they were doing wrong, but they shut those thoughts off and focused on what they were doing – in particular, keeping their lifestyle hidden from everyone else in the family. It was now that they were introduced to crack cocaine, which they smoked by adding it to the top of a bong pipe containing cannabis. Simon continues:

> We didn't know it at the time but a lot of our associates were using crack cocaine or were on heroin; their lifestyle was that of serious criminal offenders. However, even though we did get into a lot of things during that period, heroin wasn't one of them. Under the influence of these 'associates' we found ourselves drawn into committing petty crimes. At first, it was mostly for fun, to pay for shoes and clothes, but soon it was to get money for drugs.

At this stage Nick was with his first long-term girlfriend Ruth; she hated our friends and wanted them out of the house, but they were much older and much harder than we were. We were frightened of them. We couldn't stop them coming into the house. Sometimes we wouldn't answer when they knocked on the door so they would come in through the window and demand, 'Why didn't you answer?' They just did what they wanted.

In the end, it took a phone call from the police to bring matters to a head. Simon and others had been arrested for what appeared to be a car crime, and on this occasion, the police said, Nick hadn't been involved. I was devastated. Still unaware of their drug use, I wondered how on earth my sons, our sons, had got themselves into trouble with the police. What was going on here – why were they unable to lead trouble-free lives?

When their father and I went to Hampshire Magistrates' Court, we were horrified to hear what had happened. A 'friend' of Simon's had stolen a car because he wanted to go and visit his sister in Surrey. Simon and three of their friends had decided to go with him. The whole escapade ended up with all of them getting arrested for failing to pay for their petrol at a garage, at which point Simon was driving. The lad who had stolen the car had hurt his foot trying to break down a shop door. As Simon was eighteen years old whereas the others were younger, he was made an example of. I realised how deeply my sons were involved with the wrong people; it confirmed my opinion that it had been wrong to allow them to stay on their own in Bath. As parents, we shouldn't have left them to their own devices. The police were of the opinion that they were far too easily led and very naïve and that they hadn't realised what a mess they had got themselves into. But we heard no mention of drugs.

Thankfully, Simon escaped a custodial sentence, but he was given a conditional discharge, a hefty fine of £1,000 and six points on his driving licence. I was so embarrassed by the episode that I paid off the fine as soon as I could, believing that by doing so I was wiping the slate clean. We offered both sons the chance to return to Berkshire and sort themselves out. The police advised us that this would be the wisest course: to continue where and how they were living would have been a guaranteed way to secure a bed in prison in six months' time. It was, so we believed at the time, the turning point for both boys. Simon recalls what happened next:

> Dad discussed with us about moving back to live with him. We were offered a chance to live in our old family home but it was difficult because Dad had rented rooms to lodgers so we couldn't move back into our old bedroom. Nick, his girlfriend Ruth and myself were offered one room between the three of us on a temporary basis. Once we got jobs we had to pay rent and then we could rent a room off him like the other lodgers. We decided to accept this.

> By now we realised that having the freedom to be on our own was part of the problem. We were part of a larger group of people, none of whom were being told what to do because none of us were living at home. We were, without doubt, impressionable eighteen-year-olds and these so-called friends were our mentors. We aspired to their lifestyle even if it meant we would go to prison. As a result we finally stood up to these people and said sorry, you can't come into the flat, we're leaving anyway. Consequently they burgled the flat, stole all Nick's clothes

and anything that was valuable. They decided to leave a message, 'Don't mess with us' – they smashed every window in the flat and urinated in the kettle.

I believed that their own realisation of the situation they were in and their decision to return home was the best thing they had done for a long time. How I wish I could say the story ended there.

3
The Return

WHEN MY SONS were approaching nineteen, they returned to Berkshire. I breathed a sigh of relief that, thanks to their father, they would be able to move back into what used to be our family home. I believed that this was the best move for them if they really wanted to put their lives in order.

I'd wanted them to come and live with Tony and me, but we now lived in a small bungalow and Tony was concerned the tensions would be too much. Had we been able to afford a larger house, they could have had a room of their own and he would have willingly agreed. I nevertheless held tight to my belief that the worst was behind us and that happier times lay ahead.

The boys were only a couple of miles away from where Tony and I lived, which made life much easier as it meant no more long drives to Bath. We took every opportunity to encourage them to get their lives back on track. There was a real chance for my sons to put the past behind them. All of us had something to learn from our experiences in Bath. Now it was time to move on.

I was particularly happy for Nick that Ruth, his girlfriend, was still with him despite everything that had happened. I liked her very much. Perhaps one of the most astonishing things about Ruth was that she didn't hide the fact that her father, once a very wealthy man, had lost his business through heroin addiction. Tony and I presumed that what had happened to her father would be a strong deterrent for his daughter and all her friends, including the twins, against taking drugs. We felt reassured that her father's experience would make the youngsters keep well away.

I'm not sure how much Ruth had divulged to her parents about what had happened to the twins in Bath (perhaps she'd said nothing at all), but Nick and Simon were invited to go on holiday with her and some other friends to the villa that her parents owned in Malaga. I thought this was fantastic, not only from the point of view of cost but because sometimes sunshine can provide just the tonic you need to put bad experiences behind you.

And after their holiday, life appeared to be getting back to normal. The boys found jobs. First they did general bar work; a few months later, now he had some experience, Nick became an assistant manager in a local pub. Simon decided to do something different and became a junior estate agent. Both had opportunities to develop their individual careers through in-house training. It was an encouraging period: Nick gained City & Guilds and GNVQ qualifications in Catering Hospitality, Essential Food Hygiene and Health and Safety, while Simon was promoted to senior sales negotiator and his company ran a feature about his progress in the local property newspaper. I was very proud of them and how well they had overcome their difficulties. I also felt confident enough to fulfil my own ambition to study for a master's degree in Education, and I was duly accepted for a part-time evening course at Oxford University from October 1997 to July 1999.

With the twins' twenty-first birthday approaching, it seemed the right time to organise a surprise party. I contacted a number of the boys' friends and we celebrated the occasion with a supper with family and close friends. I had also arranged for some surprise guests – Nurse Beverley (for whom the twins had been pageboys sixteen years earlier), Sister Joseph and their primary school headmistress, not to mention their employers. How surprised and excited both boys were to see all these people at their family party. Photographs taken at the time show wide-open mouths and huge grins on everyone's faces. Sister Joseph subsequently wrote to me: 'It really was great to see the boys and Marie again. All three of them are a credit to you and their father.'

A few days later, as I put together a photograph album of the event, all the evidence of this special family occasion indicated that here were two young men moving forward; they had had their fingers severely burnt and had learnt their lesson. They looked healthy and, dare I say it, handsome; they appeared to be going from strength to strength. Their sister made each of them a *This is Your Life* style photographic review of their twenty-one years. Six weeks later, on Christmas Day, I gave both boys a scrapbook containing all their cards and the photos of the party. At the end I wrote to each of them: 'We are all very proud of you and the way you have come through some difficult times and yet, thankfully, we have always remained close and good friends.'

Christmas 1997 was a relaxing, positive time. All trace of the nightmarish past was behind us, or so I thought. Simon, however, gives the real picture of what was happening:

> After the court episode and our flat was smashed up, we moved back to Dad's house. Then we had a couple of years of trying to get ourselves together. Things went back to normal, more or less; we reintroduced ourselves to our

original friends, Kai, Teggie and Tomsie, whom we had left behind a few years earlier when we moved. Throughout the next couple of years we were still partying with our mates and using ecstasy, cocaine and smaller drugs. However, although we were still doing drugs, they were 'recreational'; it wasn't a constant, day-to-day thing.

Nick and I first got a part-time job working in a pool bar at a sports centre. Essentially we were just idling about, trying to figure out what to do with our lives. Then Nick got a deputy bar manager's job in a pub with the opportunity for further training and qualifications. I became an estate agent for the next two or three years. We changed our lifestyle because we were both working full-time but we were still using drugs. Drugs were part of our evening and weekend life. I was actually doing quite well, but I would binge out some weekends on ecstasy and cocaine.

We had left the crack scene behind us and the criminal associates. We did carry on, however, using all the drugs we had used before, but Mum and Dad never knew anything. Sometimes it was once a month but it wasn't a big thing, just that on a Friday or Saturday we would get 'wrecked'. A close friend had a coke habit of £500 to £600 per week, until he realised he had got to stop or he would be in real trouble. Of course Mum, Dad and Tony knew nothing of any of this.

I believed that life for my sons was going well, but the reality was quite different. Simon continued to live at his father's house, while Nick, who was still with Ruth, moved into a flat almost opposite the pub where he was working. The move to the flat seemed a reasonable and sensible thing to do, particularly as Nick and Ruth were going to share with another young couple with whom they got on very well. In fact, at first, there was no drug use at all in this flat. Eventually, however, it became a 'session house' for smoking drugs. Nigel and Anna, their flat mates, were unhappy with what was going on and moved out, while other friends moved in.

It was about this time that the boys and their friends met a man called Ricky. Simon recalls:

Not too long after our twenty-first, we were introduced to Ricky; we didn't know he had ulterior motives for meeting our large group of friends. What happened didn't just involve Nick and me but all of us, about thirty people or so, though Ricky didn't succeed with everyone.

He would come to the pub and buy everyone two drinks each at a time. Inside an hour and a half he would spend two or three hundred pounds on alcohol. Everyone thought he was a really nice guy but he was anything but a friend. None of us realised that all he was interested in was making money out of getting us hooked on drugs.

A few months down the line – and bear in mind that because of our cannabis use, Nick and I had an attitude of 'we'll try anything once' – we got into Ricky's car outside the pub in the car park. He was with a couple of friends and we had a few spliffs. There was also a joint of heroin being passed around, but we were excluded from that. We were told 'You can't do it', but this just intrigued us.

We thought it was only 'a spliff' and that we would be fine. Nick got more into it at this stage than I did. He was working in the pub and had the opportunity to do it. I was much more inclined to go to the pub and play pool and have a laugh. But that was when our life on heroin began. It didn't interest me that much at first, until all of my mates got introduced to it and stopped going down the pub. I can remember it so vividly because from a group of twenty or thirty people who met together, no one came out any more, it was that serious. Kai, Teggie and Tomsie had no choice but to walk away; they could see what was happening to all of us.

I would go up to Nick's flat and he and his friends would be sat in his bedroom 'gouged out'. Gouged is a word heroin addicts use to describe being 'out of your face'. When you gouge out you aren't on this planet – your head isn't attached to your body. Actually you're off your head, half asleep, but your body is tingling and you don't care what is going on around you. Somebody could be shot and you would probably say, 'Yes, well, so what?'

I then befriended some people who weren't doing it. But even they got intrigued and tried it, though they were sensible enough to walk away. Even the very sensible ones tried it because everyone was doing it.

After several months in their flat, Nick and Ruth split up. Their life together hadn't worked out and their relationship had deteriorated significantly; I sensed that she had met someone else though I decided not to suggest this to Nick. Once they had been inseparable – in fact, I think that at one stage, Nick had loved

Ruth more than he did Simon; Simon told me that he found it very hard to be emotionally separated from his brother – but not any longer. Nick was very upset as he and Ruth had been together for four years. But Ruth was indicating that he had no real prospects for the future and she wanted more; Nick wasn't paying her enough attention.

What none of us knew initially, including Nick, was that Ruth was herself getting involved with heroin, through a completely different source. When Nick found out that she had come across this source through her new boyfriend, he illogically believed that he might be able to win her back if he pursued the same source for his own drug use. Somehow he wanted to hold on to the remnants of his relationship, and he saw heroin as the means of doing so. Simon continues the story:

> Nick was devastated when Ruth left him. I told him to try and forget her but it was hard for him after four years together. It meant a further downward spiral for Nick into using heroin and crack cocaine, because he didn't know how to deal with the end of their relationship. When he was high on crack he broke into Ruth's new flat and set fire to all the pictures of the two of them because he was so upset.
>
> At the same time Nick and I foolishly thought at that stage we could control our use of heroin and crack. As he was so distraught I decided to move into the flat with him, only to discover that there were a lot of bills and debts which hadn't been paid.
>
> Our flat started to become a similar scenario to the flat in Bath, except there wasn't so much criminal activity. In fact

we were older now and in a position to influence other younger people, just as we'd been influenced ourselves. Not too long after this Nick met another girl, Joanna, who wasn't doing heroin but who did recreational drugs. Very quickly she got into heroin and our flat became a place for heroin smoking. All our friends who were doing 'gear' (the street word for heroin) quickly trashed it.

Mum realised there was something wrong but she had no idea that it was drugs; she helped us out by clearing all the debts, which were mainly Nick's. She thought we'd handled our money badly. One of our mates had spent the rent money, about six hundred pounds, on heroin, but Mum didn't know that.

What I didn't understand was that my maternal gestures of good-will in clearing the debts – starting when I paid Simon's court fine – and setting Nick and Simon up in yet another flat were the beginning of my own downward spiral. By continually rescuing them from the mess they had created, I was enabling them to carry on using drugs.

I kept what I had done a secret from Tony. I wanted to protect him from being disappointed in his stepsons, but I was also scared to expose what looked like another disaster. Before long I would begin to find myself trapped in the deceit and lies that go with keeping secrets from your husband to protect your children – even your adult children.

Only recently, Tony has wondered what he would have done had he been in the same situation. If it were his own child, would he have acted as I had done? He says he genuinely doesn't know, but fortunately he has never been put in that position; he firmly believes that you cannot make judgements until you are.

Due to non-payment of rent by one of their friends, they were all asked to leave the flat. Nick and Simon then moved into a two-bedroom flat a couple of miles away. Nick's new girlfriend, Joanna, joined him within a few days of their move. She was constantly round there, and, as Simon explains, all three of them were becoming more deeply involved with drugs:

> We became very friendly with Ricky and his friends. Our whole lifestyle was now focused around the heroin culture. With all the other drugs, we did as much as we could but we could pick them up and put them down on a recreational basis. When we first began smoking heroin spliffs we innocently thought we knew ourselves well; we thought we knew our limits and our capabilities, what we could and couldn't do. But when we tried to stop heroin spliffs we couldn't – it became difficult and, ultimately, impossible.

> We went from a position of not even knowing you could smoke heroin in a spliff to wanting more of a high, which we got by 'chasing the dragon', or smoking it 'on the foil'.* Actually this allowed you to do less and get higher because at the time it was inexpensive to chase the dragon compared to how much we were spending on smoking it in spliffs. It was pure agony; the more you smoked the more you became used to it and had to up the dose. That is when our lives really started to go downhill.

> In Ricky's eyes we had now reached a stage where we were interesting to him as a dealer. We had gathered a

---

* This involves placing powdered heroin on aluminium foil and heating it from below with a lighter. The heroin turns into a sticky liquid and wriggles around like a Chinese dragon. Fumes are given off and inhaled, sometimes through a tube.

number of friends, friends of friends and so on through the drug – there was now a group of fifteen to twenty of us – but Nick and I were only scoring off Ricky. He saw an opportunity and offered Nick and Joanna the chance to start selling for him, rather than having the hassle of doing it himself. They accepted Ricky's offer, which enabled them to support their habit and also make cash on the side – which went straight on drugs.

That was when things became serious. Crack came back on to the scene in quite a dangerous way, far more than when we were in Bath. Nick and Joanna now had the money to get hold of crack as well as heroin. Heroin and crack accompany each other. Crack cocaine speeds up your heartbeat and gives you a feeling of anxiety and paranoia. You would wonder why anyone would want to feel like this for a 60-second buzz which comes directly after inhaling the crack smoke. The reason why heroin is taken with crack is because, even though they are opposites in effect, heroin allows you to get the initial buzz from the crack smoke and it quickly removes the anxiety and paranoia. Ultimately it provides the addict with maximum effect from both drugs in one hit.

One of Nick's particular friends was called Mike. He was much closer to Nick than he was to me. They got on really well together, they never had a cross word. Mike was adamant that anyone who did drugs was 'scum'. In fact he lectured us about it. He had lived in the other flat for a while when Nick was with Ruth. When he discovered we were on heroin he went mad and screamed at us in the local pub, made it known to everyone how he felt.

Yet, only months later, Mike was using heroin himself. I challenged him and asked him why, as previously he had been so against it. All he could say was, 'Well, I was until I tried it, it just turns people.'

Everyone made themselves out to be so good but they were all being hypocritical to their parents because they ended up using. It was hugely frustrating because they were all wreck-heads in their own right. Maybe they weren't as engaged in it as we were but it got them all in the end.

Heroin is very easily accessible. You can score off a number of different people and even have it delivered to the house, it's that easy. I had it delivered to where I was living and just walked twenty yards up the road to collect it. That was what made me so mad and frustrated because no one thinks it's going to be a serious thing when they first start.

While this was going on, Simon was still working. One day he popped round to the house and said that he was broke. 'Could you lend me twenty quid?' he said. I had no problem with this; in fact I didn't think anything of it at all. But such requests became increasingly frequent. When I asked him if he had money problems, he explained that he had taken out loans and some HP and that he needed to consolidate his debts and try and pay everything back at £100 per month. He said he didn't want to borrow money, but he wondered if Tony or I would stand as guarantor on a loan of £4,000, because his dad had said no. I approached Tony and he gallantly agreed to help by loaning Simon the money; it was my husband's way of helping his stepson to rebuild his life.

They came to an arrangement that suited them both and no more was said about it. There was nothing to indicate that Simon needed this money for drug debts.

Meanwhile, in between Nick's shifts at work, he and Joanna were selling drugs to support their own habit. Simon wasn't spending much time with them; according to Nick, Joanna wouldn't let him see anyone else. It was very frustrating; he was glad when she went out so he could have some time with his brother.

After six months, many of Simon's friends walked away from drugs and from him and Nick, as they could see the deterioration in their own lives. These friends still had to go through the experience of 'clucking', a term used by addicts who withdraw from heroin without medical aid. Also known as 'cold turkey', it is one of the most unpleasant aspects of addiction. The symptoms manifest themselves as severe flu coupled with vomiting, diarrhoea and stomach cramps. Simon was waking up to the realisation that he had to find the means to break his habit, even if his brother wasn't going to do so. He describes how his lifestyle had become:

> I was now falling asleep at work; I remember sitting in the office while people looked in through the window and my boss coming up behind me and I was woken up. I was stunned. Things started to go seriously downhill jobwise because every day I was sneaking out at 11 am for heroin, and again at 1 pm. I needed to do it just to feel normal.

> I would get wrecked on it in the car and fall asleep for the rest of the day. I no longer had any interest in my job, in fact I didn't really care any more. I was only interested in what my friends were doing and in getting high. The

money side of things wasn't really an issue while I was working, although now I was working just to pay for my drugs. Everybody seemed to be doing the same at the time. In the early days, you could put on a front and pull the wool over your boss's eyes because you had built up his trust over the last few years when you weren't doing drugs. The last thing your employer would think was that you were on drugs.

In the end, of course, I got the sack. It became evident things weren't right because I was falling asleep all the time. I would take two-hour lunch breaks because I needed to score, I would be ill otherwise. But I had to wait around for the drug dealer to deliver to me. I would make up appointments showing people around properties and would be gone for hours. And Nick had been spotted in my car when I was in the office. Things weren't good on the dealing side for Nick, so I would pretend I'd parked my car round the corner or down the street and would meet him to give him the keys. He would take the car to go and score.

Simon's friends could see his life was deteriorating and that he wanted to get off heroin. They invited him to join them on a holiday abroad, and he accepted. I'm not sure how he paid for it. He spent five of the seven days 'clucking' as he had no heroin. His friends told me in later years that he had been so ill that he stumbled out of the apartment in the early hours of the morning and pleaded with them to take him to hospital. But it was a waste of time: he had to wait hours and they simply gave him an injection without finding out what was the matter with him. Simon recalled that he had never been so ill in his life as during that holiday. But he knew that he would go straight back to heroin as soon as he came home.

Simon had kept the truth hidden from me and the rest of the family, 'bullshitting' about why he had lost his job and why he was ill on the holiday. He felt we wouldn't want to hear that such things were happening to our sons, he didn't want us to be faced with the stress and shame it would cause. He knew that somehow he had to break the habit, own up to the fact that he was a heroin addict and deal with it. Yet the cravings for 'brown'* completely controlled his mind:

> I had the intent to get off heroin but the clucking on holiday was unbearable. I told my mates not to worry about me but to go and enjoy themselves. The minute I got back home I phoned Nick and begged him to bring me some gear. My mates were gutted. They'd seen what I had gone through and they pleaded with me not to use it. I had got through the initial sickness but there was this thing in my mind that was just craving for the drug, it was an absolute craving for the feeling of warmth that heroin gives you; it takes you somewhere unbelievable and that's what I wanted to feel like. When I wasn't doing it, my body suddenly came alive again where before it had been asleep. I could feel senses and smells – it was like being pulled out of a womb as an adult and I didn't like it.

As the millennium drew near, Nick and Joanna had spent a couple of years living very different lives from Simon. Selling

---

* 'Brown' is the street name for heroin, so called because it looks like a brown powder. Street heroin is sold as 'brown' – some people think it is not as addictive as pure heroin – but it certainly is.

drugs had made them ruthless. Heroin had changed their attitude to life, destroying their understanding of right and wrong. When a relative's flat became available to rent, Nick and Joanna decided to take it. Simon realised they didn't want him involved at all, so they could keep their dealing between the two of them. Heroin and dealing heroin was corrupting them and destroying their morals.

Neither Nick nor Joanna had permanent jobs, and their debts were building up to significant proportions, but they kept their heroin lives secret from both sets of parents. Their web of deceit, dishonesty and lies was becoming more and more skilful. They kept their distance from Tony and me without being rude, explaining that they were working long and unsociable hours temping with different agencies. When we saw them on special occasions, such as Tony's sixtieth birthday party and my degree ceremony in September 2000, they gave a very polished performance, giving the impression that they were doing well and were very happy. Physically they didn't look ill, although they often looked tired and drawn. Sometimes I noticed that their teeth were rather stained, but I didn't know that this was associated with drug addiction.

But, for Simon, life had become very difficult:

> I was in a struggle with the life I was living. All knowledge about what my life was really like had been kept from our family and I knew that would have to end sooner or later. I liked the buzz, we all did – but I wanted the pros without the cons. Deep within myself I didn't want this awful life any more. A lifeline appeared when one day Laura, an old girlfriend from the Bath days, visited me. I told her the state I was in and she offered to help me get off it, saying that I could go and stay with her in her flat. I

grabbed the opportunity with both hands. Staying where I was meant I was surrounded by drugs and I didn't have Nick any more, so I thought I would try and start a new life back there. Another friend, Matthew, who became an addict, had moved into the flat. I got on well with him, but it was impossible to get off heroin while we were together.

Of course there were masses of debts building up. I was given a five-thousand-pound handshake when I was asked to leave my job, and most of it went on drugs. I'd already borrowed four thousand pounds off Tony. I was paying him back at a hundred pounds a month and now I was no longer in a position to do so. I knew I would have to tell Mum, Tony and the rest of my family.

One evening in the summer of 2000 I received a telephone call from Simon telling me that he had bad news. Initially, I didn't take him too seriously. But his tone became more anxious, and I thought he was about to tell me he had crashed his car or he was really ill. When he said he had lost the job that he had once enjoyed so much, I was shocked. He asked me if I would come to the flat so he could talk to me face to face. He sounded very low. I became worried, but what he was about to tell me was the furthest thing from my mind. Every parent's nightmare was about to unfold.

4
Vicious Circles

I PULLED UP outside Simon's flat and turned off my car engine, bracing myself for what I was about to hear. I had been driving in a daze, asking myself why my son had lost his job when everything seemed to be going so well. It was only recently that he had been promoted to senior sales negotiator, and whenever I popped in to see him, he was always smartly dressed and confident. He had told me frequently how much he enjoyed his job and how successful he was when negotiating with vendors and buyers. I prayed that he hadn't turned to crime again. Surely he wasn't about to tell me that he had been fiddling the books or had been caught with his fingers in the till? By the time we met I felt tense and panicky and could hardly look him in the face.

Simon appeared quite relaxed. He made me a cup of coffee and sat down with me. Before I could say anything, he confessed that he wasn't in a position to pay back the money Tony had lent him. At the same time he assured me that he would have no problems getting another job and that everything would be fine. Once he was back on his feet, he would be able to resume making the payments. And then, to my surprise, he mentioned casually that he was going to spend some time with his former school friends in Bath.

I bombarded him with questions. 'Why do you need to go to Bath? Why don't you just get another job here? I don't understand you at all, what's going on? Tell me the truth, please. Something's very wrong here.'

Simon was struggling nervously to find the right words. He was agitated, embarrassed, almost desperate. He replied: 'Look Mum, I'm just going to spend a few weeks with a friend in Bath and clean up my act. I'll be fine. Don't worry about me.'

I glanced out of the window. The sun was shining and the spring flowers in the garden were in bloom. I felt sick at heart. I pleaded: 'Why can't you be honest with me and tell me what all this is about? You asked me to drive over here because you wanted to explain to me why you lost your job. Surely it can't be that bad. OK, so you've got the sack, but it's not the end of the world; there are lots of jobs out there. You'll just have to find one.'

Simon replied: 'Mum, I got the sack because more often than not I didn't turn up. I simply can't go to work unless I've got gear inside me. Most days I don't have my drugs sorted out in the morning and I have to spend most of my day trying to score off a dealer. That's why I can't work normally and why I couldn't pay my rent last month. You and Tony were great, you helped me out, remember? Mum, now you know that's why I am constantly asking you for money. I hate my life.'

I was absolutely astonished. 'What do you mean, "gear"? Are you saying you're still using drugs, Simon? I thought all that cannabis business was over a long time ago, when you got caught at school. Surely you haven't started smoking it again? Is that why you got the sack?'

Then Simon confessed for the first time, 'Mum, I'm a heroin addict.'

I felt a chill of anxiety pass through me. I realised that I must share the information with Tony, but I dreaded the thought of telling him, had no idea when or how I was going to do so. I knew how disappointed and angry he would be. Faced with this sudden, terrifying knowledge, my body felt emotionally burnt out. The steep learning curve about this destructive way of life, of which I was totally ignorant, had just begun.

As I listened to my son, certain events began to make sense. The loss of his job, his unpaid rent and bills, the times he borrowed money, particularly those requests for 'twenty quid'; so many odd, unexplained occurrences began, in a flash, to connect. As he sat in front of me, still very nervous, I realised how thin and gaunt he had become. He tried to reassure me that he would eventually be OK as he wasn't injecting heroin – only smoking it 'on the foil'. Yet again, I felt sick.

Even though the penny had dropped, my head was spinning with confusion and disbelief. I had to ask Simon whether Nick and Joanna were also addicts. Out of loyalty to his brother, Simon gave me the impression that Nick had moved with Joanna to their new flat to get away from him in order to carry on with their own, drug-free lives. As Simon later explained to me, he couldn't bring himself to tell me that all three of them were heroin addicts. Partly he wanted to protect me from further distress and partly he believed that Nick himself should tell me about his own situation. Simon had finally reached the point of telling Nick that he was going to own up and ask for my help, but Nick insisted he wanted to be kept out of the picture.

Simon was at pains to help me understand why he had decided to accept Laura's offer of help. He said that I needed to grasp certain facts: he couldn't withdraw from heroin if he remained in his current flat with someone who was also an addict. It was vital for him to remove himself from contact with anyone who could supply him with heroin while he was attempting to break the cycle of addiction.

Later that day, I listened to a conversation between Simon and his flatmate, Matthew, about his decision. Not only did I learn that Matthew too was an addict, but I also witnessed these two young men in their twenties, with their whole lives ahead of them, sobbing openly in front of me about their inability to give up their addiction. What struck me most was the amount of weight Matthew had lost and what a wreck he looked compared to the healthy young man I remembered when he first moved in. It seemed that the only thing that mattered in their lives each day was to get enough heroin to smoke to keep them going until the next day. On waking up, the whole revolting cycle of finding the money and contacting a dealer to score would begin again. They needed all this just to feel 'normal'. I was already becoming familiar with some of the street language: 'score', 'gear', 'cold turkey', 'clucking' and 'on the foil'. Only then did it begin to dawn on me how little I understood about the life an addict leads, how the savage power of addiction consumes every minute of your day, every day of your life.

Simon went on to tell me that his aim was to spend about six weeks in Bath to 'cluck it out' and to try as hard as he could to put his life back in order. Although I was out of my mind with worry, his explanation was logical and very definite. After all, he was in his mid-twenties, and it was his choice. Shocked as I was, it was a positive step that he wasn't in denial about his addiction and was desperate to sort himself out.

After giving notice to their landlord, Simon and Matthew moved out of their flat and went their separate ways. Matthew is still a heroin addict today and living on the streets. We are still in contact with him and hope he will eventually get well.

I know that when Simon went to stay with Laura he was genuinely committed to overcoming his addiction. As subsequent conversations with Laura and other friends confirmed, there was very strong support for him on his arrival in Bath, particularly from Carl whom he had known from his schooldays. Although the mental and physical cravings for heroin were massive, his desire to be 'normal' was sincere. I thought that, with his friends around him, he would recover in time, just as someone recovers from a nervous breakdown. I didn't understand how the addiction worked on Simon's brain and body. I was to learn how heroin controlled his life, ruled his daily routine. I was shocked to hear about the terrible physical pain that accompanies withdrawal and the equally terrible mental cravings linked to that pain.

Simon described his efforts to withdraw from heroin as 'hellish, extremely unpleasant sweating, chills, stomach cramps, a very painful cluck'. Friends who watched him go through this medically unsupervised process of withdrawal (not recommended by doctors) were shocked at the reality of it. Laura explained the massive determination it had taken for him to go through it. She had watched him suffer pure agony and pain, which drained him of every bit of his energy. He had been unable to sleep and vomited constantly.

I told Tony immediately about Simon's heroin addiction. It was impossible to hide it from him: I was tearful and unable to sleep. Tony didn't like to see me so distressed and although he was extremely angry with Simon, he knew it was important to me that I should support my son. To my great comfort, he came with me several times when I went down to Bath. His friends met up with us and assured us that they supported Simon in his attempts to get off this vile drug. We felt sure he was in safe hands.

Consequently, I was amazed and relieved when two or three weeks later, Simon phoned to say that he was feeling much better and that he had been invited for an interview with a Bath estate agency. He promised that if he got the job he would try and rebuild his life. Within a short time he had found a flat and started the job. I dared to believe that the worst might be over. Full of hope, I paid the deposit on yet another flat and helped him get back on his feet financially.

While some may applaud my actions as those of a loving mother, and may well do the same themselves, the reality was that I was now on a treadmill of rescuing Simon from his own actions. By continuing to clear his debts, setting up a clean slate for him once more, I was enabling him to go back to drugs. I was in the process of becoming codependent on Simon, as if I was addicted to his addiction and committed to find a way to fix his recovery. I didn't realise that Simon must first want to cure himself, and that he must do it for himself and not to please me. I thought I must be strong for him and take control of this addiction. If I was determined enough, I thought, I could make him well.

At times I felt that my love for Simon was an unbearable burden, but I felt chained to it because it wouldn't let me walk away from him. However difficult the situation, responding with love, practical support and financial help was all I felt I could do. Every time you rescue an addict, you convince yourself that you are doing the right thing. Yet, unless there is a real commitment from the addict to accept full responsibility for winning their battle with addiction, all you may end up doing as a loving but misguided parent is to release your son or daughter back into the power of their own addiction.

I was cautiously optimistic now that Simon had a job in Bath and appeared to be getting his life back on track. However, I didn't disclose to Tony the financial assistance that I had given

Simon. Tony had lost a considerable amount of his own money trying to help my son: because of his love for me, Tony had bailed Simon out with several rent debts from the previous flat as well as making him the loan of £4,000, which Simon was unable to honour. Indeed, Tony had even paid off a couple of drug dealers who were threatening Simon. I couldn't bear telling Tony I had spent more money on Simon. But by keeping things from my husband, I was becoming caught up in the dishonesty, the insanity and twisted thinking that goes hand in glove with heroin. As Tony recalls:

> I began to see my retirement money disappear; I didn't fully realise it when I started to pay off the drug dealers. I will never forget the first time I took £3,500 out of the Bradford and Bingley Building Society. I was Simon's stepfather and I bailed Simon out because I knew how terrified you were Simon would sustain serious harm. If it had been my son and someone had done this for me I would have said 'thank God someone has got Simon out of trouble'. I thought the first time I did it would be the end of drug dealers, but it was only the start.

Our joint financial losses, as a couple, were beginning to build up. I had also been manipulated into helping Nick to settle various debts, which once again appeared to have no connection with drugs. 'Blagging' money goes hand in hand with heroin addiction. Blagging is an addict's ability to manipulate others and to fabricate believable lies. Both sons became expert blaggers as they sunk deeper and deeper into their addiction.

Nick in particular was extremely proficient at blagging, always presenting plausible reasons why he and Joanna needed money here and there. When I met Nick, he would complain about how awful it was that Simon had gone down the dreadful route of heroin addiction and then he would boast about how well he was doing at work. To stop me from being suspicious of him, Nick continually reassured me of his success. Since I had helped Simon financially and given him moral support, I felt I couldn't deny the same to Nick. If I could help him out with a bit if cash, if he was short of twenty quid now and then, that was fine by me.

As a mother I acted out of misguided love, desperation, confusion, anxiety, pity. Most significantly, I had no knowledge of drugs, other than cigarettes and alcohol. The power of heroin addiction was irrelevant to me and my family. It was something I read about occasionally or heard about on the news. It was something that happened to other people but not to anyone in my family. Had I been able to learn, as a parent, about the dangers of drug addiction and its potential impact on the family, things might have turned out very differently.

When Simon began his new job as an estate agent in Bath, I believed that the situation with his addiction was retrievable. I didn't envisage what was to happen within a few weeks. Simon explained to me that he had foolishly assumed that being back in Bath would be like 'old times'. What he hadn't realised, because he was caught up in his drug problems, was that several years had passed and things had changed:

> When I moved back with Laura and then got my own flat, I thought it was going to be like old times with my school friends, before things had gone seriously wrong when we were eighteen and we had to leave our other flat. But I was fooling myself. Everyone had grown up and moved on as they had careers to follow. I ended up working, then going home and sitting on my own. I was bored and isolated. I thought to myself, if I'm going to sit on my own

I may as well do a bit of gear to forget the night away – but this time I'll keep it under control

It didn't take long to get back into the Bath drug scene – I spoke to a homeless person to find out where I could score – but the drug deals were rubbish. I still ended up driving to Reading almost daily, using the company car, in order to score off my brother, as he or his contacts had better deals.

I continued to work as an estate agent, often blagging about appointments with clients so I could be out of the office for hours, getting my gear. I was also back in with the criminal elements. By now I desperately needed money for my addiction. Along with others, I even staged a burglary at my workplace, as there was a considerable amount of cash left on the premises one day. My employer suspected it was me, but he had no proof. But I ended up getting the sack after he searched my company car and found drug paraphernalia in the boot; he thought I had a cocaine habit.

It was late September 2001 and I was at work when Simon phoned me to tell me that he had been sacked again. Despite his attempts to offer excuses, I guessed immediately that he was back on heroin. My heart sank. Should I walk away and let him sort himself out? After all, both my sons were grown men. Perhaps I should have disowned them both, but that's very hard to do if you aren't mentally prepared for it. There are those, I know, who will say that this was a big mistake, and I would agree with them. All I can repeat is that a mother's love for her children is immeasurable. I clung on to the hope that everything would be all right.

Yet another job having been lost, another flat fell apart with outstanding debts to pay. Neighbours were complaining about the company Simon was keeping. They were worried about their own safety and expressed their anxiety to the landlord. When, some days later, Simon and I had a face-to-face meeting, he had deteriorated physically and mentally since I had last seen him. It was evident that he needed urgent medical help.

Simon consulted a doctor in Bath who advised him to seek help from the community drug agencies, either in Bath or in Reading. At this time, these agencies worked in partnership, making a four-way agreement to help addicts to take responsibility for their own recovery. Once the drug counsellor had made an assessment, a contract was made between the chemist, the doctor, the drug worker and the addict himself. Support might be in the form of a synthetic substitute opioid liquid called methadone or a tablet called Subutex. Either of these could be given by the chemist as a daily or weekly prescription (known as a 'script') to combat the physical cravings for heroin.

Methadone* is a heroin substitute which stops the cravings for heroin. It is often given to addicts to help them to start the slow process of recovery by gradually withdrawing from opiates. It works by preventing withdrawal symptoms in people who have stopped taking heroin. Subutex only takes effect when it dissolves under the tongue. It does not have any effect if the

---

* Methadone is one of a number of synthetic opiates that are manufactured for medical use, in the treatment of heroin addiction. It is usually a liquid which is swallowed. It if is prescribed by the addict's doctor, it is subject to stringent controls (i.e. the correct amount and strength). It must be taken in the pharmacy in the presence (if prescribed by) of a doctor. Methadone can also be bought on the streets (as can Subutex tablets). Generally speaking, it will have been tampered with – usually concentrated or diluted.

addict chews or swallows it. Addicts attend the chemist daily to collect their tablet and remain there until the pharmacist is satisfied that the tablet has dissolved. But the waiting lists for such support were very long, months in fact. Simon clearly needed help immediately.

If you are unable to get an immediate appointment for an assessment, which at that time was the case with Simon, you are left with no choice except to feed your habit in whatever way you can. You can either pay a very high price for second-hand tablets or turn to crime or prostitution. At the time, this situation was well recognised among both addicts and the support agencies. It explains why many parents continue to 'rescue' their sons or daughters – of course I didn't want Simon to commit crime or to prostitute himself. Black market purchasing became the norm for a while. It's as near to emotional blackmail as a parent can experience.

Medical control over synthetic drugs has to be very tight and the black market prices are unbelievably high. I met several addicts 'on a script' who had found loopholes in the four-way system. If they were on a weekly pick-up from the chemist they would sell their tablets at extortionate rates (in exchange for heroin). If they were on a daily pick-up they would appear to let the tablet dissolve in front of the chemist. As soon as they were outside, providing they had managed to store the tablet in a tooth cavity, or even spit it out if the pharmacist was not observing them, they put it into a tissue and waited for it to dry. Later that day, they would try to sell their tablet to get money for heroin or would simply exchange it for heroin.

Feeling very low one morning, I took a risk. I explained the situation to Zuzanna, Katerina and Karol, three close friends of mine from Slovakia. They offered whatever help they could and personally arranged for Simon to go to a hospital in Banska

Bystrica in Slovakia for heroin detoxification, more or less immediately. He could, if he wanted to, stay for up to a year in a
rehabilitation centre out there. To me, this was an amazing
chance to 'sort it all out', particularly as it would not be half as
costly as paying for a private clinic, or continuing to purchase
black market Subutex.

I pressurised Simon to go abroad to address his addiction. But,
as I realise with hindsight, it was I, not he, who was focused on
his recovery. Had I been the addict, maybe my determination to
kick the habit would have eventually been successful, but it was
as if I was vicariously living Simon's addiction. It was Simon who
had to want to get well. It didn't matter how much effort I put
into his detox and recovery, if he didn't want to give up the drug,
nothing I did would ever work.

Eventually Simon was persuaded to go to Slovakia, but he
resisted the idea of staying long. It was Nick who talked him into
going, still carefully masking the fact that he was in the same
situation. I was so eager to help Simon that I told him not to
worry about leaving the flat in Bath. I assured him that, if necessary, I would sort out the finances. Yet again, my codependent
determination made him give in and say he would go. I didn't
pass much of the detail on to Tony. He was understandably disillusioned with both his stepsons so I avoided the subject, fearing
confrontation. Our relationship was beginning to come under
considerable strain.

Prior to the October half-term of 2001, I made myself tell Tony
that that our good friends Zuzanna, Katerina and Karol had
arranged for Simon to go to hospital in Slovakia. I also explained
that I wanted to accompany him. Tony wasn't happy about me
going but he reluctantly agreed. When he dropped me off at
Reading station I knew he was angry with me and yet worried for
me. The atmosphere between us was dreadful.

Simon had reluctantly agreed that he would try the detoxification but insisted he wouldn't stay at the rehab. He had to take methadone to get him as far as the hospital and so I gave him the money to buy it from the black market dealers to tide him over until we reached our destination. The journey by coach to Banska Bystrica took twenty-six hours. Simon continues the story:

> The detox in the hospital abroad was a nightmare. It was a 'cold cluck': I was chained to a bed and locked in a ward with bars at the window. It was very uncomfortable, silent and nobody spoke my language apart from one person who spoke limited English. I did try and make some friends because we were all in the same boat, you could see it in each other's eyes. You ended up bonding because you looked at one another without even saying a word; you all knew your lifestyle had brought you to a place like this. They were very tough times. In the end, I couldn't stand it and I blackmailed Mum emotionally to give me my passport back.

Harsh though it sounds, I took the view that this strict detox was the best approach. That was a significant attitude change for me – I was beginning to toughen up a little. As I was leaving to return to England, I handed Simon's passport to the hospital doctor. I was confident that, at last, my son was on his way to recovery, and hoped he would see sense and stay at the rehab for a year.

The night before I was due to travel back to England, events took an unexpected turn. Tony rang me to say that his father, Bernard, had died suddenly. I was devastated, not only because of his death, but also because I wasn't there to support my husband when he needed me. Once again, I felt emotionally split in two.

On the journey home I kept myself distracted from thinking about Simon's addiction and concentrated instead on what I hoped I might be allowed to say at Bernard's funeral. Mindful of the fact that Tony might not feel up to speaking, I felt this was one way in which perhaps I could help. I jotted down my thoughts on a notepad that I had in my handbag. Although I was deeply upset that Bernard had died, it was almost a relief to think about something other than drugs and heroin addiction. Remembering all the good times I had shared with Bernard helped to pass the time on the long journey.

On my return home, I concentrated on supporting Tony, helping him to arrange the funeral and trying just to be there for him without being distracted by Simon's problems. Even so, Tony later commented, with some justification:

> At a time when I really needed you, you were abroad with Simon, dealing with his problems. I was left to cope alone when Dad died; one or other of the twins always came first and I came second. How do you think this made me feel towards them at this time in my life?

Nick and Joanna attended Bernard's funeral, assuring us that they were very well and looking forward to their future together. They didn't look too bad physically, but their ability to bluff was very well honed. With Simon safely away in Slovakia and Nick giving us every assurance that everything was fine, I dared to imagine once again that the worst was over.

Simon managed nine days out of the fourteen-day detoxification before he started to make waves about wanting to come back to England. There were several telephone calls and a couple of letters that indicated in no certain terms that he didn't want to stay in Slovakia for a year. In one letter he wrote:

The truth is that I feel as healthy as I have ever felt even before doing heroin. I feel strong enough to come back to England, knowing that you, Nick and Joanna are there for me, to support me, and I don't mean financially. I do agree that coming out to Slovakia has helped me a lot and this is why I feel strong enough to come home. My other concern is that it is my birthday in November and I want to spend it in England with Nick.

In another letter Simon wrote to Tony:

I do not expect you to welcome me back to England with open arms. I know that I have to prove myself to regain your trust . . . It must be difficult for you to see Mum torn apart by her children. Mum has hidden the truth about me because I asked her to and because she was scared of your reaction.

I would like to go to Bernard's funeral . . .

I have to admit that I completely lost my temper with Simon. I sent him the following email:

Simon, many people have been willing to help you at very short notice . . . Neither you nor I can afford a private hospital in England and you cannot get off the drug yourself, so why are you being so selfish? Stop using Nick to blackmail me to get you home. Leave your brother to get on with his life . . .

You will have to stay where you are so you can survive drugs because you need discipline and structure. You must take this chance. If you come home now, who will pay your rent? Who will employ you? What support will you have if you come back now? In a few weeks you will see things more clearly if you stay ... Simon, you have drained my emotions completely – you have also drained me financially, using my kindness as a mother to your advantage. Everyone has to make sacrifices for you but you will not make sacrifices for anyone. I am completely finished with you.

In a week of sadness and distress in our lives due to Bernard's sudden death, you have only thought about yourself, your situation, your life, your wants, your needs. Tony needed me when his father died and I was not there for him because of your drug problems. Now you have pushed me to the edge.

Simon nevertheless left the hospital in Banska Bystrica after only eleven days. He made his way back to London by coach, where he met up with his sister. She was very anxious to know why he had left the hospital so prematurely, and no doubt Simon was very persuasive in the reasons he gave her. He then travelled to Reading to spend a couple of days with his father before returning to his flat in Bath. He managed to convince everyone but me that now that he was back in England he would be fine. I wasn't convinced in the least; I was sure he was conning everyone. And the very next time I visited him in Bath, it was obvious to me that he was using again. By now I had become an expert in recognising the signs by his appearance and body language. Simon recalls his situation:

When I left Slovakia I eventually came back to Bath. Mum had paid for the flat while I was away. I hadn't been back that long when I met a homeless friend who was an IV heroin user, which meant he was injecting heroin rather than smoking it. He offered me a chance to inject – but I refused. I phoned Nick and told him. He said to me: 'You know everybody who chooses that route ends up dead.' So, for the love of my brother, I didn't inject, even though my addiction had now reached the point where I was very intrigued by the idea of injecting. All my friends in Bath, except for Carl, had understandably given up on me.

The next time Simon telephoned me it was to say that his flat had been burgled. He was sure it was the work of other addicts, but he couldn't prove it. They had taken his passport and other important documents which he needed for identification at the DSS. The few possessions he owned were gone. The flat had been stripped bare. I advised him to come back to Reading and to concentrate on finding a job. To my relief Simon agreed; he gave up the flat and left with what little he had. For me it was another financial disaster as I lost the deposit yet again. Would I ever learn my lesson?

Back in Reading, Simon, now homeless, spent his time blagging a bed from various mates. And his life with heroin was about to enter a new and more dangerous stage:

I went to see my brother only to find he was hiding stuff under the pillows when I arrived. New addicts were on the scene and within twenty-four hours Nick told me he had done his first injection with them. I had always foolishly said to Nick that if he ever dared inject himself then I would do the same in front of him to bring him to his senses. We had a massive row; it was awful. I reminded him that I'd been offered the chance of injecting about a month before in Bath and that when I phoned him up and asked him what I should do he had a real go at me, saying that smoking it was bad enough. When he now admitted to me that he'd been injecting for a few weeks I said that as I was his identical twin, I didn't want him going down that path without me by his side. So I got him to do my first injection sat on the sofa in his flat. I can't remember much after that because I was out of my head.

The decision to inject heroin was a further step down a dangerous slope for Simon. His father allowed him stay at his house for a while, but he made him leave eventually as Simon, desperate to feed his cravings for heroin, was stealing money not just from his father, but also from his lodgers. Simon ended up on the streets living rough:

> Now my heroin addiction meant I had nowhere to go and no one to turn to. I was so ill from not having any heroin and I had no energy because I had no food in me. I can remember on more than one occasion standing outside my brother's flat, plucking up the courage to knock, but his girlfriend wouldn't have me in; Nick was devastated that this had to happen and I remember him coming out and apologising to me. He was always the one who would sneak me out a bit of gear; he would make me a needle of heroin and come and find me on the streets somewhere. This went on for several months. I could blag a bed at someone's house if it was my giro day but if not it was anywhere I could find to sleep: empty cars, benches and parks . . .

Soon afterwards, Simon met Dave, a much older man who lived about half a mile from Nick. Dave was also a heroin addict and because Simon was homeless, he allowed him to live in his flat. Dave, who had had enough of his own addictive lifestyle, soon took the opportunity to accept a place at a rehabilitation centre. He left his friend Pete, who was more an alcoholic than a drug addict, in charge of the flat. Simon says:

One night when the flat was full of addicts someone who was very drunk knocked on the door. He was called Colin. I didn't know that I was about to witness something awful. You see stuff on TV but this was for real. Before very long, Colin and Pete were 'washing up' heroin.* One of them wanted to smoke it and the other to inject it. Colin injected about a third of a needle full of heroin into Pete's arm and within five minutes Pete had slumped onto the floor. At first we just thought he was 'gouging out' but he slid off his chair and had a convulsion; he was going both red and blue in the face. None of us knew how to cope with the situation, as we were all high, but we called an ambulance somehow.

Pete died. When the police came they thought he had overdosed himself.

I ran to find Nick and his girlfriend and then went back; this dreadful event had a massive effect on me. I went to Nick and pleaded with him to let me stay the night there. Within two or three weeks I phoned Mum from a call box

---

* 'Washing up' involves putting heroin powder or 'brown' onto a metal spoon and diluting the powder with a small amount of water. Then the liquid and powder substance is heated to form liquidised injectable heroin.

and asked her to ring me back. I said I needed to speak to her as soon as possible. I was in a terrible state. I knew she would be very shocked when she saw me. I had had enough of this life but I didn't know how I was going to tell her that I was now injecting heroin. I wondered if she could take much more of this. God knows how she would feel if she knew about Nick as well.

5
Desperate Acts

I WAS SITTING on a bench outside a pub on the outskirts of Reading, waiting to meet Simon. Although he had specifically asked to see me, I couldn't be sure he would turn up. I was resigned to the fact that drugs would be his first priority, but I wasn't prepared to wait longer than an hour. I had a newspaper with me to help pass the time, but I couldn't concentrate on what I was reading. I kept glancing up and down the street to see if I could spot my son.

From a distance, I caught sight of a young man, who looked to be in his twenties, walking towards me. He was thin and bedraggled. He looked filthy. Poor chap, I thought, he must be on drugs. I hope to God that Simon will never get into that state. As I continued looking at the newspaper, I became aware of someone sitting on the bench opposite me. It was the young man I had seen up the street. He said: 'Hello, Mum, sorry I'm a bit late. I didn't mean to keep you waiting.' I sat there speechless. His appearance had deteriorated so much that I had failed to recognise my own son.

I tried not to show how shocked I was as we chatted. I sensed that he was trying to say something important, and gently egged him on to tell me what was bothering him. I was pretty sure he wanted money for drugs, or that he was about to warn me that he was in trouble with the police. As far as I was concerned, nothing could be worse than my son being a heroin addict, so I felt I could handle whatever he was about to tell me. But I was wrong.

There was an expression of deep regret on Simon's face. He looked around anxiously to see if anyone was listening, then leaned forward and said: 'Mum, I am sorry, so sorry – but I've got something awful to tell you. I'm a pinhead – I'm in a desperate state.' He rolled his sleeves up and showed me his arms, which were painfully thin. I didn't follow at first; I didn't know what the word 'pinhead' meant. I hadn't made the connection he assumed I would make. He pushed his arms right under my nose and I was horrified to see that they were covered in bruises and injection marks. Then the penny dropped. He was injecting heroin directly into his veins.

I had come to terms with the fact that Simon was a heroin addict but I would never have believed that his addiction would get to this point. The very thought of him sticking needles into his veins terrified me. That type of procedure should be left to the medical profession – that Simon was prepared to risk doing it to himself was beyond me. Until then I hadn't realised that once you become addicted to heroin you inevitably end up being a 'pinhead'. I felt choked with emotion, yet I held back my tears because I didn't want to draw attention to myself. Whatever society's attitude to heroin addicts, whether adopted through ignorance or lack of understanding, for the mother of an addict it's exceptionally hard to be faced with a situation as desperate as this.

Once again, my immediate thought was to do everything in my

power to help Simon get back to 'normal'. I couldn't accept the sense of helplessness that I felt. I erased the sorry sight of my son on the streets, desperate for his next 'hit' of heroin. I pushed to the back of my mind the knowledge that his craving for heroin was his single focus on waking and that it consumed every minute of his day. I fought an emotional battle as my love for him conflicted with anger. Common sense urged me to walk away – but I couldn't. My heart ached with sadness.

I bought Simon something to eat and drink as it was obvious that he hadn't eaten a decent meal for a long time. Foolishly, I also gave him money for heroin, as I knew he would have to find it somewhere, whether through crime or by 'ticking it on'* with a dealer who might trust him to pay later. I asked myself how anyone would want to live like this. This wasn't a day for blame and recrimination. It was a day for realising that I was powerless to take away his cravings for this vile drug.

Simon agreed to let me take photographs of him. I believed that one day he would overcome his addiction and would use the photographs to deter others from going down this destructive route. Photographs don't lie; they present a powerful truth. They visually describe the destruction of the human spirit by heroin addiction.

When I left Simon, I was near despair. I have no idea where he stayed that night. When I arrived home, it took all my strength to call a number of drug helplines, begging them to tell me what I should do. There was no one to turn to for guidance except a voice on the end of a phone line. I wondered how many other mothers were going through the same experience. At that moment I would have given anything to be able to talk to another

---

* 'Ticking it on' is the street term for 'buy heroin now and pay later'. Dealers do this with addicts so they can build up a debt with them.

mother, or a group of people who knew what Tony and I were going through. But I had to be practical. I had to start somewhere. The helplines advised me to set boundaries for Simon, to detach myself from him but to let him know that I still loved him. The advice was always the same: 'Let Simon hit rock bottom, make him face his responsibilities and deal with them.' Has Simon hit rock bottom? I wondered. Have I?

I began to worry how I could share this latest crisis with Tony. There was no joy in our lives any more: I lived in a permanent state of anxiety, fear and exhaustion, all centred on Simon. I knew Tony would be furious. I guessed he would avoid any long discussions and would be of the opinion that Simon had no one but himself to blame. And how could I share such news with my friends and colleagues? How could I confess that my son was sticking needles full of heroin into his arm? I resolved to keep it a secret from them for the time being because I was so ashamed.

Nevertheless, I confessed to Tony that evening how desperate Simon's situation had become. His reaction was much as I had expected. He was furious and deeply disappointed. Tony and I had conflicting views about what course of action we should take. He felt that we had done enough to help Simon, and Nick too (even though we didn't know about Nick's addiction at this stage); he believed the best thing to do was to cut ourselves off from Simon immediately. But no one else now wanted to have anything to do with Simon – as his mother, I wasn't ready to abandon him too.

Now that Simon lived on the streets the only way I could make contact with him was by mobile phone. Even that depended on whether he had a place to charge it up – that is, if he found anyone to give him a bed for the night. During the day his mobile was switched off, but sometimes it worked in the evening. Every contact, therefore, was hit and miss. The sad alternative was for me to search the streets and look for him. My friend Rosemary remembers those days only too well:

> You hadn't told anybody what was happening, and then you thought you would tell me just a little bit. I was horrified. I don't know how you coped because you came to school and you looked totally professional. Sometimes I was worried that you were stretched to breaking point but you did it because you had hope that you might be able to get Simon better.

Unexpectedly, there was a sudden glimmer of hope. Simon contacted me in the spring of 2002 and pleaded for my help to get him on to a detox programme again. He asked me to go with him to see his doctor to find out if this would be possible, and I made phone enquiries to various organisations up and down the country offering private and NHS detoxification and rehabilitation. The local NHS detox unit had a very long waiting list so I asked for information about private clinics. The doctor told us that there was a private hospital called Detox 5 for which Simon might be eligible. It offered a five- to seven-day opiate detoxification programme for inpatients, using non-opiate-based sedatives and pain relief medication to alleviate the symptoms of withdrawal. To my relief, the doctor put Simon on a daily methadone prescription to tide him over until a place at Detox 5 became available, which he hoped would be in about three weeks. I hoped that with the prescription, Simon wouldn't have to commit crime in order to get drugs.

By now I had found the confidence to share what was happening with a small circle of friends. A short-term but welcome practical offer of help came from Stephen and Marion, who were in the process of selling their house. They agreed that

Simon could live there until he went to Detox 5, although they emphasised that the place was completely empty. The house was in Basingstoke, Hampshire – quite some distance away – but I hoped that it would at least keep Simon off the streets. I was so grateful for their generous offer. Rosemary recalls:

It was very early spring when you told me about Simon injecting heroin. You said your friends had offered Simon a place to stay because he was homeless. My brother had gone to New Zealand and so I had his huge Volvo. When Simon moved in, my husband and I packed the car with a fold-up bed, kettle, toaster, TV and microwave as we had a lot of student paraphernalia in the garage. We then followed you to the house in Basingstoke. I remember it was completely empty and you were going to stay with Simon in the living room and sleep on camp beds.

This was the first time I had met Simon. He was very polite and extremely grateful. I just did what I could to help you both. Simon explained to me that there was a chance he could get a place in Detox 5 and he thought if he could keep clean for a couple of weeks, using methadone rather than heroin, he would get in there, but you, Elizabeth, were just living on hope. I don't know how you did it; driving to work and then back to Basingstoke. You would have your supper with Tony and then go and see Simon, sometimes staying overnight, then drive to school, all the time smiling and pretending everything was normal. I think it was absolute hell for a fortnight or so until you got him into Detox 5.

I explained to Rosemary how essential it was for me to continue working. The school was my refuge, a place where I could put my problems to the back of my mind and concentrate on teaching. But when school ended at 4 pm, back crept my anxieties. After a full day's work it was exhausting to drive from High Wycombe back to Reading, then on to Basingstoke every day. But I felt Simon needed my support and besides, I wanted to keep an eye on him. I took him food to heat up in the microwave as the house was miles from any shops. I didn't leave him with any money in case he used it to buy drugs.

One lunchtime at work, I felt so tired that I made an appointment to see my doctor, Dr Mike Davies, that evening. I was frequently waking up around 3 am and was unable to go back to sleep. My hopes and worries kept going round in my head and I often got up exhausted. My visit to the doctor gave me the chance to speak not only about Simon's addiction but also my increasing suspicions about Nick. I told him that I wasn't sure whether my mind was playing tricks on me but that, lately, Nick and Joanna's behaviour had made me very suspicious. Nick, as Simon had done, was forever asking to borrow 'twenty quid', always giving a plausible reason – for petrol, food, something like that. At the same time he seemed to be avoiding contact with the family; he only got in touch with me when he needed money – even though, time after time, he had assured us that he was working, or at least temping. I suspected he might be 'blagging' money for drugs, but I convinced myself that he needed the cash for some other reason. I couldn't bear the thought that Nick was on the same destructive path as Simon. The doctor was extremely supportive when I shared my worries with him. He realised that I was at my wits' end and immediately arranged for me to have weekly counselling.

I can't speak highly enough about the importance of counselling in these circumstances. What a relief it was to confide in a person who was completely detached from my situation and non-judgemental. That I could go back week after week became crucial to my survival. I was able to open up and pour out all my worries to Anne, my counsellor. I trusted her implicitly. There were times when I was very low, but as difficult and distressing as the situation was, I kept on regardless because I found the counselling so beneficial.

When I drove to Basingstoke to see Simon one evening after school, he told me how grateful he was for the time he had spent in Marion and Stephen's house, as it kept him from living on the streets. Although the past months had been a terrible time for us both, I knew I would never be able to abandon him. He says:

> When Dr Graham put me on a methadone prescription, Mum bought me £200 worth of heroin to see me through until I got into Detox 5. She did this because I was worried that I wouldn't be able to cope on methadone without 'clucking'. I'm sure I had a needle fixation as well.

> Mum thought Nick and Joanna were OK but she had the wool pulled over her eyes. It was so frustrating for me. I really wanted to say: 'For God's sake, can't you see what they are up to, Mum?' They came to Basingstoke and took half my gear, saying that I owed it to them anyway because I got it free from Mum. They left me clucking. Heroin turns you into very, very nasty people and it was awful to see what had become of us all. Dr Graham had said quite firmly to me, 'If your mother is going to pay for you to go to Detox 5, you should do the right thing by her.' I wanted to, but mentally heroin takes you to awful places. I couldn't help myself at that stage.

Detox 5 would accept Simon for his opiate wash-out only if he had the opportunity to go on to a rehabilitation centre for aftercare. Prior to his being accepted at Detox 5, I had discovered, quite by chance, that there was a drug and alcohol rehabilitation centre within a couple of miles of my home. I went to find out what the centre was like before I told Simon about it and then, in March 2002, arranged for him to go and see it. The visit made me realise that there was help out there for him, as I met many addicts who had been in the same situation, if not worse.

Simon's first appointment at the rehab centre was on 18 April 2002. He was interviewed by Tom Ward, the referrals coordinator, and had the chance to meet other residents. I remember Tom asking, 'Do you really want to do this, Simon? It's an eleven-month programme to which you would have to be fully committed. Don't try to make your mum or anyone else in your family organise everything for you if you aren't going to stick with it.' What he said once again brought home how much effort I was putting into rescuing Simon from his addiction, rather than letting him take responsibility for himself. It was part of my co-dependency; I felt as if my own life was on hold while my whole being was focused on helping Simon get well.

The majority of the residents were government-funded, but red tape meant that Simon wasn't eligible for such funding. So, once again, I said that I would pay for him. My friend Rosemary reminded me:

> You told me about Simon getting a place at Detox 5 and then going on to the rehab. I asked you where you were going to get the money from to pay for all this. I don't think you dared ask Tony, since you and he had lost so much money already. You were just going to get yourself further into debt. Who else could you ask? People generally don't have £3,000 easily available.

But because I was recently divorced, I had some money and I didn't need to ask anyone's permission, so I went and got a cheque payable to Detox 5 from the building society. I realised the sense behind your plan with the detox and the rehab, but it shows how your vision becomes clouded and how desperate your acts become when you rescue an addict, the depths to which parents, and particularly mothers, will sink to help their children. It must have been hard and so shameful for you as a mother to practically end up begging friends for money, as I know you did on more than one occasion.

On his admission to Detox 5, Simon weighed seven stone. I took a photograph of him because he was extremely thin and weak. The medical records which were faxed to Detox 5 show that he had previously used crack cocaine, ecstasy, LSD, marijuana and cocaine and tried unsuccessfully to cold-turkey several times. Before Dr Graham put him on methadone, he had managed to reduce his dosage to 0.5 to 1 gram of heroin daily, the bare minimum he could exist on. He was injecting himself three times a day just to avoid becoming extremely ill. In financial terms this cost him £40 a day – but it was nothing in comparison to the £300 to £400 a day he had been paying previously.

Simon explains what happened to him:

> Detox 5 is a sedative based five-day programme where the addict is sedated for four days allowing the body to detox-ify all the chemicals in it. Because you are asleep or sedated, the opiates are flushed out of your system without you feeling the desperation and pain of 'cold turkey'. On the fifth day, before you leave, you are given a tablet called 'naltraxone' which flushes the last traces of opiates

out of your system. This was a very brutal experience as I was unable to control my bowel movements. I had to be held naked over the toilet as I was too weak to stand up.

For the following week in rehab, I was unable to move without help. Any addict who went out onto the streets without support would start again very quickly to take the pain away.

During the time Simon was in hospital he was heavily sedated so I didn't visit him. And he has little recollection of Friday 3 May, the day he was collected from the hospital, as his sedation made him drowsy and unable to control his limbs. How I hoped when I left him that this would be the beginning of an eleven-month journey to his recovery. Armed with a certificate from Detox 5 saying that his body was opiate free, I drove Simon back from London to Hare Hatch, near Reading, to Yeldall Manor Rehab.

The first four weeks of the programme were an assessment period. On his arrival Simon was expected to shower. His clothes and personal effects were searched for drugs. Personal radios, televisions, video and tape machines, record players and mobile phones were not allowed. Any literature which was deemed to be objectionable or counterproductive would be taken from him. It would be a disciplined, tough regime. Contact with the family, either by letter or by phone, was not permitted for the first two weeks.

I gave much thought to how I could motivate Simon to stick with the programme and not give up as he had done when he went to Slovakia. Relieved that there were rules regarding contact with family members, I decided to give him a copy of a poem called 'If' which hung on the wall of my classroom. I had often read this poem to my pupils to motivate them to believe in themselves, particularly at examination time. Knowing how much power his heroin addiction had over his mind, I wanted Simon to hold on to the belief that he could free himself from it, could have a better life – *if* he really wanted it.

> If you think you are beaten, you are
> If you think you dare not, you don't
> If you'd like to win, but think you can't
> It's almost certain you won't.
>
> If you think you'll lose, you've lost
> For out of the world we find
> Success begins with a man's will
> It's all in his state of mind.
>
> If you think you're outclassed, you are
> You've got to think high to rise
> You've got to be sure of yourself before
> You can ever win a prize.
>
> Life's battles don't always go
> To the stronger or faster man
> But sooner or later, the man who wins
> Is the one who thinks he can.

At the end I wrote: 'To Simon, love Mum, May 3rd 2002'. It was the best I could do to help him find the motivation he needed. Other friends offered to send him letters of encouragement and support. Sometime earlier I had taken Simon to meet Liliane, a close friend of mine, to see if she could talk some sense into him. She was one of the few colleagues at work who knew what was happening in our lives. I still have the letter she wrote to him: 'Delighted to hear that you have taken the first step to recovery. I sincerely hope that this is a new stepping-stone for a more purposeful life in front of you . . . The greatest gift you could give to your mum and Tony is to be free from drugs and totally abhor your previous life.'

I hoped that Simon would at least make it through the first four weeks. I knew that the key factor was motivation. I wondered how other addicts like him adapted to living in a disciplined and structured environment when for years their lifestyle had been so chaotic. In the end I resigned myself to the fact that it was down to Simon to succeed. I had done everything possible to help him.

After a few weeks Stephen and Marion, the couple who had let Simon use their home in Basingstoke, also wrote to him:

> We have been thinking about you and praying for you. We know that you have been through a difficult time and we respect your desire for recovery. Thank you for leaving our house so clean and tidy. The detox in hospital must have been very unpleasant but well done for going through with it. The first fortnight at the rehab must have been tough as you are not allowed contact from your family but it sounds an amazing place where you can get well. Thank God they have accepted you. Hang on in there, Simon, you can do it.

It was now mid-May and I was sitting in the garden. The weather was warm and beautiful and for the first time in ages, I felt I could relax. Now that Simon was safely in the rehab centre I could allow myself a little peace of mind. The anger and resentment which had gradually built up between Tony and myself was still there but that day, as the weather was so warm, we had decided to have a barbecue with our neighbours. I was looking at a card I had bought and which I intended to put in the post for

Simon the next day. Every line said all I wanted to say to both my sons. I basked in the warmth of the May sunshine, thinking about the hopes and dreams I had for my boys. Would they ever be fulfilled?

I can't explain the reason why – maybe it was because my boys were so much on my mind – but I picked up the phone and rang Nick to ask how he was, as the last time I had spoken to him he had mentioned that he was not feeling too good. To my horror, Simon answered the phone.

Tony saw the expression on my face and realised that there was something wrong. Before I knew what was happening, he had whisked me into the car and we were on our way to Nick's flat. Tony recalls his 'slightly diluted' version of that evening:

> I was spitting bullets when Elizabeth told me that Simon had left the rehab. She got in the car with me to go and find him. I thought I was going to explode. When we got to Nick's flat I told her it would be best for her to go and wait in the pub down the road, as she wouldn't like to see me lose my temper with either of her sons. When I saw Simon I picked him up and slammed him against the wall. His brother told me to stop it and that it was his flat and not to behave like that. Yes, there were other people in the flat as well, but I didn't care. I said: 'If you lot can handle a raging OAP, go for it!' I looked Simon in the face and said: 'What sort of a man are you, legging it out of Yeldall? Have you got no backbone to see it through?' I said a lot of other things to him which I'm not proud of, but Simon understood exactly what I meant.

Simon tried to explain to Tony that he had left Yeldall because his grandmother, Lawrence's mum, had died; although she had been ill for a long time, he claimed he hadn't expected her to die. And, he said, he didn't want me to pay for him when the other residents were government funded. But a few days later he admitted:

> Nan's death was a plausible excuse which allowed me to walk out of there. As much as I appreciated what everyone at Yeldall was doing, I couldn't see myself staying there for eleven months. I thought that if I was going to let Mum down, I might as well let her down after two or three weeks rather than after six months or eleven months. I didn't want to build Mum's hopes up. Another major factor was that Nick was also using heroin, which of course Mum didn't know. I knew that, regardless of what state I was in when I walked out of Yeldall, if Nick was still on gear, eventually I would use again.

> There was a massive incident with Tony that day. He thought I'd just left to deliberately get back on drugs. He came round to Nick's flat and he was absolutely raging. He said he'd come round to sort me out and he picked me up and held me against the wall. It was very shocking – I couldn't believe how strong he was. And what he said to me isn't repeatable. Because of that, I have to say, I was even more determined to prove to him and Mum that I really did want to get off drugs. I just didn't want to do it at Yeldall Manor.

Surprisingly, Simon found a job working in a local pub. He had nowhere permanent to stay, but various friends let him sleep on their sofas. He began to look healthier, stronger and more like himself. I started to relax.

It was almost May half-term. I knew that I would be away in Prague all week for my school's annual music tour. To give me some peace of mind while away, I paid for Simon to go into bed and breakfast accommodation for that week. At least I wouldn't have to worry that he might be on the streets. By the time I returned, Simon had found a room in a house with friends who weren't on drugs. Yet again I paid the deposit and the first month's rent for him. Simon recalls:

> During that week I saw Nick occasionally. I knew I couldn't spend much time with him because I would end up using his drugs. The problem was that I kept on looking better while Nick kept on looking worse. Everyone who knew me at the time was saying there was something seriously wrong with Nick, so I gently tried to persuade him that the best thing he could do was to own up and tell Mum what had happened. I knew she would forgive him in the end because she loved us both and she would be less angry if she knew than if she didn't. His life was getting worse and worse and I impressed on him that there was no point lying to her any longer.

When I returned from Prague, Simon told me that he had decided to go back to the estate agents where he had worked and ask his boss for another chance. He said that he would be totally honest; he hoped his boss would see by his appearance how well and determined he was. It was obvious that my son wanted to get his life back on track. To my surprise, there was a girlfriend in his life. Could things finally be looking up? His former employer did give him another chance, which was wonderful news. Clearly what Tony had said to him on the night he left the rehab had made Simon determined to prove him wrong.

By July 2002 Simon had kept off heroin for almost three months. He had a good job and a nice girlfriend called Anna, who was aware of everything that had happened to him. Maybe, just maybe, the nightmare was coming to an end.

6
Lady Heroin: Learning to Die

I will seduce you and make you my slave,
I've sent men stronger than you to the grave.
You think you could never become a disgrace,
And end up addicted to poppy seed waste.

So you'll start to inhale one afternoon,
Then you'll take me into your arms very soon.
And once I've entered deep down in your veins,
Your life will never be quite the same.

You'll need lots of money as you've been told,
For, darling, I am more expensive than gold.
You'll swindle your mother without thought or fear,
You'll let your child starve if it gets you the 'gear'.

You'll mug and you'll steal for my venomous charm,
And feel true contentment when I'm in your arms.
The day when you know the monster you've grown,
You'll silently promise to leave me alone.

You'll think that you've got the mystical knack,
Well, sweetie, try getting me off your back.
The vomit, the cramp, your guts in a knot,
Your trembling nerves scream just for one more shot.

Hot sweats, the cold chills, the withdrawal pains,
Can only be stopped by those little grains.
There's no other way, there's no need to look,
For deep down inside you'll know you are hooked.

You'll give up your morals, your conscience, and heart,
And you will be mine till death do us part.

(Written by an unknown prisoner)

Back in 2000, when Nick and his girlfriend Joanna decided to move into a flat together, Tony and I and Joanna's parents had done our best to help them set up their home. They made a lovely couple and seemed very much in love, and I dared to hope that theirs might be a serious and lasting relationship; after all, Nick had stayed with Ruth for four years.

Tony and I wanted to support Nick as best we could. When we changed our car that same year, Tony sold our old one to him for next to nothing. Before long Nick had a crash and the car was a write-off, but when Bernard, Tony's father, passed away, Tony came to Nick's rescue and gave him many items from the house, including his father's car. As the stepfather of my boys, he always did his best for them. He hoped that having a smart car would help Nick and Joanna lead a stable life.

When we met Nick and Joanna socially, we never spoke about drugs. At times Joanna did appear a little possessive of my son, but doesn't that sometimes happen when two people are in love and settling down in a new home? There were three particular occasions when Nick and Joanna met Simon and other family members and our friends: Tony's sixtieth birthday, my fiftieth birthday and my graduation from Oxford University. My memories of these happy times are captured in the photographs I took. But I misinterpreted one vital clue: the brown stains on Nick's, Simon's and Joanna's teeth. I believed they were nicotine stains, as all three smoked cigarettes. I even remember suggesting, jokingly, that they should invest in decent toothpaste. In fact the brown stains were caused by smoking heroin. Would most parents be as ignorant as I?

Nick and Joanna had lived together for some time when they came to see me, confessing that they had got into 'a bit of a financial mess'. They admitted that they had no money to settle their domestic bills. Inevitably Joanna's mother and I came to their rescue. Neither she nor I dreamt that, far from rescuing our children from financial difficulty, we were enabling them to continue their drug use.

When, in 2001, Simon sought my support, Nick and Joanna hid behind the pretence that they were clean and stable, at work and at home. And as Simon was so open about his own addiction and so loyal to his twin, I felt I could trust him; it never occurred to me that he would lie to protect his brother. I have realised since that heroin is synonymous with dishonesty, concealment, fabrication and carefully planned lies; I have learnt from bitter experience how heroin undermines trust. But I believed Simon when he told me his brother wasn't doing drugs. After all, Nick and Joanna looked well and appeared to have a bright future ahead of them. Nick often told me how much he was enjoying his work. Did he lie to protect me because he was ashamed? Would it have been better or worse if he had told me the truth when Simon did? I will never know. But what a dilemma for Simon to be in; to have to choose between being loyal to his brother or to his mum.

Perhaps deep inside I knew all along that, given their attachment to one another as twins, Nick would inevitably be involved with drugs in a similar way to Simon. Maybe I didn't want to believe it; maybe I did believe it but couldn't accept it. I felt suspicious of Nick and Joanna – there were a number of events that didn't add up – but at the same time I also felt guilty for thinking in this way. Was my mind playing tricks on me? Was I imagining that Nick was on drugs just because I had seen what heroin had done to Simon? It had been so difficult to cope and to try to come to terms with Simon's addiction and to experience the destructive fallout on Tony and myself. With so much damage to our relationship, surely it couldn't happen all over again?

I don't remember the precise date when it finally dawned on me that Nick was also an addict. Seemingly insignificant incidents would occur, to which I gave little thought at the time, but which later left me with doubts and unanswered questions. Looking back, there were many carefully contrived 'blags' to get money. For example, Nick would turn up unexpectedly at my gym or even at my school just to ask to 'borrow twenty quid' – in fact he was forever wanting to 'borrow twenty quid' – yet I didn't associate this with drug-related behaviour. He always had a plausible reason for needing the money. He constantly expected me to lend him money because he was in debt – but he always assured me it would be all right when he got paid. How easily I fell for it. I was lulled into lending Nick twenty quid far too often. Simon explained to me:

Nick used to put blusher on his face so that he looked well. Time after time you had the wool pulled over your eyes by Nick and Joanna when they went to meet you. It frustrated me that everyone looked down on me when Nick was so heavily into it. It made me really angry that I was getting so much stick from everybody. If the police had raided Nick's house, he might easily have had a ten-year prison sentence.

All the elaborate lies were a decoy to draw me away from suspecting that Nick and Joanna were up to their eyes in drug use and drug dealing.

Mundane events such as meeting up for a drink gradually stopped happening. Nick became very unreliable and secretive. I sensed his lack of responsibility for his actions; there was an air of aimlessness about him that I couldn't understand. Having witnessed the gradual transformation in Simon's behaviour at first hand, I began to realise that Nick's behaviour was mirroring his brother's. Common sense kept telling me that if my adult son was in charge of his life, and was holding down his job, there would not be the repeated requests for 'twenty quid'.

Several incidents confirmed my increasing suspicions. One evening, when Nick and Joanna came round for supper, Nick asked if he could use the phone in my office, which is at the other end of the house. 'Help yourself,' I said. Not until a couple of days later, when I went to buy some petrol, did I notice that my bank card was missing from my purse. When I got home, I looked everywhere for it but without success. I cancelled the card, scolding myself for being so careless. A couple of days after that, I went to the bank to get a mini-statement and to find out when I could collect my new card. What a shock I had when I saw that approximately £200 had been taken out of my account, at a local hole in the wall, on the very day that Nick had been at my house. It didn't take long to put two and two together.

I remembered that, on the evening Nick and Joanna were with me, he mentioned that he had run out of cigarettes, and popped out to buy some. Could he have accessed my account then? But he didn't have my pin number. I discussed with Tony what I should do and we decided that, for my own security, I would report the matter to the police, rather than accuse Nick outright. I told my son what we were about to do, saying that the police were coming to the house so that I could seek their advice. I held my breath and waited, but Nick didn't react at all.

When the female police officer arrived, she explained that Nick was an adult in his own right and she couldn't divulge any information about him to me, due to data protection. But when I raised the subject of drug use with her, she said that it wasn't at all uncommon for heroin addicts to steal from a member of their family, and that, more often than not, mothers were the prime targets. Long after the officer left, Nick admitted to us that he had stolen my card because he owed somebody large amounts of cash. He refused to tell us who that somebody was. I felt violated and sickened that my own son could steal from me.

I remembered an earlier occasion when I had called round to Nick's flat for a coffee. It was a warm sunny day, so we sat in the garden chatting. I had left my handbag and coat on the sofa in the lounge. When I got home and took my purse out of my bag I thought some money was missing. I couldn't be sure who the culprit might be, but I felt uneasy that several pounds had disappeared. I had no proof, but I suspected that Nick or Joanna were the culprits. On the other hand, they weren't the only people in the house, it could have been any one, I kept telling myself. I tackled Nick and Joanna outright, but they emphatically denied any involvement.

In July 2002, while I sat in my garden, I put my thoughts on paper:

HOW A MOTHER KNOWS
A mother knows her son is a heroin addict

When

He asks for food and there is no evidence of any food or a food
bill

When

He wears a shirt in hot weather and covers his arms.

When

He says he has been working on a building site in hot weather
and there is no evidence of a tan

When

He asks to meet you at seven o'clock in the morning and asks for
money for an electricity bill

When

He gives a fake address where he is staying

When

He asks other people to lie for him

When

His appearance rapidly deteriorates

When

He doesn't get his hair cut and he begins to smell

When

He leaves the washing-up for three weeks

When

There is constant disbelief in your heart

When

You know he is a liar, a thief, a shoplifter, an addict, a drug dealer
and

When he is dead.

In my head and in my heart I knew the truth and what was to
come. I had reached the point when I could no longer fool myself.

I needed to face the brutal truth. Both my sons were addicts and both of them could die.

My real wake-up call came quite by chance, when I came upon the poem 'Lady Heroin' (a prisoner's poem passed round many prisons in England, which appears at the beginning of this chapter). I read the words over and over again, forcing myself to face the truth. Every word, every line mirrored my experience – except, as yet, for the last line. The words sent a chill down my spine. And the truth of the words 'You'll swindle your mother without thought or fear' hit me hard. Even worse was the brutal realisation that my sons had given up their morals, '[their] conscience, and heart'.

But I had stood by Simon, who finally seemed to be getting his life back. Now it was Nick who needed me, and I knew in my heart that I would be there for him as I had been for Simon. How could I stand by one twin and walk away from the other? Having made up my mind, I phoned Simon to tell him the lying game was over and that he need no longer cover up for his brother.

Simon was relieved but not surprised when I spoke to him. He said he had repeatedly told Nick and Joanna that it was 'bloody obvious' they weren't going to get away with hiding their addiction from me for much longer. He had urged them both several times to go their separate ways and to own up to their parents as soon as possible. He thought his recovery would prove that it was possible for them to get well too. I listened to my son with pride and admiration and drew strength from his determined words. With him at my side I knew that Nick would have to face the truth. I was no longer alone.

Within an hour, Simon and I were knocking on the door of Nick's flat. I was in no mood to listen to any more lies, as Nick sensed immediately from the tone of my voice. Having Simon at my side gave me the strength to look Nick straight in the eye and say: 'You're on heroin, aren't you, Nick? You have been all the time, ever since Simon first told me about his addiction.'

For a moment there was silence. Then Nick turned to Simon and raised his hands in defeat. To my surprise he said, 'Yes, Mum, I am.' Immediately he and Joanna broke down in tears. He looked ashamed but almost relieved that at last his addiction was out in the open. The confrontation I had expected hadn't taken place.

I looked at Nick; he was pathetically thin, pale and sickly. He looked back at me and said: 'I've got nothing left, Mum; my life has never been as bad as it is now. I can't hide the truth from you any longer. I can tell by the look on your face that you know. All the way through my addiction I've tried to hide it from you but I'm sinking fast. It's my own fault, I know. I've gradually lost everything, including all my friends and family. I've done the dealers over as well as my addict friends because that's what the addiction has done to me – it's turned me and Joanna into very nasty people. I'm frightened for us both.'

My emotions were frozen as I glanced around. Nick's and Joanna's flat was filthy. Piles of dirty plates and cups were scattered everywhere, the washing-up hadn't been touched for weeks. There was bacterial growth on some of the crockery, and maggots had hatched. Then I noticed that most of the electrical appliances such as the microwave and fridge, and the record player that Tony had given them from my late father-in-law's house, were gone – sold for heroin. The car Tony had passed on to Nick was also gone. I always kept my camera with me since Simon had told me he was injecting, and I took photographs of Nick's filthy flat so that he could eventually see for himself, if he ever became well again, how low he had sunk. Simon and I put some of the crockery into the bins in the garden as it smelt so awful.

Distressing scenes followed. Joanna and Nick were in a highly charged emotional state; despite everything they had done together as addicts, deep down they cared for one another immensely. Once they had been in love, but they had exchanged that love for the love of heroin. When I put it to them that they both urgently needed professional help and hospital treatment, they clung to one another, panicking because it meant letting go of their comfort zone. The only thing that mattered to them was to get heroin into their arms; to be confronted with changing their whole way of life within the next few days was over-whelming, even though they were well aware of how badly they needed help. They realised that, if they were ever to get better, they would have to part.

When I insisted that Nick must go to hospital as soon as possible, Joanna panicked even more. She too had hidden every-thing from her parents. 'If Nick goes into hospital, where will that leave me?' she screamed. 'How will I cope on my own?' Nick was frantic with worry for her but he knew how badly he needed help himself, and all three of us advised her that she should be sensible and own up to her family. Simon repeated several times that it had become obvious to everyone who knew them that something was terribly wrong. Nick tried to persuade Joanna to confide in her mother, but without success; in the end I phoned her and asked her to come round to the flat as soon as she could.

Simon said: 'Look, Nick, this is the best thing for both of you. Now you can get help and get out of this dreadful situation. Just a few weeks ago you and Joanna sat in front of me in tears, telling me how you'd never been as low as this. Take your chance now and accept all the help you can get. It's been a massive fight for me mentally but I'm doing well. You can get better if you want to.'

I explained to Nick that, because I suspected he was injecting heroin, I had already telephoned a private hospital in London and the NHS to find out if there was a place available for him in a detox clinic. How many times had I played this scene with Simon in the last few years? Perhaps, because I knew what lay ahead for Nick, I was fully aware that the best thing I could have done was to walk away, but I loved him too much to do that.

Within a few days, Nick and Joanna's relationship had collapsed. Joanna's mother took over her daughter's care and soon booked her into a west London clinic.

Now I had to break this latest dreadful revelation to Tony. He was already aware that I suspected Nick of stealing from me, so the blow would be softened. But it took all my strength to do it. Tony had already done so much for Simon (including paying off drug dealers) and now his expectations would be shattered once again. Did I have any right to hope that he would continue to stand by me? This wasn't what he had signed up for when he married me. His reaction was blunt: 'What you've just told me about Nick puts me in a very difficult place. You want my support and so do your boys, but I'm trying to cope with serious financial loss, if not bankruptcy. We've already remortgaged the house. I'm trying to hold my own life and our marriage together. The loss of my money, our money, has serious implications for both of us.

'I'm also trying to cope with my own emotions. The support I've been trying to give you all has drained me of my own strength. Don't forget I'm not getting any support from anyone, only lies, deceit, selfishness and a total lack of understanding of what I'm going through. And remember I've also had my father's death to cope with. This drug experience has taken me into a world I wouldn't wish upon anyone – I feel like this marriage is over. But I'm not prepared to see my stepsons wreck your life and destroy you too. Do what you have to do to help Nick, but don't expect me to be happy with it.'

I had Tony's support, however reluctant, but I knew how emotionally fragile he was. Our marriage was near to breaking point.

On the morning of 8 August 2002, my sons and I boarded a train to Paddington to take Nick into the Florence Nightingale Hospital. By then he was a physical and mental wreck. I had taken many photographs of him, and the one which proved to be the most shocking was the photo of him standing on the station platform, side by side with Simon. It highlighted the massive physical difference between the pair of them. Simon, still heroin free, had put on plenty of weight as his appetite had returned. He looked remarkably fit and relaxed; there was even a sparkle in his eyes. By contrast, Nick looked dreadful. No one would have taken them for twins now, let alone identical twins. When he was weighed that day, it turned out that Nick was only half of Simon's body weight.

My feelings were mixed as I sat in the waiting room of the smart private hospital. Earlier that morning I had drawn out the last of my savings (£11,560 to be exact) to pay for Nick's treatment. I remember how vulnerable I felt as I closed the account with all my savings gone. I realised how angry and frustrated Tony felt about me doing this; both of us had already parted with thousands of pounds. Yet I pinned my hopes on this one chance of helping Nick; I had seen Simon come through and I believed with all my heart that his brother would come through as well.

Nick was admitted later that morning and we were told he would be under the care of a consultant psychiatrist, a full-time substance misuse specialist who ran the inpatient drug and alcohol detoxification unit. After we were advised about visiting restrictions and how much contact we were allowed with Nick, either on the phone or by letter, we left Nick and the consultant together.

As Nick began withdrawing from heroin, he became highly emotional. He cried uncontrollably at times. Nevertheless, when I was allowed to visit him, I felt I was getting to know my son again. I recorded many of our conversations. It was important that Nick could confide in me, and he was able to be honest and truthful with me for the first time in years. Heroin had possessed him, sapping his emotions, every thought and every feeling. Before going into hospital, he had even lost the ability to cry. Heroin had robbed him of everything; all he thought about was his next fix. He had lost his self-respect. But I had already gone through a similar experience with Simon and nothing I heard from Nick shocked me – yet.

Nick talked to me openly about his addiction and particularly about 'snowballing', which is when addicts put heroin and crack in the same needle. This combination of drugs made him para-noid, he explained. He would crouch in a corner of a room alone, with all the lights off; if someone walked past, even if he just saw a shadow, he felt he was going mad. Aware that he was heavily dependent on drugs, he constantly worried that the police would catch him or be waiting for him outside the flat. He admitted that in the past, whenever I gave him presents or vouchers or cash, he had exchanged the lot for heroin or crack.

He explained how many addicts 'blag' housing benefit, or sponge off the government. He had been claiming about £500 a month rent from various government departments such as the DSS. Such handouts were invariably spent on heroin. He confided in me how an addict with a good job had passed his work security card to him and Joanna, so that they could access a well-known company and steal palmtop computers, laptops – any electronic equipment which could be sold for heroin.

Nick also confessed that he and Joanna had frequently committed fraud:

> Dealers would give us credit cards in exchange for our daily fix of heroin. This type of deal is well known in the

world of heroin addiction. The 'agreement' is that we, the addicts, buy clothes with the credit cards we're given, forging a signature or pin number. After a certain period of time, we take the clothes back to the shop to try to get the money back. We have to wait for a few days for the funds to clear on the cards. If successful, we keep half the cash and our dealer takes the other half. So, for example, if Joanna and I had spent £1,000 on credit cards, we would keep £500 and give the dealer the other £500. Our share would go straight into our arms. We were caught by the police recently and I know for sure they'll prosecute us later this year. We were even reduced to selling drugs for a small-time dealer to feed our habit – it's known as 'dealing for the dealer'– that's how bad things have got.

Shocking things had gone on in his flat, more dreadful than any parent could imagine. But Nick and Joanna had made sure that the truth stayed hidden from their families:

We had a very good relationship with one of the main dealers in Reading, who was selling massive amounts of crack cocaine and heroin. He asked us to deal for him. This was why I had no need ask you for money like Simon did. We were well catered for, as we worked for a dealer to secure our regular fix.

There were long periods when we didn't need financial help from you, or Joanna's mum, whereas Simon was without a job and was pleading for you to help him. I certainly pulled the wool over your eyes, Mum; everyone assumed I had a good job and was able to look after myself and Joanna and pay our bills. This was the image of respectability we portrayed to everyone. We were living a lie and conning people. But as time passed our addiction became so chaotic that we went from one dealer to another and ended up owing a lot of people significant amounts of money. The problem was that much of the time my addiction was so bad that me and Joanna had 'laid the drugs on' previously and spent the money before we even got it.

Once, when Simon and I were visiting Nick in hospital, both my sons told me of an incident with a well-known cocaine dealer. Nick began to tell the story:

There was a coke dealer that Joanna and I knew; now and again we bought an occasional gram of coke off him. We befriended him over a couple of years and then, when we had the opportunity, we stupidly stole all his drugs. It happened when we were invited round to his flat one day. In his lounge there was a tray with probably a couple of ounces of cocaine in it and another tray filled with 'skunk'.* There were about ten designer gold watches on another tray which must also have had about £15,000 cash on it. Joanna asked if she could borrow the coke dealer's car to nip down the shops but instead she went to get a copy of the front door key cut. Later that evening, when Joanna and I were back home, we phoned him and he told us he was out with mates. We seized our chance and drove round to his house, used the key to get in and stole all his drugs.

---

* Skunk is a type of herbal cannabis. It is very strong and artificially modified, with a powerful smell. It contains much more THC (the ingredient that gets you high) than ordinary cannabis.

Simon continued to tell me about the horrifying episode:

> The cocaine dealer eventually beat the hell out of Nick. I
> took him to hospital because he had about twenty lumps
> on his head where the coke dealer's mates had hit him
> with crowbars and truncheons. I made sure he didn't go
> to sleep but he couldn't walk because his leg was very
> swollen. Nick had been given a severe beating and if it
> hadn't been for adrenalin kicking in, so that he managed
> to escape and get to his flat, I'm sure these blokes would
> have beaten him to death. It was awful to hear his
> screams and cries of fear, I knew my brother was running
> for his life. At the end of that confrontation, Nick and me
> and another friend stood there with kitchen knives, trying
> to fend the coke dealer off. The three of us would have
> stabbed him in self-defence if he'd come anywhere near
> Nick after what he'd done to him already. I'm sorry to
> frighten you, but it was a very serious incident.

On another visiting day, Nick confessed how he and Joanna were
eventually reduced to 'cutting up' large amounts of heroin and crack
cocaine. They became part of a chain of 'workers' that began with
the main dealer. To agree to 'cut up' was a massive risk. The main
dealer never risked keeping large quantities of drugs on his own
property, but used addicts like Nick and Joanna to store the drugs
for him. They were so desperate for their drugs they would do anything to get them. Had Nick been caught with such a large amount,
a long prison sentence would have been inevitable. He and Joanna
cut up heroin and crack using electric scales before handing it on
to other dealers who were part of the chain. They would cut up nine
'bars' or ounces of heroin each day for the head dealer. The street
value of a bar is roughly £9,000 to £10,000.

They were so desperate for their fix that they shaved off small bits of heroin and crack to feed their habit – their addiction had increased to the point that they were ripping off the main dealer. Joanna was paid as a driver, and Nick for keeping the drugs in their flat and for cutting up the heroin. When the heroin and crack were ready to sell, they passed it to others in the chain who had cars. They would go and sell the drugs to addicts on the streets, who were at the bottom of the chain. Nick recalled:

> Anyone who agrees to cut up for a head dealer takes a serious risk. But you do it because then you don't have to worry where you're getting your next fix from, or how you're going to blag money for drugs or commit crime or steal from friends and family. That's where my crack psychosis started, Mum, because I had crack in abundance in my flat. The psychosis, the effect of crack, made me repeatedly sweep the floor or get down on my hands and knees to search for lumps of crack. Then I smoked what I found on the floor using a crack pipe. Sometimes it was enough for twenty or thirty pipes, but I would inject as well as smoke it.

> The paranoia and psychosis came on after I had used the drug. It made me feel anxious to get more and more of the same feeling. The anxiety came over me about every thirty seconds or so. Once I accidentally smoked a Sugar Puff which I found on the floor because I convinced myself it was a lump of crack. You may think that's funny, but that's how desperate crack made me.

Nick told me there were many violent scenes with dealers, particularly when they discovered that Nick and Joanna had 'ripped them off'. On one occasion Joanna was viciously 'backhanded' by a dealer. She was quite petite and the force of the blow sent her flying right across the room. She landed on the floor and when Nick went to her defence, the dealer, a big man with huge hands, held him by the throat until he turned blue in the face. Nick confessed:

> I thought I was going to die. There are many vicious dealers on the streets today. They have no mercy for anyone who crosses them and they don't hesitate to hurt or kill, although they're likely to contract someone else to do it for them. In Reading at the moment, it's mainly Jamaican 'yardies' that are in control of big-time dealing. Because Joanna and I fell out with some of these dealers, they're now making serious threats to sort us out; the dealers are calling in our debts.

When Nick owned up how much he owed to drug dealers, I was quick to remind him that the debts which had accrued on the flat needed to be addressed too. Joanna's mother, Paula, had already begun to sort them out. I showed Nick the letter she sent me:

> Please find attached all the bills I can find so far. The main ones missing are to do with NTL and the water rates. I will keep hunting. I have enclosed two copies of everything and I have tried to summarise on the spreadsheet everything I am aware of. I just hope nothing else comes out of the woodwork.
>
> Please discuss with Nick with regard to which bills he thinks should be shared between them. I have taken an

overdraft to clear as many as possible because they are affecting my other daughter's credit rating as they were renting her flat, as you know. It is obviously not fair on her if she is penalised, and when she gets new tenants, understandably I don't want them confronted by debt collectors. Please could you also ask Nick if there are any bills outstanding?

The easiest way to settle the bills is if you or Lawrence can make the appropriate payment into my account. Total amount outstanding so far is £6,245.00.

Can you imagine how shocked I was? I explained to Nick that Tony was fully aware of the debts connected with the flat and that although seething with rage, he had gallantly suggested that whatever Nick owed could be covered between us and Lawrence. 'Despite what you may think – and, yes, I know I get very angry with your sons, bloody furious in fact, who wouldn't in my shoes? – I'm an honourable man,' said Tony. 'I think I should meet Paula and discuss the debts and see what's the right thing to do. Nick and Simon aren't my sons and I'm sick to the back teeth of them both, but as their stepfather I'll try and do what I can. It isn't acceptable to allow Paula to pick up the tab for all of this £6,000-plus drug mess. Maybe if I speak to Lawrence he'll meet me halfway.'

Unfortunately, when Tony approached him, Lawrence said Nick must sort it out himself. I often wonder if Tony and I should have adopted the same attitude.

But, as I later told Nick, Tony did meet Paula. They went through all the relevant paperwork: outstanding rent, unpaid electricity and telephone bills, unpaid water rates, unpaid council tax, various loans with three loan sharks, repairs to the flat, fraudulent use of Paula's credit card, redemption of sold goods; and so the list went on. As Paula's letter had indicated, Nick's half stood at over £3,000 – all because of their heroin addiction. And that was only scraping the surface. There were also the debts owed to dealers. Nick knew only too well they would start to close in on him as soon as he left hospital.

Despite these grim prospects, I shared some happy moments with Simon on the way to the hospital. I remember having a good laugh with him as we went into Marks and Spencer's near the hospital one day and tried on some hats. At last I was having fun with my drug-free son and I savoured every moment. It was great to see Simon looking so well and being so supportive. I felt confident that if he had managed to get this far, so could Nick. We both believed that seeing Simon doing well would inspire Nick to stick with it.

Two major issues would have to be addressed when Nick left hospital. Apart from the possibility that the drug dealers would pursue him for money, with no money available for long-term rehabilitation there was the problem of where he was going to live. I would have given anything to have him living with Tony and me, but I knew I couldn't trust him yet. He and Joanna had agreed to go their separate ways, so he couldn't go back to the flat. And no one else would take the risk of letting him live with them. Perhaps the statement that shocked Nick more than any other was that his father, Lawrence, had made it clear to him that he had accepted that Nick was going to die and there was nothing he could do about it. But that's the price you pay if you become a heroin addict.

I worried that if Nick was homeless again, it would only be hours before he used heroin. Simon thought the best thing for Nick would be to get a full-time job to keep him out of mischief, and Nick himself knew he needed to pick up the threads of his life as soon as possible. To get him out of Reading, I offered to pay for him to go in a bed and breakfast hotel in Wokingham. While Nick was still in hospital, Simon saw a room to rent in a large house in the same town. The landlord agreed to let it to him and, full of good intentions as always, I found the means to put down another deposit by charging it to my credit card.

Now that Nick was ready to leave hospital, I was full of hope. He was discharged on 16 August 2002 into the care of our GP, Dr Jones. I felt confident he was in safe hands. The alcohol and drug addiction team presented Nick with a special certificate which said: 'On behalf of the Florence Nightingale Hospital and the ADU team we would like to present you with this memento of your continuing recovery.'

As Nick was leaving the hospital, I took a photograph of both my sons. It was amazing to see the difference in Nick after such a short stay in hospital. My sons still didn't look like twins – their weight difference was obvious – but Nick had a sparkle in his eyes and a smile on his face. Mercifully, the depressed, lifeless facial expression I had photographed on the train going to the hospital was gone; it was amazing to see the difference now that he was physically opiate free. But I knew that mentally he had a long struggle ahead.

Nevertheless, when I read the copy of the letter the consultant had sent to Nick's GP, I began to feel what it might mean to be happy again. I call it 'my letter of hope':

> I have been asked to report on Mr Nick Mills's recent drug history. Mr Mills voluntarily presented himself to this hospital on 7th August 2002. I am charging him into the care of his GP today, 16th August 2002. He gave a five-year history of dependent heroin addiction. He underwent inpatient detoxification using lofexidine and

became completely abstinent from all drugs of abuse as determined by clinical examination and by urine tests. He has been prescribed naltrexone, an opiate blocking drug which will be supplied by his GP and supervised by his mother. For as long as he takes the drug he is completely protected from relapse to heroin use as the drug blocks the actions of heroin in the body. He has also commenced an agreed plan of psychological and social rehabilitation including attendance at aftercare meetings at this hospital and he is willing to go to Narcotics Anonymous meetings. At present he is fully compliant with his treatment plan.

We returned to Wokingham, and after I had checked Nick into the bed and breakfast hotel, Simon took us both to see his room in the house nearby and meet his girlfriend, Anna. He had done quite a good job of making the room look homely, and he felt that seeing the room and meeting Anna would be an incentive for Nick to stick with his recovery process. It was the middle of August and there were two weeks before the autumn school term started. Perhaps I could reassure Tony that the worst was over. I so hoped it would be possible to save our marriage. He and I might even have some quality time together.

At the end of that long day, Simon pulled me to one side and said: 'No one knows more than me what you've gone through, what me and Nick have put you through. Seeing me do well and getting back to work should strengthen Nick's determination to succeed. But remember he's never really tried to give up heroin before, and I've tried many times to get to the point I'm at now. I went through a lot of different stages and disappointed you many times.

'The only other time Nick attempted to give up was when he and Joanna tried to go cold turkey and then they got friends to deliver drugs to them because it was so painful. This is going to be a really difficult period for Nick – he'll have mental cravings and there are loads of temptations out there. But we can pull together to help him; I know he can do it, but you know as well as I do he has to want to do it for himself.'

I understood exactly what Simon meant. I also knew that Nick would ultimately have to face the drug dealers' debts. For the present both my sons were off heroin, and that meant the world to me. Yet Simon's experience and his words of caution about Nick made me realise that I must keep my feet on the ground. I had a mother's hopes but an observer's doubts. Who could blame me?

7
A Slowly
Unfolding Tragedy

TWO THOUGHTS WEIGHED on my mind. First, where would Nick eventually find a permanent home? I had no choice but to accept that, given time, this would sort itself out. Second, I dreaded the drug dealers causing him serious physical damage. I tried not to dwell on this too often, but it was difficult to push it to the back of my mind. Thinking of how the drug dealers would 'sort him out' when they found him led to many sleepless nights – the heartache and constant worry of Nick being maimed or even killed wouldn't go away. Ideally, he needed long-term residential aftercare, but that wasn't possible unless I paid for it privately, and now all my money was gone. Nick had a long way to go.

During the time Nick stayed in bed and breakfast accommodation, we often talked about the lows he had sunk to because of drugs. One morning he told me about the 'handbag runs' which addicts sometimes resort to. He said:

> I can't believe the things I've done. I've sunk to the point where I even became part of a trio of bag-snatchers. My mate Phil, another addict, would grab a lady's bag and run off with it. Joanna and I would then go to the lady to check if she was OK. We needed to know she wasn't hurt but we also needed to make sure she couldn't identify Phil. We always asked, 'Are you OK, love? Did you see who did it? Can you give us a description?' Once we'd checked she was all right and couldn't identify Phil we would leave. We would meet up with him and take any cash out of her bag to buy heroin. That's what heroin has done to us, it's made us sink to the lowest of the low.

I expressed my disgust when Nick told me about this shameful activity, yet in a way I felt easier that he was able to get it off his chest. I made it clear to him that it was yet another reason why he must make up for what he had done in the past, stick with his recovery and live a decent life.

By chance a room soon became available in the house next door to where Simon was living. I suggested to Nick that it might be sensible to rent this room; it would probably be much more secure than living in a bed and breakfast or a hotel. I hoped that if he moved into a house he could meet a group of drug-free people, which might give him a further incentive to rebuild his life.

I didn't realise it at first, but a man named Andy Smithfields owned both houses. When I realised this room could be rented from the same landlord as Simon's, it seemed an even more sensible proposition. Andy liked to meet all his prospective tenants before they signed a tenancy agreement. As he later told me:

> When I met Simon, it would be dishonest of me to say that there weren't one or two things that led to a certain apprehension on my part. There was a twitchiness about him, an anxiety, and an edginess which got my antennae flapping. This was compounded by the fact that he was very keen to have the tenancy. I was also unconvinced about his financial position and by his story about what he had been doing before. Having later met you, Elizabeth, it allayed some of my fears. Of course one says whatever is necessary to defend one's children, particularly if you believe that they are about to make a new start in life. I suspect that's what you thought about Simon.

> You agreed to take on certain responsibilities as guarantor; I can't honestly say that the situation was one with which I was totally comfortable, but I do love to try and give young people the benefit of the doubt, even if they have got themselves into difficulties. I believe that everybody should have a second chance, particularly in this case as the support you were giving was clear; my impression of you as a mother meant that I decided to give Simon that chance and so I agreed to sign the tenancy agreement with him. When you called me a short time afterwards and said that his twin brother, Nick, had just come back 'from travelling abroad' and would I be prepared to take him on the same basis as Simon's tenancy, I guess I thought, 'In for a penny, in for a pound.' Simon's tenancy hadn't given me any problems at that stage, so I agreed to take Nick too.

Nick moved into a room in the house next door to Simon in September 2002. He had very few possessions as most of them, except his clothes, had been sold for heroin. Like Simon, he had a clean room, bathroom and shower, cooking facilities in a shared kitchen and the chance to start again.

Thankfully, Simon had got his old job back and was enjoying being back at work; he had settled back into estate agency work with ease and was doing his best to impress his boss about how committed he was to putting the past behind him. Nick could see how enthusiastic Simon was when he left for work in the morning, but he too needed to find a job as soon as possible. Occupying his time productively and putting some discipline and structure into his life was essential for his recovery.

Simon reminded Nick that when he left Yeldall in May 2002, he had grabbed on to all the drug-free people he knew from his school days, particularly Teggie, Tomsie and Kai. He suggested Nick should try and do the same. In fact Simon surrounded himself with all his old friends. They met regularly a couple of times a week, and they were keen to support both Simon's recovery and Nick's. But, as Simon confided to his friends, he was concerned that Nick was living so close to him. He didn't think it was fair to have the responsibility for his brother when he himself was trying to stay clean. 'Neither is it fair for Mum,' Simon insisted, 'to pay hundreds of pounds a month for him to live somewhere. It's important that Nick gets a job as soon as possible to occupy his time and to pay Mum back.'

Simon and I spent the next month worrying ourselves silly, talking regularly to Nick to prevent him from buying drugs. We even took him back to London to the Florence Nightingale Hospital where he could attend the weekly aftercare programme. We did our utmost for him, given that I was now back at work and Simon was trying hard to re-establish himself with his old employer. However, as we feared, being on his own too much was Nick's main problem. Mentally he was pulling his hair out for drugs.

Simon spotted an advert in our local paper for part-time bar staff at a country pub within walking distance of where they lived. He encouraged Nick to apply, and Nick got the job. Although it was mainly evening work, at first it was very encouraging. But, as Simon recalls, things soon began to slide:

> One day, Nick rang me at work. In fact I was just about to finish and lock up for the night. Nick told me he had scored drugs, he hadn't done them but he said he desperately wanted to do them. He couldn't cope mentally, that was the problem; he was struggling to live without drugs, it was tough for him because that lifestyle was all he knew. I automatically phoned Mum and we agreed to go and meet him.

> I think Nick ringing me was his plea to me to say, 'Simon, I want you to do drugs with me, I don't want to go down this route but I can't stay drug free, I can't do them on my own.' I told him how much money Mum had spent on us both, and asked how could he possibly want to do this to her. I knew that he didn't want to hurt Mum deliberately, but mentally he just couldn't cope with normal life without drugs. It was all he had known for years.

Simon and I dropped everything, got into our separate cars and met Nick in a pub near where they lived. By the time I arrived, Simon had already laid into Nick verbally. He wasted no time and snatched the drugs off Nick, grinding them into the pavement. Overheard by several people, they had a row. We both reminded him what his life would be like if he went back to heroin, though I believed he had already taken some drugs without telling us. I went to bed that night feeling more secure about Simon's recovery and far less secure about Nick's. As Simon reveals, things weren't so simple:

> The next day when I came home from work, I went to Nick's room to see him. He had a guilty look on his face and I said to him, 'What's wrong, what's wrong?' He pulled out four needles full of heroin. Waving them in front of me, he said, 'I'll do it, if you'll do it.' Angrily I said to him: 'Why are you doing this to me, Nick? You know how well I'm doing, I've been clean for several months. I'm really trying to sort my life out.'
>
> But the more I argued with him the more my attention turned towards the needles. Furiously, I said: 'Look, you idiot, you do realise that if you or I do this, every part of what I've done these last few months, all this money Mum's spent on both of us, everything will just be ruined. Inside a month I'll lose my job, I'll be back on the streets and Mum will disown us.'
>
> We both knew what was going to happen if we did drugs again, but the heroin was there in the room, just sat there, in front of us. It was like sticking a bottle of vodka in front of an alcoholic and letting him stare at it all night. If the drugs had been taken away from both of us at that moment I don't think I would have relapsed. If someone had flushed them down the toilet, I don't think I would have touched them. But Nick had already made up his mind that he couldn't cope with life without being on

heroin. I was really struggling at that moment. I wanted to do it but I didn't want the life of a heroin addict. I knew that if I touched drugs I would end up coming back after work the next day and day after day, for more drugs.

I remember sitting there, so upset that I was doing this again. But I put the stuff into my arms and so did Nick. All the help and support Mum had given us, the detoxes she had put us through, and inside thirty seconds it was completely ruined. We'd put ourselves back to square one. That's the problem with heroin – if it's there in front of you as blatantly as it was that day, it's very difficult to say no. I was in tears when I injected heroin into my arms again, knowing I was going to go downhill and yet accepting it. Sticking the needle into my arm, knowing I had just wrecked my life again, wrecked Mum's life again, the guilt was awful.

Unaware that both sons had relapsed, I continued to believe that they were doing well. I thought Simon, who was in a stronger position mentally, was setting Nick a positive example. I was aware that Nick was struggling, but I hoped that, as he now had a job, he wouldn't give in. Never in my wildest dreams would I have guessed what was already happening.

However, by the time Simon got his pay cheque at the end of September, he and Nick had used heroin a number of times. In fact, on some days, Nick collected Simon's car from work to go and get the drugs they needed. At lunchtime they smoked £40 worth of heroin and even injected while sitting in the car. Simon said:

Nick was really on my case, because as soon as I had any money I was supporting his drug habit from my wages as well as trying to support my own. But I just couldn't ditch my twin brother. Once again, heroin put us on a different planet, it stole our lives. We ended up trapped in a cycle of destruction. It completely took over. Most of the dealers we ended up scoring off on a regular basis didn't touch it. We had no control over anything, but heroin had complete control over us.

It was now the middle of October 2002 and my friends Janet and David phoned to ask how the boys were getting on. I had known Janet and David since 1969, from our student days at Liverpool University. Since then, we had met regularly two or three times a year. They had known Nick, Simon and Marie since birth and they had two sons of their own, a few years younger than my children.

I had spoken in confidence to Janet and David several times on the phone about my sons' drug problems. I knew I could trust them implicitly, and they were always very supportive. It was good to be able to update Janet with what I believed to be positive news. She suggested that I bring the boys for supper one evening, and the following week Simon met me after work, we collected Nick from his house and I drove the three of us to London. I remember telling our hosts how pleased I was with their progress. We had a very good evening; indeed, Janet remarked to both my sons that despite their physical and mental scars, she felt they were genuinely trying to put their lives back together.

When we left Janet and her husband that evening, she and I felt confident that everything was much better than it had been for a long time. How naïve we were. As Simon explains:

It wasn't a thing we did every day. We genuinely told ourselves, if we use heroin again we will lose everything.

We knew from past experience that that was the way it would go, but we told ourselves we would only have the one hit, we would just try it to get the feeling again as we knew that one hit would be brilliant. That was what we craved. It was gradual, we didn't say, 'Let's go and score every single day.' It was four or five days before we next picked up the drug. The clucking didn't kick in straight away because you can get away without clucking if you don't do heroin every day.

We didn't want to arouse suspicions, we didn't want that life, but we wanted to get away with doing the drugs. We secretly persuaded ourselves that it was OK to have one hit every now and then and that we could get away with it – nobody would be the wiser and we would just have to live with the guilt. But reality kicks in pretty fast, and soon you know you can't stop because you have become physically and mentally addicted again.

These were still early days in their relapse; I should have realised that if they started using again neither of them were going to openly admit to it, but as yet I hadn't spotted any warning signs. Yet, although Simon was working and Nick was doing part-time bar work in the evening, the lying game had started all over again. Secrecy and lies would be their priority whenever they saw me.

In the meantime Nick had received a summons to attend Newbury Magistrates' Court on 5 December 2002 to answer the charge of dishonestly receiving stolen goods. As he reminded me, this was what he and Joanna had been arrested for earlier in the year. While he was in hospital he had confessed to what he had done and was advised to get a solicitor to represent him in court.

The solicitor who took on his case was very down-to-earth. When I went with Nick to see her, she explained that as it would be his first time in court, a prison sentence was unlikely – but that the possibility should not be dismissed. She advised us to ask our friends and family to write letters of support about his progress which could be presented to the magistrates on the day of the case. She would argue against a prison sentence and would recommend to the magistrates that they deal with Nick by means of a Community Rehabilitation Order (CRO) or probation order. The thought of Nick going to prison terrified me – but perhaps, with hindsight, it might have been the best thing that could have happened to him.

When I spoke to my closest friends about the impending court case, without exception they offered to write letters of support. Nearly all of them had met Nick after he had left hospital and had encouraged him never to touch heroin again. In good faith, Janet put her beliefs to the magistrates:

> We are fully aware of Nick's past drug addiction problems, and the very unfortunate behaviour which was associated with it. A few weeks ago Nick came to our house for supper and we had a long chat with him. It was evident to us that he is now trying desperately hard to put his life back together, and that he very much regrets his past actions and all that he has put his family through. He is now working part-time and hopes to go full-time as he has many debts to pay and he does not want to lose his job . . . When you sentence Nick we would ask you to bear in mind the anguish his family has suffered already both financially and emotionally, particularly his mother. Nick has the support of many friends and family members and is determined in his attempt to rebuild his life.

Similarly, Rosemary wrote:

> It appears that Nick has now fairly and squarely faced up
> to the wrong he has done. He voluntarily participated in a
> detox programme in August of this year and he has vigor-
> ously stayed away from heroin and anybody associated
> with it and he now has a new job. I have observed the
> relationship between Nick and his mother: she has
> supported him all the way and while his mother's support
> is a key factor in his recovery Nick has to take on board
> the responsibility for his own recovery and accept the
> sentence of the court.

My great friend and colleague at school, Stuart, wrote:

> I have known Nick for over three years and I have
> followed the fortunes and otherwise of Nick and of all the
> family over these years. I know it has been a very great
> ordeal for his mother who has fully supported him and
> his brother. She has often shared her worries with me
> about both her sons but I can say she has given Nick
> unequivocal support, financially and maternally. In fact
> there is an excellent network of friends working on their
> behalf as we all want to see Nick find his way again and
> be fully rehabilitated with his life and future career. Nick
> is genuinely repentant about his past drug-associated
> behaviour and I would like to see him being afforded the
> opportunity to pursue his career path with forgiveness
> and without judicial prejudice. It is clear to me that his
> family and in particular his mother have suffered a great
> deal of emotional stress and financial loss, so I do ask you
> to show leniency for his and his family's sake.

Nick's solicitor collated the letters of support in preparation for his case, and on 5 December I went with him to the Magistrates' Court. I felt utterly ashamed as I listened to him and Joanna plead guilty to the charge of dishonestly receiving stolen goods – but this is the reality of where heroin takes you.

After his solicitor had given all the facts to the court, my heart was in my mouth as the three magistrates adjourned to consider the sentence. I kept telling myself to keep my dignity and not to break down if he was sent to prison. After thirty minutes, maybe longer, I listened as the chairman of the bench gave Nick a three-year Community Rehabilitation Order (CRO). He was also ordered to report weekly to the local probation service. Embarrassed though I was that this was happening to my son, I was relieved that he had escaped a prison sentence. I comforted myself by thinking that at least he was off heroin. Maybe the CRO would bring him to his senses.

As we drove back from the court along the M4 towards Reading, Simon rang my mobile to see what had happened to Nick. He said he hadn't gone to work as he was so worried about his brother. What I didn't know was that he had been sacked some weeks earlier – and what was more, that Nick had also lost his bar job. Simon recalls:

In the very early stages of our relapse we became friendly with a new dealer. At this point I had a company car, and Nick and I didn't look like street addicts. Nick had bumped into the dealer a couple of weeks ago when he had broken down in his Transit van. He helped him by using my company car to tow him up a steep hill, but this broke the clutch and the car was abandoned. When it was collected and the boot was emptied, drug paraphernalia was found. Andrew, my boss, came round and said, 'Come on mate, you know you aren't turning up at work, you're doing drugs again, aren't you?' Then he pulled out a needle. I tried to blame it all on Nick to save my job, but it was too late. But I knew right from the start it was going to go downhill like this.

In trying to keep their relapse and recent job losses hidden from me, Nick and Simon had placed themselves in a near impossible position. However, the power of addiction, reinforced by their closeness and loyalty as twins, meant that they would protect one another first and foremost. I doubt that Nick and Simon were at all aware of how difficult it was for Tony and me to cope; everything was once again veiled by the drugs they were taking.

Since Nick had come out of hospital three months earlier, Tony had found it very difficult to be convinced that the boys were doing well. I kept him up to date with what was happening, telling him about their jobs, our visit to Janet and David, Nick's court case, but Tony had distanced himself emotionally from my sons. Understandably, he was cautious about meeting them or even letting them come into our home. I began to take the view that perhaps the least said about them, the better. I never stopped holding on to that tiny glimmer of hope that Nick would finally come through and overcome his addiction just as Simon had done. But the strain on our marriage continued; I always found myself torn between my love for my husband and my love for my sons.

After Simon was sacked from his job, he had a stroke of luck. Another estate agency with which he had registered when he had left the rehab in May, and who were unaware of his drug background, rang him and offered him a job. He explained to me that he had already decided to find a job that offered better career prospects and the chance to earn more money. He accepted the position, knowing full well that his addiction meant he wasn't going to last long there. Once more, he frequently made up appointments with clients just to get out of the office and feed his addiction. Usually he met Nick and lent him his company car. Jason, a new dealer who had just arrived in Reading, had asked them both to sell drugs for him. Nick and Simon abused the company car so much through selling heroin day and night that eventually it broke down.

Simon soon discovered that he wasn't the only addict working for the company. Another employee frequently appeared to be 'gouging out' at his desk in front of Simon. After a few days in the job, he and Simon ended up on an appointment together and, from then on, they regularly used heroin in his car. Eventually, their boss found out what was going on. He wrote to them both, expressing disgust and disbelief that they had behaved in such a way, and they got the sack. They were to return their company cars within twenty-four hours or the cars would be reported stolen.

Nick's court order meant that he had to report weekly either to his probation officer or his substance misuse officer. So, on 12 December, one week after his court case, Nick reported to Berkshire Probation Service. Although neither of my sons had been able break the news to me or Tony, he explained to his probation officer that he had lost his bar job and that Simon had lost two estate agency jobs. By 17 December, during Nick's second appointment, he told his probation officer that he and Simon had managed to secure temporary Christmas jobs as waiters in a hotel round the corner from where they lived.

In fact, between Christmas and New Year, Tony and I had a meal at the hotel. The boys had told us that they had taken on extra evening work as waiters and as it happened they were working a shift the evening we ate there. They dared not confess to us that they had lost their jobs, but they glossed over the fact by concentrating on how much they were enjoying their temporary Christmas work, because it meant they were earning extra money to supplement their wages.

Neither Tony nor I felt able to invite my sons into our home for Christmas lunch that year. I found it very sad – it broke my heart that they weren't there on Christmas Day and I counted the hours away. But our trust had been shattered too often. Despite my belief that all was well, we couldn't take the risk.

And, by 14 January 2003, Nick and his brother had been sacked by the hotel manager, as he told his newly assigned substance misuse officer:

> We were still well enough to work before Christmas. Thank God, we both got jobs at the hotel – they desperately needed Christmas staff and we had previous experience of silver service waiting. We only lasted till 12 January. We got the sack because we were nicking the tips, stealing out of the tills behind everyone's backs. This was the only way we could get money for drugs, that's how bad it's got. Halfway through a shift, we would go into the loos and inject a snowball of heroin and crack. We had to calm ourselves in the toilets because the hit was so strong.
>
> Eventually the head waiter set me up by putting a £10 note under a napkin and waiting for me to put the money in my pocket. I was sacked. They said Simon could stay but because he defended me they told him to go as well. We're worried sick about telling Mum we are using drugs again. Both of us have a tenancy agreement with the

landlord. Mum has helped us so much, she has paid deposits on both rooms and she is our guarantor. We have got nothing, no rent, no money, everything has gone on drugs.

The magistrates had made us fully aware that it was essential for Nick to comply with the Community Rehabilitation Order; failure to do so meant that the probation service would report him for breaching the order. He would have to return to court for resentencing, which could end in a prison sentence. However, having complied with the order at first, soon Nick was reporting only irregularly to his probation officer and substance misuse officer. The probation officer later told me:

Nick was very likeable. At first he complied with his court order but things began to go wrong. It doesn't take long to see through our professional eyes that there were too many excuses, that there was something else going on. It was amazing how Nick and Simon tried to get their stories to tie up. Sometimes they got tied up in knots, and there were times when they were both very crafty. Behind it all Nick realised that he had to get off drugs if he was going to do anything at all with his life. But it was the draw of heroin and he just couldn't manage it.

He found it very difficult to walk away from the environment that he had got to know, and with his twin brother also being a drug addict, it was really hard for both of them. They loved each other to bits: neither of them were going to walk away, they followed each other everywhere. Nick was the more headstrong of the two, in my opinion anyway; many people thought Simon was the more sensible one. At times they were full of support for each other, but they would also blame each other.

When he started his CRO, Nick said his intention was to get a job. He said, 'I've got to get a really good job, because I've got to pay my mother back. I love her so much.' We tried to persuade him that because of the heroin it might take a lot longer than he realised. He said he had several years' experience in the drinks industry and he knew exactly what to do as a bar manager, but he wanted to get a much better job. He was interested in becoming an electrician, but it was again that dreadful hold that heroin had over him. Constantly, week after week, we would say, 'Have you done anything about a job?' And he always would answer, 'No, but I will, I will.' He had many excuses. They seemed plausible but there was no evidence to back them up.

By mid-January 2003, I knew something was wrong. Something about Nick was niggling at me. Physically, he didn't look too bad, although I had noticed that both he and Simon were thinner. I had sensed something wasn't right when we attended the Magistrates' Court in December, but I think I was so relieved that Nick wasn't sent to prison that I didn't want to suspect him of anything else. And I wasn't convinced that Simon, as he had said, had taken the day off work because he was so worried about his brother. Surely if that was the case he would have attended the court?

One minute I kept telling myself that I was imagining Nick and Simon were back on drugs and the next minute I was chastising myself for even entertaining the possibility. I had been very busy at work in the build-up to Christmas and I thought perhaps I was letting myself get worked up over nothing. In my mind, I kept going over the times earlier in the autumn when I had met the boys or spoken to them on the phone. They'd seemed stable and well. Was it all a pretence? Surely I wasn't so stupid as to allow them to pull the wool over my eyes again? What about the time when they had met Janet and David? Surely Janet would have told me if she thought they were back on drugs? And what about all those letters written to support Nick when he went to court? Surely Nick and Simon hadn't kept up the pretence of doing well at work and sticking with their recovery, when all the time they were back on heroin? I didn't want to be suspicious, didn't even want to think about the possibility of them going back on drugs. I didn't want to accept they had both relapsed.

Towards the end of January, Andy Smithfields, their landlord, rang me and asked if he could meet me, as he had some concerns regarding my sons. We arranged to meet in a local pub. I realised this might be a very awkward meeting, as Andy knew nothing about their previous drug history. And so it turned out.

When I got there Andy explained to me: 'There are some problems with non-payment of rent, and I feel I have to make you aware of my worries as you're their guarantor. Late autumn last year I saw Nick and Simon about their overdue rent and they reassured me they would pay their rent as soon as possible.

'The usual period of promises elapsed – "It'll be there tomorrow" or "I'll pay you next week". As I was getting very concerned about the situation, I went round to see them about Christmas time or just after. I was struck by the squalor Simon was living in. I hadn't seen them for some while because they'd kept a low profile, and I couldn't help noticing how they'd changed in appearance, the degree to which they'd deteriorated.

'Recently I've been getting a lot of reports from other residents that food is going missing from the fridges in both houses. Then my payphone went missing. Of course I don't want to believe either of them would steal deliberately from me or my other tenants, but I'm sorry to have to tell you, Elizabeth, that I've gradually become aware that there are drug issues which are bringing visitors on to my premises, unsavoury characters that I suspect are responsible for a lot of this. I've started to get extremely concerned because of my responsibility to my other tenants.'

As I listened to Andy I knew I had to make a decision. Either I had to pretend to be shocked that he could dare to suggest my sons could be involved with drugs or I had to tell him the truth. As I opened my mouth to speak he continued: 'If you're unaware of the consequences of drugs, Elizabeth, this may be a very sharp learning curve. The financial issues are quite serious. But my other concern is for Nick and Simon's safety and their health, as well as the welfare of my other tenants.'

At that moment all my suspicions were confirmed. Nick and Simon were heroin addicts again.

Andy deserved the truth. What would be the point of me lying to him? Even though I knew he had every right to throw the boys out if I told him the facts, I felt that he was such a decent, good-hearted person that I had no choice. To my relief, when I had explained to him the pitiful scenario, he said that he felt inclined to let the year's tenancy run its course, providing the boys shared one room. In this way he could at least rent the other room to someone else. He said: 'Elizabeth, this is clearly a very stressful time for you and the family. I can see all of this is having a deep effect on you and obviously it must be affecting you and Tony very badly. I also genuinely feel sorry for your sons. They both seem to me to be extremely personable and to be people who could make a great success of their lives if drugs hadn't taken hold of them.'

As guarantor for Nick and Simon, I had to honour my obligation and pay the unpaid rent, a considerable amount of money.

They had told Andy that they had applied for housing benefit, which presumably had been spent on drugs. To his credit, Andy did everything he could to help my sons. I was very touched by this, given that he only knew them in his professional capacity. He even took the trouble to speak with Nick's probation officer, as he didn't want to see Nick and Simon homeless and sleeping rough. Until the end of August, at least they had somewhere to live. Months later he told me:

> I suppose I believed there could be a solution, but I was unaware just how drugs had gripped your sons. I thought there was hope for them. It was a very painful period of time for me, one fraught with worry for yourself, the boys and the safety of my other tenants. It was probably the first time I've come across a situation where I felt absolutely powerless. In the end there was nothing I could do, no words, no gestures, nothing had any effect. It was a very sad experience. I was very angry about the system that enabled all that to happen to them, very angry with the people who supply drugs. It makes my blood boil.

All that Andy had told me was confirmed when I confronted the boys. The many sleepless nights, racked with pain and worry, when I hung on to a thread of hope, had come to nothing. And still the spectre of reprisals from the twins' drug dealers, old ones and new ones, kept haunting me.

After meeting Andy, I felt physically sick and emotionally exhausted. But my next task, and my biggest worry, was yet again to tell Tony about Nick and Simon's new debts. By now he and I were at breaking point, financially and emotionally. Within a couple of days he gave me an ultimatum: 'It's either me or your boys.'

8
Tough Love

I WAS FULL of anger and resentment towards Tony. I couldn't believe he'd asked me to choose between him and my sons. How had it come to this? I despised him for placing me in such a position. Yet, on the other hand, because of my continually 'rescuing' my sons, I had overlooked the fact that Tony was also a victim and was suffering too. He too had cashed in all his savings to bail his stepsons out. I knew this hurt him far more than he openly admitted. I realised how much he loved me, how much he really cared for me; how terrible it must have been for him to witness his wife, time and time again, experience disappointment and fear because her sons were heroin addicts. I couldn't expect Tony to feel the same about his stepsons as I, their mother, did. But why now, on top of all the anxiety and stress, did my husband have to present me with this ultimatum?

Tony tried to explain: 'I'm in a difficult situation – between a rock and a hard place. As I've said to you previously, I want to support you and the boys. I'm trying to take it on board that I'll be working till I'm seventy-two – there can be no retirement for me, we'll have to remortgage the house because of all the drug debts. The way we're living is destroying us. Heroin addiction hasn't just changed the boys' lives, it's changed everything in our lives too. It's very hard to cope emotionally, let alone financially. Can't you see we have nothing else to give Nick and Simon? We're on the road to ruin.'

Listening to what Tony was trying to explain to me, it should have been obvious that there was nothing else to give to my sons. Several times in the past I'd had to come clean to him what a huge debt I had accrued by helping the boys. Had I been able to think clearly and be more logical, I might have been more sensible much earlier, but I wasn't able to do that. Perhaps I was just unwilling to recognise the hard truth that, sooner or later, I would have to choose.

To walk away from my sons was surely impossible. But whom should I choose – my husband or my sons? I couldn't contemplate making such a choice. Or was I just being bloody stupid? I agonised through the night.

I continued to seethe with rage for several days. I was angry with myself, with my sons and with Tony. Unable to sleep, I wondered night after night how many other families go through a similar nightmare. Do they have someone to talk to? Where does one find help? Is there anyone who can offer guidance or understanding on how to cope? Is it really about just walking away from those you love? How do other mothers, other parents, cope with these emotions? How do you emotionally separate yourself from those you love?

The only place where I could find any peace of mind was at work. There, I could escape from the anxiety of heroin addiction for several hours by focusing on my work with the children. They were my lifeline to normality. I no longer wanted to go home after work. The atmosphere between Tony and I had become unbearable. I went to stay with my friend Rosemary and her husband Steve. I needed some space to escape the pressure of Tony's ultimatum. Rosemary recalls:

> It was an awful time for you and Tony. You didn't have anywhere to sleep when you left. Steve persuaded you to come and stay with us but you had left the house with nothing to wear, you didn't even have a toothbrush with you. At the time you said you weren't going back to Tony for anything, so I went with you to Marks and Spencer's and you bought a few clothes to wear for school. You were plodding around, hardly talking, you were like a zombie and I could see you were struggling with so many thoughts in your head after school.

> Eventually you did go home, because you knew what you had to do. But I have to say that I agree entirely with what Jo, a recovering heroin addict, told me when she later heard your story. She said to me, 'What that couple went through, you wouldn't wish on your worst enemy. Many addicts don't realise or even think about the impact of their addiction on their families and the lives of their families. Their story certainly had a massive impact on me. It really hit home to me the damage and worry I caused to my parents and close family. Elizabeth and Tony must have gone through hell.'

When I eventually returned home to Tony we both knew the truth. Nick and Simon's addiction made it impossible for them either to understand or care about the impact it had on anyone in the family. The only thing that mattered to them was where their next needle full of heroin was coming from.

I struggled to find the emotional resolve to walk away and let them hit rock bottom. Yes, I admitted to Tony and to the few close friends who knew about the situation, I had repeatedly taken pity on my sons because of what many may argue was misguided love for them. By secretly paying off debts, by paying for detoxification and rehab, by cashing in savings and insurances and getting more and more into debt, I had embarked on a voyage of personal destruction. And inevitably Tony had been drawn into the cycle.

It's plain to me now that I didn't know how to focus on myself or Tony any more because I had spent all my time focusing on my sons' addiction. I believed it was my responsibility as their mother to stand by them no matter what. Without exception, mothers who have subsequently spoken to me about this situation have said that, in my place, they would have done exactly the same. At last, however, I came to the realisation that I needed to choose Tony rather than my sons. Nick and Simon's situation was hopeless. We needed to focus on ourselves if we were to survive as a couple.

But, if I responded to Tony's ultimatum by deciding to put him first, could I really find the peace of mind to live a normal life with him, without being consumed with guilt that I had turned my back on my sons, without feeling deep resentment towards him? Somehow I had to find the emotional resolve to do so.

Then something quite shocking happened, finally helping me to make my decision. One afternoon during the February half-term of 2003, still in an angry mood with everyone and perhaps even 'playing for time' to delay my response to Tony, I agreed to give Nick a lift to meet his probation officer. I was still making sure Nick got to his appointments on time, in order to comply with his Community Rehabilitation Order. When I picked my sons up, Nick sat in the front passenger seat and Simon was in the back. I could see from the minute Nick got into my car that he was in a terrible state. His speech was slurred as if he was very drunk.

As I was driving, I became aware of Nick putting his right hand into the top pocket of his shirt. I thought he was about to take out his cigarette lighter. With one eye on the road and one eye on Nick's hand, I caught sight of a needle. I demanded to know why Nick had brought a needle into my car. Then, as I drove, Nick found a vein in his left arm and injected in front of me. I will never forget those few minutes as he lifted the skin on his arm in search of a vein to dig the needle into. It was repulsive and terrifying to see my son do this to himself.

My eyes darted between the traffic on the road and the veins in Nick's arms. I felt icy cold and at the same time I broke out in huge beads of sweat. My head spun. I felt as if I was about to faint and be sick. I heard Simon say angrily: 'Nick, you shouldn't have banged up in front of Mum, it's not fair to put her through seeing you do that. What the hell are you thinking of?' Nick didn't reply. He was out of his head as the heroin circulated through his veins.

I was lost for words as we drove into the car park near the probation office. As I brought the car to a halt, the boys got out. But I held on to the steering wheel with both hands, put my head forward and breathed deeply to stop myself from being sick. I reflected on my many recent conversations with Tony. One in particular came to mind.

'Have you forgotten about the times I went out and paid the drug dealers off?' he asked me. 'Let me remind you, I'm embroiled in this seedy world too. Sometimes I withdrew thousands of pounds a day to pay them off. I drew out £3,800 from one bank to make up a payment of £4,500 to one dealer. That wasn't the only policy I had to cash in. I went to meet a dealer once with £2,000 in my pocket and handed it to a runner because the dealer wouldn't meet me. The very last one I paid off for Nick was when he assured me it was a loan he had forgotten about and I said to the guy, "Don't let him borrow more money from you."

'We've both been emotionally blackmailed by the twins. I know we weren't actually being physically threatened, but if the twins didn't pay off their drug debts, we knew they would get beaten up. And the dealers might find out where we lived because they still wanted their money. The dealers never showed themselves to me face to face – although, as you well know, I always took an iron bar with me to protect myself. But one night they saw my car registration number and I wondered whether they would be able to track us down. I made it clear to a runner once that I would retaliate if they attacked my family. And if that doesn't make you realise why I've given you the ultimatum "it's either me or your boys", I don't know what will.'

As I sat in the car, I muttered to myself, '"It's either me or the boys." I've made my decision.'

Inside the probation office, I asked for a glass of water and tried to pull myself together. I told the probation officer what I had witnessed. I realised, as I sat waiting for my sons, that no matter how much love and support I gave Nick and Simon, only they could get themselves better. No amount of money, love or support would ever cure my addicted sons. I remember very little of the rest of that day other than the quiet acceptance that my help had been counterproductive. Hard as it was, I had to let go. As I said goodbye to Nick and Simon when I dropped them off, I knew I wouldn't be seeing them again until they themselves had made the effort to change. And I had to change as well.

Over the following weekend, sitting in the warmth of the spring sunshine in my garden, I picked up my pen and wrote:

Tough Love

One day, it just happened
The hope died, the dream was gone
I realised I had done everything
There is now nothing more I can do.

Thousands and thousands of pounds
Lost to drugs, to dealers and to pins in arms,
Our house about to be remortgaged
So many times our lives have been wrecked.
My decision to break with my sons was made.

It's been like I imagine it to be in war
A battle, but charging at your own life to save it
And yet, trying too, to save the lives of others.
Eventually you win or lose.
I have lost everything – except a mother's love for her sons.

I lay my head upon the pillow so many times
Water – can you call it 'tears'? – pours from my eyes
In my mind I plan their funerals, choose the music,
The hymns, the readings and who I will ask to be there.
The dream has gone, I knew it would in the end.

I remember, through flashbacks, those certain special times
The day they had their first bikes, the times we went skiing,
The love, the cuddles, the laughter
The mother I was, now replaced with an inner scream of pain
As I know my sons are near to death.

They know, whenever they die, that I loved them –
I cared for them, I did everything I could for them
But my dreams for them have already died
In pain, not ever really to be cried.

I didn't tell Tony straight away that I had made my decision. I wrote a letter to my sons first, and a few days later I felt strong enough to talk to Tony about it. I vividly remember the look of sheer relief on his face when I told him I had made my choice. We talked a great deal about the future. Together, we rang British Telecom and arranged to change our telephone numbers so they couldn't keep blagging me or Tony for help or money. Together, we made an appointment to see the manager at the building society to remortgage our house. Together, we listed all the debts, financial losses, cashed-in insurances surrendered by Tony to heroin dealers. The total at this stage was over £70,000. Dreadful though it was to face up to it all, at last we were working together to try to rescue our marriage, our home and our love.

But as Tony said to me later in the week: 'Don't think that tough love is the answer to all your prayers and everything in the garden is going to be rosy overnight simply by posting a letter to them. Your decision to exercise tough love isn't going to work overnight, the change you make has to be an ongoing process for both you and me. Make no mistake about it, we still face a dreadful future financially, for how long a period I don't know. I think the biggest obstacle you face is to regain my trust. But perhaps, just perhaps, tough love is the start of a journey for us both to begin rebuilding our lives. I have no intention of leaving you because I still love you and I feel a certain amount of responsibility to support you in the best way I can, but we'll just have to see what happens in the end.'

A couple of days later, I posted the letter. I didn't expect a reply; I wondered whether they would even open their post. As I put it into the post box at the bottom of the road, I felt an overwhelming mixture of emotions, but I knew that I meant what I had written:

I have decided to write to you rather than speak to you on the phone or in person. A letter can sometimes say far more than a meeting or a phone call. The time has come for you both to sort your lives out and face up to your problems and sort them out for yourselves without me being in the picture at all.

As your mum and your friend, I have given this a great deal of thought and in arriving at my decision I know it is borne out of love for you. Only you can sort out your lives, not me. I cannot do anything more to help you. I cannot keep you off drugs, only you can do that, it is your choice, not mine.

I am sure you both know that I will always love you and what I am doing now is an act of 'tough love' to walk away from you and let you stand alone to conquer your addiction.

I have never been able to walk away from you before. A mother doesn't do that to her children, whatever their age. I learnt that from my own mother. On the contrary, I have tried to understand you both, to support you financially and to help you overcome your addiction. Foolishly, I have even enabled you by giving you money for drugs because I felt sorry for you when you were clucking. I helped you to get into hospital, in Slovakia and to the Florence Nightingale Hospital, into the Detox 5 hospital and Yeldall Rehab. It was the wrong thing to do. You have to want to get better and do it all for yourselves.

I have sacrificed my own savings, my time, and nearly my marriage to Tony. I gave my moral support and now there is nothing left for me to give you except this act of tough love; I would tell all parents in the same situation to do the same. If it was not for Tony standing by me, I do not know where I would be right now. What it has done to him is terrible and, even worse, his pain and emotions have gone unnoticed. Your addiction has consumed our lives too.

I hope that you will both be able to find the way forward in future years. I hope that you will be able to find work and lead a drug-free life eventually. Many people do recover from addiction. I was speaking to someone today from Narcotics Anonymous and he has been clean for five years and now works for them.

I don't want you to end up homeless or in prison. If you do sort your lives out I hope that you will get in contact. Tony and I would like nothing more than to have a happy relationship with you both. That is all we have ever wanted.

I do wish you well but please do not contact me again until you are off drugs, whether that takes months or years. Hold on to the fact that you have been and always will be loved.

Simon and Nick did receive the letter. They tried to phone me at home, not realising that our telephone numbers had been changed. So they rang me at work. As soon as I heard Nick's voice say, 'Hello, Mum', I put the receiver down. It was very upsetting to do this, but my resolve was firm.

Tough love was also about learning to give much more of my

time to Tony, particularly to listen to how he felt and not just to focus on my own hurt. It was about making him feel that he mattered and recognising the added strain brought to him, as an only child, by the sudden death of his father. Following years of estrangement, our marriage had brought Tony and his father much closer – and there was a further blow when Tony discovered that a relative was contesting his father's will because Bernard had included Tony in it. He wasn't gong to inherit millions of pounds, but it would have helped to redress his financial losses. Thankfully his three aunts and his uncle had a 'whip round' for him from their own inheritance.

I also needed to understand that Tony didn't have as many people to turn to as I did. I had a counsellor on whom to offload all the problems and anxieties I faced. He said that his lifeline and his beacon of hope were our elderly neighbours, Bob and Phyllis. They had listened to his moans and groans, his thoughts and concerns, and had helped him get through. They never took sides, but he gained strength from their willingness to listen to him, their understanding of how he felt.

Tony had felt on several occasions that our marriage was over because of the drugs. But he was sure that if I meant what I said, we would pull through. He couldn't leave me to cope with two young men who were emotionally destroying me, but he couldn't see them as his stepsons any more. He had to detach himself from them. As he later explained:

> I know I've been accused of not giving you emotional support. But what do you do when everything around you is lies, deceit and cons because of drugs? Your life starts to fall apart, your marriage and your finances are in shreds. I know it was tough for you when I gave you the ulti-matum. But I took what I considered to be the best course

of action for both of us. My back was against the wall, they weren't my children, and their own father had disowned them. My emotional support was there if you looked for it, but I saw practical support like trying to hold everything together as more important at the time, in that way at least there could be something there for us at the end of this.

What more could Tony have done? Tough love was also about understanding that his emotions and his sanity too were in turmoil. We needed to reach out and support each other, be determined not to lose everything. It was hard to hear, but Tony felt I hated him. He told me how isolated he felt, how little inner strength he had left. But he had hung on to his love of music, his bloody-minded determination and, despite everything, the love he had for me:

> Even though there was deceit and lies from all three parties, without holding on to these things, I really don't know what I would have done. I did go off the rails a bit now and then with drink and I'm sorry for being volatile, grouchy and cantankerous. It was because I had no support from my immediate family. I felt on my own and when you've had a few years of things going on behind your back, it's really draining. If I hadn't had the strength to deal with our demise, in the best way I could, I may have done the unthinkable and topped myself. Now I can hold my head up high and even feel some pride in what we achieved together in the end.

The knife of heroin addiction had sliced a big wound into our marriage, but maybe now the healing process could begin.

Simon explains how he and Nick reacted when they realised I had decided to let go of my sons and the problems of their addiction:

> When Mum cut us off us Nick and I were dumbstruck. We gave up on ourselves because we were so disappointed that we had relapsed. Only a few months ago we'd both been off heroin, but once we had the opportunity to start again, inside a short space of time we were addicted once more and in a worse situation. We knew Mum meant what she had written and that she wasn't going to spend twenty or thirty thousand pounds to bail us out this time. The realisation that we had lost her support hit us hard; the fact that she didn't want to know us any more, didn't even want to speak to us, really upset us. But at the same time, the drugs were making us say, 'Oh, f––– it.' We accepted that we were going to die young because of the lifestyle we were living as addicts. We used to say, 'We won't be alive when we are thirty-five.'

Now that I finally had the strength to exercise tough love and focus on myself and Tony, I also had to accept that I would be completely in the dark about what might happen to my sons. I no longer knew what they were doing or how they were living. I could only hope and pray that they might eventually come to their senses and find the will and determination to give up heroin and put their lives in order.

Despite the shock that I had severed contact with them, they later explained to me, their sole concern the day they read my letter was to find a way of getting their drugs, now they could no longer blag money from me. Inevitably this brought them into contact with the homeless scene in Reading. They got to know drug users living on the streets, as well as new dealers. On the street, the way to make money for drugs is by thieving from supermarkets, stealing handbags or mobile phones. And they became reacquainted with their former dealers. Nick recalled that it didn't take long before they were 'invited to start a business' with one of the main dealers in the area and began to sell thousands of pounds worth of heroin a day for him. Simon explained to me what had gone on:

> During the period when you cut us off, there was a massive escalation in our drug dealing. You need to understand how the big dealers think. The reason our dealer wanted Nick and me and our other addict friends working for him is because we were all 'bang on the gear', completely addicted. That meant we knew all the other people on it too. Therefore other addicts knew they could come to us for their gear at any time of the day or night. In fact we were earning a hell of a lot of money when things were going well with the main dealer. Sometimes we could make six to seven thousand pounds a day selling heroin for him. At the time we loved it because, for every grand we gave him, we got a couple of hundred quid for our own habit. We were literally working twenty-four hours a day selling drugs and injecting heroin and crack cocaine. We didn't think about anything except drugs. We just went with the pace of that life. We only had a couple of hours' sleep in three or four days.

When addicts begin to 'work' for a dealer, they regard it as a weird kind of privilege. The dealer sets his addicts up by creating a mobile phone number for them, and sometimes a place to deal from. Then he provides them with a bag of heroin and a bag of crack cocaine, advising them that once they are halfway through the bags they are to ring him for more. Within a couple of hours, the dealer will deliver more heroin and crack, and collect the money which his 'dealer addicts' have made for him. As long as the money is handed over immediately, the addict's habits are well looked after. Nick and Simon's dealer used to put them up in hotels and even hired a car for them so they could deliver the drugs. Simon recalls:

> It seems incredible now, but we were chuffed if we got a good workload from our dealer. It was sheer relief to us both; not only were we kept, but our habit was taken care of as well. We didn't have the worry of trying to go and steal. The problem was that every bit of money we made went straight into our arms. We didn't think about making 'real money'. Every little bit went on drugs. We just wanted more and more. We were working twenty-four hours a day, seven days a week and we never switched the phone off once. We were even asked to be 'mules' by our dealer but we refused.

Not long ago, I met one recovering addict, a woman named Olivia who had known both my sons during this period. I spent several hours talking to her and she reiterated everything Nick and Simon had told me. Olivia worked for the same dealer as the twins, and ultimately she became a 'mule', carrying drugs back-wards and forwards from Jamaica to Britain.

Her heroin addiction meant she, like many others, would do anything to get their drugs, taking huge risks with their own freedom. As a 'mule' she agreed to fly to Jamaica to collect a suit-case full of heroin and bring it back to the UK. She told me that it was the most stupid decision she ever made. She was caught at

the airport with five kilograms of heroin hidden inside the suit-
case:

Drugs were professionally built into the suitcase. I'm
convinced I was set up as a decoy because there were
several of us involved. When the others walked into the
airport, they weren't stopped, they got through customs.
But I was arrested immediately. I was carrying drugs
worth £95,000 a kilo, it had to be half a million street
value I had in my case.

My dealer asked Nick and Simon many times to be mules
for him, he was constantly on at them both to go as their
flights and hotel would be paid for. But they wouldn't do
it. Thank God they didn't. When I went, I got put in a
hotel with the others. We were the only people there, it
was crazy, horrible. I hated it. It's not part of my life I want
to think about now. It's madness, the things you do for
heroin. The big dealers try to put this risk on anyone they
can, anyone who will bring them back enough gear so
they can make loads of money.

Olivia and I talked for a long time about what happened to her
after she was arrested. She ended up with a prison sentence of
three and a half years, which she served in a Jamaican jail. There
she learnt a lot about the life of poor Jamaicans:

I'm not making excuses for them but you need to know
this. What people don't realise is that some Jamaicans
come over to this country to earn money to send back to
their families. They see drugs as a means of supporting
their families. They set themselves up in a flat or bedsit

from where they work as a drug dealer, they may not necessarily live there in case they get caught. Ten pounds here is worth $1,000 in Jamaica.

They come over here to send the drugs money back because they can't buy a house out there. They have to build a house themselves and this is how they start out. They buy a little plot of land and then build the house on the land. That's what all the money that they earn from drugs goes towards. Their families have nothing. They live in sheds and huts. You've not seen anything like it, it's awful.

When I was over there I got to know several of the prison officers, they were my friends more than the inmates were. Once, when I was cleaning, I got talking to them. They've literally got nothing out there, just a little plot of land and a couple of hundred quid. Even one of our wardens was a mule. She never got caught, but she later died of cancer. She used to take the flights every year, make the money and go back over – that's how she was building her house. She told me that herself. But that's the side of life tourists never see, they don't realise it even exists.

On the one occasion that Simon, Olivia and I met together, they told me of the dark days with Nick at the height of their addiction. Both were at pains to emphasise how violent and ruthless drug dealers, and particularly the Jamaican yardies, are. Olivia said: 'They're the kind of people who wouldn't think twice about raping anyone. Nick, Simon and I knew one girl who was deliberately filled full of crack cocaine by a dealer and raped. He held her hostage for days, he even raped her friend. This happened in a council flat, so he was milking the system even more – he was claiming benefit for the flat while he was earning half a million to a million quid a year from dealing drugs.'

I was horrified to learn that one dealer who was owed a considerable amount of money by Nick and Simon had told someone to kill them both. As Simon explained: 'Because of our addiction we got deeper and deeper into ripping off our dealer. We stole hundreds of pounds from him over a period of about six months. We stole all his customers and undercut him, we sold them heroin and crack cheaper than he did, or in bigger bags, until we could get some money. We stole £15,000 in cash from him and converted it into drugs. There were police chases as well. We were chased by undercover police who turned up when we were meeting people to deliver drugs. Once I hid under a car to avoid a police helicopter. They used the arc-light to search gardens to find us. I legged it but Nick hid round the corner.'

Olivia went on to confirm the story: 'Yes, it's true; the same dealer rang me repeatedly to ask where the twins were. He kept saying to me, "I know they've stolen it, I know they've stolen it." I heard he'd contracted someone to go and kill them, literally to go and shoot them. And he would have done, believe me. These people just don't care.'

And Simon added: 'The dealer said, "The next time I see Nick, he is a dead man." That was the worst period in our lives. I think I lost about five stone in four months from doing heroin. I went from being quite chubby when I was in recovery to skin and bone. At the time we protected the family from understanding just how serious the whole thing was. But when you're actually living it, it's not that serious to you.

'Heroin addiction is so selfish; it's all about just getting your gear at the end of the day. You're prepared to do anything to earn that money and the more money you can earn, the more gear you can get. And when you get it, you don't think, "Well, I might need money in the next few hours." As soon as you've done your hit, you're wasted, then you're back up, awake and you've got to get more money for more drugs.'

Olivia interrupted: 'We had lots and lots of forged notes. We sent Nick to another dealer with them to buy lots of heroin and crack. Nick handed them over notes and came back to the flat. We were all sticking together by then. This dealer put a price on our heads because of all this forged money.'

Tough love meant that I could only imagine from one day to the next what would become of my sons. The phrase 'tough love' was easy to say, easy to convince myself of, but it was tough for me as it went against all my instincts. Slowly, however, I trained myself to accept that it was their responsibility to sort themselves out. Had I known the depths to which they had sunk, I am not sure how I would have coped. Simon explained later:

Our lives deteriorated dramatically over the next few months. We had seriously annoyed our main dealer and he wouldn't let us work for him. He delegated the responsibility to other people because he didn't trust us any more, although there was the odd day when he let us deal. We lived among the down-and-outs and even guarded the prostitutes' houses when they were doing sex for drugs. We talked to the prostitutes to make sure they were OK.

Things picked up a bit when we started dealing for a smaller dealer, though we were only selling £500 to £1,000 a day rather than £5,000 upwards as we had done for our main dealer. But that didn't last long. Another dealer said he would shoot us both when he found us. Once again, we smoked and injected all our dealers' money and drugs, so we had no money to give him for what we had sold. We owed him massive amounts.

Once, in June 2003, we tried to contact Mum. We stuck a note through her door and asked her to meet us at the bottom of the road. Nick said he'd taken seventy valium tablets and told her he'd tried to commit suicide. This was a blag just to get money out of her, but we used to take valium regularly, usually ten to fifteen tablets, and then inject on top. We did it to escape reality, because we couldn't cope with the emotional wrecks we had turned ourselves into.

It had got to the point where we couldn't walk around Reading because the dealers wanted us. We had to be very careful where we went for our own safety, even the street users would grass us up for heroin if they spotted us. Nick and I were really scared that we couldn't go into Reading to score. We were reduced to hanging around with an addict who was in a real mess, but we were in a real mess too. We started befriending people who looked dreadful and we really went downhill. Now we were the nobodies, the down-and-outs. We had nothing, no motivation to get on with our lives. We'd completely given up on ourselves and Nick had accepted the fact he would go to prison because he had failed to comply with his Community Rehabilitation Order. We stole from shops on a regular basis – baby clothes, booze, food. Anything we could get to sell for heroin.

It was now July 2003. Almost six months had passed since I cut myself off from my sons. I faltered in my resolve just once when, by chance, I saw Nick and Simon sitting on the side of the road in the gutter, near Wokingham. I pulled my car over to see if they were all right, simply to check that they hadn't been injured in a road accident. I never told anyone but Rosemary what I had done because they were both in an appalling state from 'clucking' as they did not have any heroin – they were vomiting, sweating and very ill.

I went to a cash machine and gave them some money and then I drove off. I can't put into words how I felt about my sons lying in the gutter, the guilt I felt about giving them money for drugs. When I told Rosemary, it was the only time she ever got angry with me. As she explains:

> I was really cross with Elizabeth for doing this. I told her that she should have driven on and ignored them, to which she replied, 'What would you have done if they were your children, Rosemary? Would you drive past if you saw your son or daughter lying in the gutter?' I realised if I was totally honest that I probably would have done the same.

> I didn't know what to say to her; I don't know how she kept her sanity. It was absolutely shocking what heroin addiction did to her and Tony.

The next day I wrote:

Six Months On
July, six months on
A myriad of emotions, yet
Still the love never dies. Why?

How painful it has been,
Yet, always I hold in my heart
that tiny glimmer of hope for change.
My photographs capture their
Slow demise towards death.
Filthy, ragged, dirty sons
Possessed by cravings, possessed by needles
Lying in the gutter –
No longer are they recognisable as my sons.
Frozen emotions.
At times I am walking in an empty body,
Unable to breathe from the maternal stabbing,
Release me from this motherly love
Will change ever come?

In mid-July, Andy Smithfields contacted me to remind me that the tenancy agreement on Nick and Simon's room was about to run out. If they had nowhere to live, they would be on the streets. He had a new tenant moving in on 1 September, so he asked me to ensure that the room was vacated by 31 August. Andy had held on to his belief that perhaps he could help Nick and Simon to change, although in the end he too realised that nobody could help them, that the desire to change had to come from them. But it was his request that, in late July, brought me back into contact with my sons.

I had no choice but to visit them. I couldn't really face it; I intended to pin a note to the door to remind them about leaving and then just go. Seeing them in the gutter some weeks earlier had been bad enough, it was hard to imagine what they might look like now. Would I see any evidence of change? I doubted it very much, but inwardly I hoped and hoped. I knew that I must maintain my resolve not to rescue them or try to fix things for them. This wasn't the time to succumb to emotional blackmail or to feel sorry for them.

When I found them in their flat, the 'reunion' was charged with emotion. We went together over the road and sat outside a pub. They looked awful. Words cannot adequately describe their appearance, but the pictures I took of them speak the truth. It seemed that they had finally reached rock bottom.

After I reminded them about vacating their room, Nick told me that he had been summoned to attend Slough Magistrates' Court, as he had indeed breached the Community Rehabilitation Order. His probation officer wanted to see him the next day, so a full pre-sentence report could be prepared for a later court hearing. Like everyone who worked to support Nick, she was a dedicated and committed professional; indeed, he told me on many occasions how much regard he had for her and how hard she and others had tried to help him. She wanted to recommend to the courts that Nick should be referred to reside at a probation or bail hostel as soon as possible and that he should be given a Drug Treatment and Testing Order, commonly known as a DTTO. She believed a DTTO was appropriate because he was addicted to heroin and committed crime to pay for his drug habit, but wanted help in making changes in his life in order to escape from drugs and crime.

If passed, a DTTO would sentence Nick to serve his punishment in the community under the supervision of the National Probation Service. He would be ordered to stop taking drugs and offending. Treatment would be given for his drug problem and he would be tested regularly for drug misuse. Health staff, including doctors and nurses, would work closely with probation staff to help him. The courts would regularly review his progress and set him targets. But the courts could only sentence Nick to a DTTO if he agreed to it.

Both Nick and Simon told me that they had recently been to see a drugs counsellor at a Reading prescribing agency. Nick said: 'Life is dramatically worse for both of us. We've realised we must do something – there must be a way out of this without involving you, Mum, emotionally and financially. That's why we've been to get ourselves on to the NHS Subutex Programme. It's our first attempt at recognising that we have to do something for ourselves.' He hoped to start his Subutex programme if he could get into a rehabilitation unit near Swindon run by the Salvation Army, or if he went to a bail hostel, it would be supervised there. He was due back in court on 15 August. 'I could end up in prison,' he said.

They had been to the homelessness department at the local council offices to ask for help, and Simon said that they had also been to see Mandy Goodliffe, the Cranstoun worker dealing with accommodation for addicts. Set up as a charity in 1969 to meet the needs of people like Simon and Nick who have drug and alcohol problems, Cranstoun Drug Services is now part of the network of local community drug agencies. It offers an opportunity for people to focus on rebuilding their lives. Simon was keen to tell me that he was also going to see a rehab in Bristol. Both sons knew that they must try to get into separate rehabilitation programmes.

I wanted to throw my arms round my sons and tell them they could come and live with me and everything would be OK – but I knew I couldn't do that. There was so much I wanted to say to them but I didn't know where to begin. They repeatedly told me, 'We're so sorry, Mum. This isn't us, we aren't like this, it's the drugs that have done this to us.' As if I didn't know. I felt heart-broken. But I knew tears couldn't solve their addiction. I cried privately, later.

Before I said goodbye, I told Nick and Simon that Ruth, a work colleague, had offered Tony and me the use of her caravan in

Cornwall and we had decided to accept the opportunity to have a break together. We were off the next day for ten days, our first chance of a holiday together for a long time. It would be good to walk by the sea, along the cliff tops, to breathe in fresh air away from the stench of heroin. We hoped to walk, visit antique shops, go to the Eden Project and the Lost Gardens of Heligan, enjoy ice creams – and laugh. A year earlier I couldn't have done that, but tough love meant I was changing.

We arrived in Cornwall on 3 August, and for the next ten days we did all we had set out to achieve. But each night, as my husband slept, I lay awake, once again wondering when it would all end. I trained myself to prepare for every eventuality. 'How long will it be before Nick goes to prison?' I kept thinking. 'How would I keep that a secret from everyone?' Night after night I had to remind myself to focus on reality – heroin kills and it could well kill Nick and Simon. 'Think through how you'll deal with this when it happens, when they die,' I muttered to myself. 'If it doesn't happen, then it will be a bonus.'

Halfway through the holiday my mind turned to Nick's impending court case, which was to be heard the day after we returned from Cornwall. 'Should I go?' I asked myself. 'Should I witness him sent to prison? Will he be ordered to live at a probation hostel? Do I keep out of it? What might other mothers, other families do if they were in the same situation?'

Unable to sleep, I got up in the middle of the night and wrote the following letter:

My name is Elizabeth Burton-Phillips. I am the mother of Nicholas Stephen and I would like to come to court on Friday 15th August. To be honest, I'm scared to come to court but if I do, I can tell you what drugs really do to families, many families, like mine. I am in the invidious position of being the mother not just to one heroin addict – my son Nicholas – but also to his identical twin brother, Simon. Their addiction to heroin has been ongoing since just after their 21st birthday in November 1997, nearly six years.

I would like you to consider the whole picture concerning my son's heroin addiction. I hope that this family information, together with the pre-sentence reports which have been put together by the probation service, will enable you to reach a decision today. I see a very bleak and short future for Nicholas and indeed his brother Simon.

My sons come from a very ordinary, middle-class, educated family background. I have 31 years' teaching experience, their father has a background in engineering and IT. Both sons have been well educated, achieving nine GCSEs, but drugs meant they did not complete their A level courses. Until heroin addiction entered his life, Nicholas wanted to train to be an electrician or to work in electronics.

As a mother, my experience and my family's experience of heroin addiction means I have seen both my sons become liars, thieves, and in Nicholas's case a criminal. This is not easy for any parent to accept – but it is the truth. I believe that the real victims of heroin addiction are my family, who have been devastated by what has happened to them emotionally, financially and psychologically. This is what drugs do to families. Like terrorism, drugs destroy lives.

A combination of panic, desperation to help, lack of knowledge and complete naïvety has created this nightmare and hardship at a time in our lives when we should be looking forward to retirement. We have cashed in all our savings to clear their rent debts and unpaid bills, and most distressing of all, my husband has paid numerous debts to drug dealers in order to avoid violence towards ourselves or my sons. I should add that we were not successful in the latter as both sons have been on the receiving end of violence from drug dealers. To date the financial fallout from this addiction is over £70,000. I say this with absolute confidence as my husband (Nick's stepfather) and I had to remortgage our property in March this year in order to rescue ourselves from the spiralling debt caused by their addiction.

I foolishly believed that I was helping my sons by solving their debt problems. When I took pity on them, I damaged their recovery. In fact, I was merely enabling them to continue a habit. The decision to withdraw from my sons' lives, so that they face up to this situation and learn to deal with it themselves, was very hard to make. It will possibly be difficult for you or others who have no experience of heroin addiction to understand but the strain and pressure on my marriage had become unbearable. But it was the right thing to do as now they realise that the road ahead cannot be taken for granted and only they can put this situation right.

I am unable to have them in my home because I know from experience that they will steal from my purse, steal my credit card, or personal belongings to pay for heroin.

This is why I emphasise that I believe that the real victims of heroin addiction are often the mothers and families of the addicts who wait and watch as this drug eats up every part of their lives, personalities and, as we have seen in the media, brings total misery to the lives of all those who love them. Never a day goes by when I do not quietly consider how I will be able to deal with both their deaths from this dreadful addiction. This is not exaggerating, merely keeping in touch with reality.

I appreciate that, as magistrates, your prime responsibility is to deal with Nick as the law allows you to. All I can ask is that you look at the wider picture given to you today by myself as his mother, and by the pre-sentence reports. What drugs do to families is unbelievable. It cripples them in every way you can imagine.

Thank you for taking the time to read this letter. I can only leave the matter and decision in your hands.

I stared at the words I had written. Should I tear the letter up? Should I post it to the court? Or should I go and watch my son being sent to prison if the magistrates felt that was the shock he needed? What would I do if I were a magistrate hearing Nick's case? Would the next step of Nick's terrible journey really be prison? I fell asleep agitated and fearful.

9
Stigma and Shame

WHEN TONY AND I returned from our holiday in Cornwall, I was still in a quandary as to whether I should attend Nick's court hearing. I didn't post the letter that I had written to the magistrates, but I didn't throw it away either. I was very cautious about the possibility of being drawn back into the cycle of co-dependency from which I had tried hard to break free. During the last few months, I had changed my behaviour and I was determined not to relapse. Life for Tony and me was slowly improving and we were looking after each other. That had to be my key focus.

At Tony's suggestion, I voiced my concerns to Nick's probation officer and solicitor. Both gave me their professional opinion of the likely outcome of his case. After speaking to them, I decided that I would attend the hearing; the only thing that would ease my anxiety was to be in court and to hear the end result myself.

As advised, I took my letter with me and gave it to Nick's solicitor who, in turn, passed a copy to the magistrates. I could only offer Nick moral support. Tony understood how I felt, but he didn't want to come with me.

The three magistrates who heard Nick's case placed him on bail and ordered him to live at a probation hostel in Berkshire. He was given the weekend to get his belongings together, say his goodbyes and prepare himself for the move. From Monday 18 August, he was to reside at the hostel under a curfew: he had to be in at night no later than 11 pm and he could not leave before 7 am. The chairman of the bench informed Nick that he would be assessed by the staff for his suitability for a Drug Treatment Testing Order. If he was found to be suitable a report would be presented to the court for their approval and implementation. While at the hostel, sixteen milligrams of Subutex, the opiate blocker, would be administered to Nick daily by the staff.

The magistrates made their expectations very clear to him: if he adhered to all that was expected of him, this was an opportunity for him to get his life back on track; if he failed to comply, he would be arrested, brought back to the court and resentenced. His probation officer advised the magistrates that she had arranged for him to visit the Salvation Army drug and alcohol rehabilitation centre in Wiltshire near the end of August to meet the staff and other recovering addicts. It would be an opportunity to assess if this was the most suitable place for him to begin his long-term rehabilitation.

It was shameful to witness my son's life and freedom in the hands of the legal system. Yet I knew that Nick had to face up to his problems and take responsibility for them. He had failed to comply with his Community Rehabilitation Order and he couldn't expect to get away with anything else. Thankfully, he had finally acknowledged that his drug use was out of control, and he had done something about it by applying to the local drug prescribing agency to be accepted for the Subutex programme.

Simon attended court to support his brother. When the case had been concluded, I gave them both a lift to Wokingham where they returned to the room they shared. Simon recalls:

> We had spent so much time together as addicts that we had become very close as brothers. It was very hard when we knew that there was now no choice, and we had to disperse. Rightly or wrongly, we had battled through a lot of our addiction together. When Nick went into the probation hostel, we didn't go a day without trying to see each other. I bought a weekly bus ticket with my giro money. We would usually meet near the hostel because Nick had curfews that he had to keep.

Three days later, when Nick left the room he shared with his brother for the hostel, Simon attended a meeting with the Cranstoun drug tenancy worker. He hoped that, with their support, he might be given temporary accommodation by Wokingham Council. If no emergency accommodation was available, unless he could find a squat with other addicts, Simon would be on the streets.

Simon started his Subutex course two days after Nick left. As with all controlled drugs, a record was kept of the time and date of its administration. Failure to turn up for more than three consecutive days meant that the agreement Simon had entered into with the doctor, the chemist and his drugs worker would become void. His experience at the chemist's was mixed. He told me that while some pharmacists, particularly our local family chemist's, were supportive and encouraging to patients in recovery, whether they were taking Subutex or methadone,

I went into labour quite convinced that I would give birth to another baby girl, a sister for Marie. Lawrence and I had even chosen her name. When the doctor told me that I was going to have twins, I was so surprised. I think the delight on my face is evident after the birth of my identical twins, Nicholas and Simon.

above left I was so proud of my beautiful boys with their golden hair on their first day at nursery. By the end of that memorable day Nicholas (on the right) had managed to get his head stuck between two rungs of a chair. I was asked to wait at the door of the nursery while the nursery staff sawed him free!

above right The boys were thrilled when they got their first school uniform, especially when they could wear a tie – although it took ages for them to tie the knot. Sister Joseph, their first infant school teacher, said they were 'lovable rascals' and she could never tell them apart. Many was the time the boys swapped their name badges to confuse her.

above left At the start of his GCSE course at his public school in Bath, Nick was a handsome, healthy and happy teenager, very popular with the girls. He did not enjoy academic work as much as his brother, his mind was more on the girls. Sometimes they even went on each other's dates to see if the girls would notice.

above right This picture of Simon reminds me of his report at the end of his first term. His housemaster said he was smart, unfailingly polite, helpful, good-humoured and popular, and he had put in a very strong academic performance.

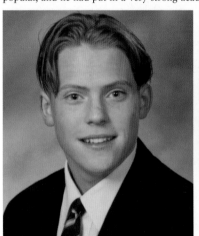

above left Having achieved eight GCSEs, Nick went on to the sixth form to study A levels, eventually hoping to go on to university. But he always struggled with his academic work. Would any mother sense that her son was already heavily into smoking cannabis and other recreational drugs if he looked so healthy and handsome?

above right A young baby-faced Nick, very much in love with his first serious girlfriend, Ruth.

ick and Simon were happily overwhelmed on their 21st birthday when one of the
surprise guests arrived. It was none other than their nursery nurse, Beverley, and the
expression on their faces shows both delight and surprise. How could I have possibly
known that within months they would both be heroin addicts?

left Here's the proof that teenagers
and young adults can successfully
keep their parents in the dark. At
first sight this picture of Simon and
Nick taken at the golf course looks
quite an ordinary picture of my
two sons enjoying themselves.
Behind the smiles however, was a
deadly secret, as they slid deeper
and deeper into their heroin
addiction.

Tony, Nick, Simon and me outside the Sheldonian Theatre. It was a really special day for me – my Master's Degree ceremony at Oxford University in October 2000. Nick, on the left, looks quite happy and healthy, but looking back with the knowledge I have now, all the signs of drug abuse are there with Simon – deathly pale, losing weight and ill-fitting clothes.

The evening of my fiftieth birthday meal in October 2000 – which by coincidence was the same day as my Master's Degree ceremony.

'I am so sorry mum, but I am a pinhead – I am injecting heroin', Simon told me. The memory of this day will be etched upon my life forever. This is every mother's nightmare, every parent's nightmare. How do you react to the news that your beloved son now lives on the streets and is injecting heroin into his veins?

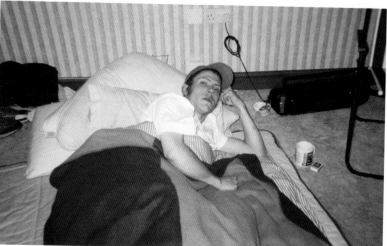

I always took my camera with me whenever I went to look for Simon and Nick when they were homeless. Here I captured Simon sleeping rough at Stephen and Marion's empty house in Basingstoke. Hidden under the sleeping bag were several used needles which Simon did not want me to see.

Nick on his way to hospital for his first attempt at heroin detoxification. Heroin has reduced him to a physical and mental wreck. His facial expression says it all – depressed, lonely, desperate.

above left Nick and Simon standing side-by-side at Paddington station the day Nick went to the Florence Nightingale Clinic in London to begin a detoxification programme. Who would ever have thought they were identical twins? As Simon begins to recover and look well again, Nick's decline is only too obvious.

above right A happy day with every sign of hope: Nick holds his 'opiate free' certificate given to him by the staff of the Florence Nightingale Hospital. Both my sons were now heroin free – but within weeks Nick and Simon would be using heroin again.

bove left Where has my son Nick gone? Tough love means you have to let the addict hit ock bottom, but it was heart-wrenching to photograph Nick in this state. To witness our son homeless, filthy, unshaven, with bruises and injection marks all over his arms as just awful.

bove right What can a mother say when she sees her other son like this? Having seen imon make what appeared to be such a good recovery, it was shocking that I did not ecognise my own son when I found him on the streets.

ere Nick and Simon were arranging to meet their drug dealer in the car park behind larks and Spencer in Wokingham. Make no mistake about it; drug dealing can take lace anywhere, any time.

A treasured memory for Simon and me – a photograph of Nick and Simon taken on the eve of their 27th birthday. Even though I believed they were off drugs, the grip heroin had on both of them meant they had become 'giro junkies': they used heroin whenever they got their giro cheques. Within three months, Nick would be dead.

above Every time we visit Nick's memorial stone at the cemetery, it is a fierce reminder that drugs can and do kill. A mother and stepfather lost their son, a sister lost her brother, and an identical twin lost his soul mate. (Photograph reproduced by kind permission of Andrews Photography, High Wycombe.)

above right A new beginning for us all – Simon, Tony and I are now great friends again. After so much dysfunction I feel we have survived and can look to the future as an ordinary family. (Photograph reproduced by kind permission of INS news agency, Winnersh, Reading.)

others had an 'attitude' about administering to the addicts. Some would even make family members feel outcasts.

One mistake which I suspect many families make is to assume that if your son or daughter is taking an opiate blocker like Subutex, then they will have no further desire for heroin. I certainly believed that to be the case. If a daily tablet takes away the cravings for heroin, then why on earth would a heroin addict have any further need for the drug? But it isn't as simple as that. As Simon explained to me, synthetic opiate blockers take away the physical cravings, but they are no 'miracle cure':

> Heroin has a powerful grip over any addict's mind. So the battle is with addicts' mental desire for the drug and the needle fixation which often accompanies their mental cravings. If you've abused heroin for many years, as Nick and I did, it's not easy to stop smoking or injecting the drug simply because you are on an opiate blocker. The physical cravings are eased by Subutex but it's the raging war with the mind that is far harder to win and overcome for the rest of your life. Perhaps the best thing about Subutex is that it helps you to stop committing crime because the physical need is so much less. You can start to think about the mess your life is in and begin to try and put things right.

Just before August bank holiday weekend, thanks to the support of Mandy, the Cranstoun tenancy worker, Simon was allocated six weeks' emergency homeless accommodation. Drug addiction had finally reduced both my sons to homelessness. I agonised once again about how much practical support I could give, but my conscience told me it wasn't wrong to give Simon a lift to his emergency accommodation the next day. All he possessed in the world was contained in one small carrier bag. Every time I tried to express how I felt a lump came into my throat. On the way home, I sobbed uncontrollably. I couldn't even bring myself to talk to Tony about it that evening. And next day it was the start of the new academic year – I would be back on the treadmill of hiding the shame from my colleagues.

Simon told me what happened next:

> Before I started my Subutex course, I was in a desperate state. After Nick went to the probation hostel I was arrested for stealing two bottles of vodka which I was going to exchange for heroin. When Nick was at the hostel, there were two girls living round the corner who dealt all types of drugs to the residents. I hoped I could get some gear from them in exchange for the vodka. Dealers aren't stupid. Where better to set up dealing drugs than near a hostel with lots of recovering addicts who are going to be easily tempted?

> It wasn't too long – towards the end of September – before Nick breached his order by using drugs on the premises. He ended up spending the night in the police cells at Reading Station. He was allowed to ring me from the police station. I didn't have Mum's phone number so I couldn't tell her. I panicked a bit and in the end I rang his hostel and asked them to ring her. I wasn't sure how she would react but I felt that she would prefer to know than suddenly find out he was in prison; I knew Nick was on very thin ice.

When the hostel rang to give me Simon's message, Tony was out. As Nick had been arrested at the hostel on Friday evening, he was to appear at the magistrates' court on Saturday morning, and I rushed down there to see what would happen to him. Many recovering addicts who have spoken to me since have said that it would have been better to stay at home and let Nick face the problem he had created. Yet, some addicts who have been in prison felt it was better for their family to be in court and to hear the sentence for themselves. Should I have exercised the toughest possible love and turned my back on Nick completely? As I drove, I asked myself, 'Am I being really stupid? Am I taking a backward step by going to court again? Accept what happens to him and just let go. Even better, turn the car round and go home.' But I couldn't do it.

Being in court when you believe your son or daughter is about to be 'banged up' is a pretty emotional experience. I watched as Nick was brought up from the police cells, flanked by two officers, to face the magistrates yet again. Despite the Subutex, as yet he hadn't been able to stop his drug use completely. I accepted that, this time, it was the end of the road for Nick. Surely prison was now the only option. The duty solicitor pointed out to the court that Nick's assessment for a DTTO had not yet been completed by the hostel and more time was needed; he asked permission from the magistrates for Nick to be released on conditional bail for one week until a decision could be made about his future, which would happen on 13 October.

And to my amazement the court agreed to bail – though only if Nick stayed with a member of his family. Had Nick's potential prison sentence simply been put on hold? I wondered. I couldn't take him home, so he moved in with Simon and slept on the floor in his room for the next few days. It was a very anxious time for Simon as he wasn't supposed to let anyone share his room.

Eventually, in mid-October 2003, Nick was made the subject of a twelve-month Drug Treatment and Testing Order. It was, in effect, a one-year sentence for breach of his CRO. Furthermore, he was sentenced to live at a different probation hostel in Berkshire for four months while awaiting accommodation at the Salvation Army rehabilitation centre.

Three key workers got to know Nick well during this period. Francesca, his key worker at the second hostel, recalled:

> Nick was very engaging in key sessions. I found him very easy to chat to. He was a good communicator, very like-able, decent and good-hearted. I can honestly say that he was one of the nicest people I have ever key-worked here. He was trying hard to address his drug problem.

For a long time I had seen these qualities in Nick only rarely. That was the son I remembered, but his love affair with heroin meant that his personality had changed almost beyond recognition. Yet Francesca emphasised that Nick got on well with all the residents and staff. He was closest to his brother, she said, but he also had a good relationship with other residents at the hostel. She described what it was like to work with him:

> When we gave Nick his daily Subutex tablet we would sit him down in the induction area and wait with him until it dissolved. Then he would sign the book and tell us what he was doing that day. He often chatted about his mum and dad. He told me all about his past, his brother and sister. He did mention that he was no longer in contact with his sister. He was very, very close to Simon, his twin. Simon spent a lot of time in the hostel visiting him. Once I got Simon mixed up with Nick and called Simon into the office thinking it was Nick.

Nick enjoyed reading Harry Potter and playing Scrabble. His bedroom was the subject of many a discussion – he wasn't the tidiest of people, to say the least. Neither was he good at getting up in the morning. When the staff did a curfew check, a hand would appear out of the covers and wave.

He had plans for the future; he wanted to become an electrician. He told me many times how much he was looking forward to going into long-term rehabilitation. It was his goal to turn his life round by the time he was thirty. He did want to change, but sadly heroin had a mighty grip on him. It was stronger than anything else, including his love for his mother and his family. But for a drug abuser who was trying to turn his life around, he had a very good rapport with all of us. He was quite open and honest about his position.

Nine days after moving into the hostel, Nick began a twelve-week structured day programme with Cranstoun Drug Services in Reading. After he had attended for about a month, Sandra, his key project worker, wrote the following report:

This is the first progress report for Nicholas Stephen, usually known as Nick. He was assessed as suitable for the Twelve-Week Structured Day Programme at Cranstoun Drug Services on 6th October after he was given the Drug Treatment Testing Order by the court. He attended two drop-in sessions until a place was available on this day programme. Nick started the programme on 22nd October. He has attended groups on harm minimisation, relapse prevention, maintenance, drugs and the law, high risk situations, relaxation and support groups.

Nick has discussed many matters with his key worker here, including triggers, patterns of drug use, alternatives to using drugs, thoughts about his suitability for rehabilitation and plans for the future. He is honest and acknowledges the links between drug use and crime.

Nick's drug test results have been very mixed. He has several positives and several negatives. He is on a Subutex prescription which he is finding effective. However, he hasn't been able to break the pattern of using heroin on giro day with his brother. This is an issue which Nick is working through both in group and in key work sessions but he is adamant that he will be able to break the pattern.

If the level of commitment he has shown so far on the programme continues, I see no reason why he will not be able to address the reason for his drug misuse and offending behaviour.

As this report indicates, the twins were still unable to resist doing drugs together. After six weeks Simon had to move from his one-room accommodation to an emergency hostel just round the corner from Nick's hostel. Simon described this move as a 'backward step', as there were several heroin users living there, but there was nowhere else for him to go. He explained:

The homelessness department did make me aware of the situation, but it was either there or the streets. I was sharing a room next to a heroin user and within two days, I used as well. Nick was round the corner now at the hostel and even though we were both on Subutex, when we got our giro money, we would then go and have a hit of heroin.

But despite his inability to stop using heroin, Nick continued to charm the professionals looking after his case. It was Danielle, his key worker from the probation DTTO team, who perhaps got to know Nick the best. She covered some of the cases in Reading and Nick was part of her caseload. After the assessment of Nick's suitability for a DTTO was finally agreed, the probation team at the Crown Court sent him to his first appointment. Danielle told me:

> When I first met Nick, I thought what a lovely looking guy. He was a polite young man. My impression was that he was an intelligent young man as well. From the very moment I met Nick, I got on well with him. I looked forward to working with him. He was down-to-earth and I liked that about him. He was chatty.

> At his first appointment, I went through his assessment and told him what was expected of him. I explained to him that he would have to attend the Cranstoun Structured Day Programme for twelve weeks. It was quite an intense programme when you are doing the amount of drugs he was doing at the time. It was on Monday, Wednesday and Friday from 10.30 am to 3.30 pm. He was already on Subutex when I took him on.

Danielle clarified that it was a condition of Nick's DTTO that she saw him once a week, usually on Thursday afternoons. Each time she tested him for drug use. Occasionally, Nick admitted he had used drugs and would willingly sign a form to declare this. She told me that he was honest about his use, and the judge could see from the paper that he was being honest. Danielle used to look forward to seeing Nick because he was never impolite, regardless of his mood. The only time he was like 'a bear with a sore head' was if he had had a row with Simon. Even so, he never missed his appointment.

Danielle realised that Nick's only coping strategy if anything went wrong in his life was to use heroin and then kid himself that he would now be able to deal with what had happened. For example, there were issues about overdue rent at the hostel which he dealt with by using drugs. But instead of being able to cope he became depressed; his anger and frustration with himself was turned inwards, precisely because he had used heroin again.

Nevertheless, Nick progressed quite well with the Cranstoun Day Programme, as is evident in the following report written about him by Danielle in early November 2003:

Introduction
Nick was made the subject of a twelve-month Drug Treatment and Testing Order on 13th October 2003. He is currently residing at a probation hostel in Berkshire awaiting accommodation to become available for him in a Salvation Army residential rehabilitation centre in Wiltshire.

Attendance, Participation and Attitude
Since this order was made, Nick has attended five appointments at the structured day programme. He has adjusted well to the group and he makes valid comments, demonstrating his communication skills. He failed to attend an appointment on 27th October due to sorting out his benefits but he was expected to return in the

afternoon. Nick did provide evidence on this occasion but his absence that day resulted in him missing his key work appointment for the next day as he was unaware of the allotted time, but he did attend the drop-in service instead. Unfortunately Nick missed another appointment the following Monday on 3rd November due to a 'family issue'. I have discussed this with Nick and I am awaiting a decision from the Senior Probation Officer as to whether warning should be issued to him for an unacceptable reason for absence.

Nick has attended four appointments with the DTTO team. He is honest about his drug use and he discusses openly how to address issues surrounding his recent relapses and the effect this has on him. He is punctual and he uses appointments to assist him with his rehabilitation. Nick has to attend an appointment with the prescribing agency on 7th November to discuss his recent relapses, which he has to address as a matter of urgency in order not to jeopardise his script of Subutex.

Comment on Nick's altrix/urine test results
Since the order was made, Nick has submitted fifteen drug tests. He has registered negative four times for cocaine and four times for heroin. On two occasions Nick has declared that he has used heroin and crack cocaine by signing a statement of use form. Nick has discussed his recent relapses with me and at the structured day programme.

Summary of Nick's overall progress
Nick is an excellent communicator and he is a good

listener. He has the ability to address his drug habit and to commit to a drug-free life. Nick needs to attend all his appointments at the structured day programme with Cranstoun and the DTTO team in order to avoid a breach, as there have been two incidents when he has not fully committed himself, which may result in a warning.

Objectives for Nick's next review
To attend all his appointments with the Cranstoun Structured Day Programme
To attend all his appointments with the DTTO team
To attend all his appointments with the Berkshire Prescribing Agency
To submit to a minimum twice weekly drug test
To make contact with the Salvation Army rehab for an update of details for his place
To produce negative drug test results

But it is clear from this report that Nick was struggling with the discipline expected of him. Danielle spoke to her line manager on one occasion for guidance because she was under considerable pressure to breach him from the structured day programme as he was not coping with the required discipline and attendance. She recalled:

If you have one failed appointment and you don't produce evidence of absenteeism such as a doctor's certificate or a job interview, you receive a final warning. He was quite good at producing his evidence most of the time. But I could see he was completely chaotic so I tried to get him to take a step back and look at this opportunity he had. He was forever rushing but with nowhere to go;

he had this or that thing on his mind. I wanted him to slow down as I felt he tried to do too much.

A lot of the support agencies were struggling with the fact that Nick and Simon triggered each other's drug use. But, at the end of the day, they were still brothers, identical twin brothers. They loved each other enormously but they were in a vicious circle together. Simon would get his giro one Monday and Nick the next. We tried to put things into place so that they avoided each other on those days or avoided going together and would then meet up later on, perhaps. We discussed the idea of money management. Nick was intelligent, he knew what he had to do, but getting him to do it was another task. When he got his giro, nine times out of ten he would bump into a drug dealer and he and Simon would go and have a little heroin party together. It was his routine with his brother.

The 'family issue' to which Danielle had referred in her report may have been when Nick accompanied me to an outpatient visit I made to our local hospital. My GP had sent me to see a specialist about a stomach disorder that might be a stomach ulcer. I thought that whatever it was, it was likely to have been caused by worry and anxiety. I was warned that after this type of stomach investigation I might feel 'a little wobbly', and it was recommended that I bring someone along with me who could remain with me afterwards until I felt well enough to go home.

I told Nick about this when I visited him at the hostel one day, and he offered to come with me. Our relationship had improved considerably since he and Simon had started their Subutex programme. I was cautiously beginning to have a little more contact with them. Nick was starting to look quite well again;

both he and Simon had put on some weight. Yet although I felt his desire to accompany me was genuine, I didn't want him to come at the expense of his attendance on the structured day programme. Only when I had established that he wouldn't be missing his appointment did I accept the offer.

When he met me at the hospital, he looked clean and smart. I was almost proud of him because outwardly he appeared to have improved so much. It just felt normal to be out with my son who didn't look like a drug addict any more. I didn't dare hope for more, but I was grateful for that tiny taste of normality.

At the hospital, I had a procedure known as a 'gastroscopy', which involved passing a lighted tube down the oesophagus to inspect the lining of my stomach. I didn't feel too good afterwards and it was comforting to have Nick there – It was one of those rare occasions when we did something together as mother and son. It reminded me of the occasion when Simon and I had gone into Marks and Spencer's and tried on hats, when Nick was in detox at the Florence Nightingale Hospital in London. Francesca told me:

> I had quite a long chat with him about this one day. He used to talk and discuss his drug use and his family issues with me in his key work sessions. I remember, he hadn't had a very good week, and he was worried about his mum as she had a health scare; in fact he thought she might have cancer. He was very, very relieved when his mum got her results and he found out she was going to be OK – he really was happy. It was coming up to his twenty-seventh birthday and Nick and Simon were hoping she might meet them so they could have a meal together. It was the first time Nick would have done that with his mum since she cut him off nine months ago. He

really wanted to celebrate with her that she was not seriously ill.

Danielle also recalled how frequently Nick discussed his relationship with me. She explained that Nick fully understood how much he had disappointed me – and indeed other members of his family. He was aware how hard I was trying to encourage his recovery. Every time he used heroin on his benefit day, he knew he was being deceitful, not only to himself but to me as well. She said:

> I asked Nick if I could meet Simon once, as he was as much a part of his life as was his heroin. I did find it useful to meet his twin. A couple of times Simon came with Nick to appointments. It was interesting, and they were such characters. Sometimes I could just sit and watch them, I didn't need to say or do anything. They would bicker like an old married couple. Simon would say to Nick, you've got to do this or you've got to do that. And he would organise him. To be honest, it was nice to see the warmth of their relationship as twins. What was so hard to observe was that two young men were also doing so much damage to one another. That was really painful to witness.

Despite their periodic lapses, Simon and Nick were still keen to knock their heroin addiction on the head. They tried harder and harder, using it only at weekends – or every ten days. Simon eventually decided to move out of the emergency hostel because so many of the other residents were using heroin. He went to stay with another addict, Martin, who was also on Subutex, as he felt this was a better position for him to be in than in the company of regular users.

By the eve of their twenty-seventh birthday, Nick and Simon had been on Subutex for almost three months. When I met them, I was pleased to see that they both looked considerably better physically. The discipline at Nick's hostel meant that he had to wash and shave every day; both my sons had regained their appetites and had begun to take a more positive interest in their appearance and their future. Even then, unbeknown to me, they were still using heroin. Martin, Nick's senior probation officer, said:

> We tried all sorts of different tactics to change this pattern but it had become quite a routine. I certainly remember them hiding this from you, and we thought we could rectify it each week by trying to find a plan not to relapse. We really wanted to crack it and get it sorted and it was felt that you didn't need to know; that it would be better to tell you as an afterthought, and then they wouldn't feel so bad. But we never sorted it satisfactorily. They were buying food and they were eating, but there was this ongoing weekly lapse.

But I felt just a little more confident about their long-term recovery, and believed that the twins' birthday might be the time to give them a sign of encouragement. Although Tony declined to come with me, I met them on 19 November for a meal. Afterwards, I told the boys about a new group that I hoped to join. I explained to them that back in August, when I was at the doctor's surgery, I had met Rosemary Sturmer in the waiting room. The only reason that I had taken notice of her was because I heard her mention the word heroin. My hearing antennae switched on immediately and I listened as she asked the receptionist if it would be possible to leave some leaflets she had with her for patients to read. My curiosity increased; I decided to go and speak to her and ask for one of the leaflets.

It was now that I learnt for the first time about 'Crack it!', a support group for those affected by someone else's drug or alcohol misuse. Rosemary said that the group would begin to operate in the autumn. It would be organised and run by local Christian volunteers, and would offer support to those caring for family members or friends who used drugs or alcohol.

I couldn't believe what I was hearing. The thought of a local support group only a couple of miles from where I lived seemed like a dream come true. I was excited to hear that I could even attend regular informal meetings which would offer me confidential support and practical information. Rosemary said: 'We hope by the time we start to have a large stock of leaflets that explain the consequences of using drugs or alcohol. We want to offer anyone who comes along a chance to offload. We aren't drug counsellors, except for one of the team, but we hope to offer a sympathetic ear, support, hope, and contact with other services, teaching sessions and access to other drug information. It'll be available for anyone who is worried or who is interested in finding out more about drugs or alcohol that a friend or relative is using.'

At long last, I thought, I might have found a lifeline. I wanted to jump up and down with relief that I had come across someone I could talk to about what drugs do to a family, what they had done to my family. I was sure that Tony would want to come along as well. I told my sons: 'Today I had a phone call to invite me to the first Crack it! meeting next week. Maybe, like you, I can find some support for myself and Tony. There's lots of support for addicts but family members – mums like me and stepfathers like Tony – just don't know where to turn.' I couldn't wait.

10
Giro Junkies

ATTENDING MY FIRST Crack it! meeting towards the end of 2003 was my most significant step forward throughout all the years of Nick and Simon's heroin addiction. Yes, I had spoken each week to Anne, my counsellor – but now I had come across a support group specifically dedicated to the one thing that had ravaged our lives for so long.

I would encourage any family member or friend worried about alcohol or drug use to take this first step – even more so if you are the carer of an addict. Go along to a group if one is available; take time to offload your worry and anxiety. Making that vital first step can be enormously daunting, because by doing so you may for the first time be facing up to the truth and admitting that there is a problem. But for myself, by the time I walked through the front door of Bearwood Hall, Sindlesham, near Wokingham, where the first meeting was held, I knew only too well that there was a massive problem – and I was determined to talk about it.

At my first meeting, I met four trained volunteers: as well as Rosemary, there were Jacky, Pam and Tom. It was therapeutic simply to feel that I no longer had to live with a dreadful secret. I continued to attend Crack it! twice a month; the time and opportunity to talk about how I felt kept me going from meeting to meeting. I was accepted without judgement or criticism, which gave me the confidence to maintain the boundaries I had imposed on Nick and Simon.

In time, Tony began coming along to the meetings. He met Derek and Sandra, grandparents of a similar age to him, which made it easier for him to talk about how he felt. Anyone who attends support meetings like these knows only too well the emotions experienced by families involved in addiction. They are clearly expressed by Andrea, a grandmother who regularly attends Crack it! and has two sons, one of whom is a heroin addict:

> When first faced with knowing that someone you care about is a drug addict you are liable to be swamped by a mixture of emotions and questions. Firstly, it is probably shock. Maybe disbelief – you don't want it to be true.
>
> Confusion – how could it have happened? What to do about it?
>
> Very likely misplaced guilt, especially if you are a parent. Is it something you have done or not done? Should you have realised sooner? Could you have prevented it?
>
> Distrust – how long has this been going on? Have I been lied to? Is that where some money has gone?
>
> Fear – where will it all end?
>
> Embarrassment – who else knows, or how can I keep this to myself?

Grief – as you realise the person you care about is not the same any more.

Isolation – as you avoid people and social situations where innocent, awkward questions might get asked.

Helplessness – what can I do, who can help me? All this can be overwhelming, depressing and intrusive in your lifestyle but YES, there is help and hope, which must never be relinquished.

Tony and I were able to talk about our disappointment and anger with other parents and step-parents. Members of the group learnt to support one another through the difficult times each of us faced from week to week. Not everyone attended consistently, for some it was enough to come only once or when they needed it. I talked to other mothers or fathers who came along about my hopes for the future and how I did not dare risk believing that it would all come to an end one day.

Many times I shared with Jacky, Tom, Pam and Rosemary how difficult it was to have not just one, but both my sons on heroin. I kept them up to date with any news I had of Nick and Simon, especially when Simon decided to move out of the hostel because of the heroin use there. I told them that he had begun to spend time with another man in his twenties, who lived at a crisis centre, a refuge for people who are trying to resolve a difficulty in their lives. Simon explained one day:

I was hanging around with a bloke called Richard who lived in a crisis house in Wokingham. Pam, the lady who ran it, didn't like me at all until she got to know me a bit. Then she realised that I did really want to get well, as did my brother. When she offered me a place at the centre just before Christmas 2003, I was so grateful to her. I made a lot of progress and tried to make a go of getting well. When I thought about it, my life was a hell-hole, mixing with down-and-outs, prostitutes and needles. It was a hectic, horrible, nasty lifestyle. Living in squats, stealing for heroin – who would want to live like that?

The grip my addiction had over me meant I was still a 'giro junkie' and, of course, so was Nick, even more so. Using heroin wasn't a daily thing – we had the tablets to stop the cravings, we didn't need to do it on a daily basis – but when we got our giro money, any time we could get a bit of cash together, we liked to treat ourselves. We would 'gouge out' on monster sessions, but less frequently. We were actually staying off drugs for four or five days a week; Nick had been living a lifestyle of injecting two or three hundred pounds' worth of heroin a day in his arm and he went from that to occasionally injecting £150. Mum didn't realise – nor do most parents – that most addicts on Subutex tablets still continue to do drugs when they get their giros. However, despite this we were still really keen to knock it on the head; gradually we tried harder and harder and we ended up just doing heroin once a week.

Pam Jenkinson, the president of the crisis centre, already knew of the 'addicted twins'; the room they had rented from Andy Smithfields was just a few yards away. She knew Simon a little, as he used to visit another resident at the house. Some months later, she bumped into Simon at the local railway station when he was on his way to visit Nick at the probation hostel. She was amazed at the transformation in him. The Simon she had known earlier had looked seriously ill and very dishevelled; now, she was pleased to see, he looked much better. Pam recalled that Simon visited the crisis centre again a while later and that he was a totally different character, neat, clean and well spoken. She continued:

> I hardly knew Nick when he lived up the road from the centre, I hadn't seen him in the way I had seen Simon. But then Nick came to the Christmas party in 2003. I asked him and Simon if they would help me move a piano the next day. The day of the 'piano move' was one of the few occasions when we actually sat down and had a drink. The twins helped me bring in a piano which had been donated to the centre; it was very hard work and they had to carry it in. They tried everything; they had to come through the Lady Balfour room. Simon made a cup of tea for Nick and he used bleach to clean the cups. Nick said, 'You can't make a decent cup of tea, Simon!' They were like an old married couple. I was roaring with laughter so I said, 'I have got something a bit stronger than tea. Let's have a drink.' So we sat around and chatted and it was really nice. Bringing in that piano conjures up the fun I had with Nick and Simon. When you've done all the hard work moving something as big as that, what could be nicer than to have a drink and a chat?

Towards the end of 2003, Pam indicated that she might be willing to let Nick live at the crisis centre until a place became available for him at the Salvation Army rehabilitation centre. As Nick and Simon spent so much time together, she thought it might be best, when a free room became available, to offer it to Nick. This presented Danielle, Nick's DTTO key worker, with a dilemma. She recalled:

> He came to his appointment just before Christmas and explained that he might be able to go to the crisis centre and live with his twin Simon. What do you do? They were both grown men, both adults, they wanted to live together so it was an opportunity for them to be more independent. Nick wanted to get out of the hostel as he hated the curfews. I was in a predicament with this option, because on the one hand that was what he wanted, yet on the other hand, it was all turning a bit sour at the probation hostel, because Nick wasn't paying his rent.
>
> He was so excited about the idea of going to the crisis centre. I spoke to the person in charge of the structured day programme at Cranstoun; in fact, we had a number of chats about it. No one in the professional teams seemed keen for him to go there, but I didn't want to put barriers in his way. Yes, there were potential triggers for further drug use if he and Simon were together all the time – but then, there were potential triggers if Nick stayed at the hostel.

The professionals had to decide whether it would be sensible to allow Nick to live at the crisis centre, or whether in the long run it would be better for him to remain at his probation hostel. His probation team discussed this at great length; their opinion was not to block it, while for Danielle it was exceptionally difficult to know the right thing to do. But at Christmas 2003, Nick was permitted some home leave from the probation hostel. With Pam's permission, he went to stay with Simon at the crisis centre.

By now, both my sons had attended several Sunday services at the local Baptist church at Sindlesham, where they were given much encouragement for their recovery. Several members of the church community, particularly Pat and Ed, took an active interest in the boys, inviting them to supper and encouraging them to rid themselves of their addiction. Nick and Simon attended this church, as I did, on Christmas Day 2003. Their Christmas card to me that morning simply said 'Thank you Mum for everything you have done and thank you for being there for us'.

It remains a sad memory that neither Tony nor I felt that we could trust the twins enough to invite them into our home at Christmas. I was prepared at least to have them to Christmas lunch, but Tony was adamant that for the time being we should maintain some of the boundaries we had set. However, I went into the new year with an open mind, thinking that this could be the year that Nick and Simon would free themselves from their heroin addiction.

On 12 January 2004, it was agreed by the professionals over-seeing Nick that he could leave the probation hostel and live at the crisis centre. When he moved out to be with Simon, Danielle and Francesca were well aware that some of the staff were concerned whether it would work. In order to reaffirm her commitment, as Nick's next review approached, Pam wrote the following letter to the magistrates' court:

I am writing to confirm that Nicholas Stephen is currently residing at the Wokingham Crisis Centre House. We are a charity and therefore he will be able to live here free of charge as a guest of the Crisis House for one year – during which time he will receive our ongoing support for staying free of drugs and crime, getting his life back together, seeking work and eventually seeking move-on accommodation. The Crisis House is a mental health facility and is free from the drugs culture. As part of our support we are administering prescribed Subutex tablets to Nicholas on a daily basis.

Nicholas has settled well with us and he is participating in our charity work. I am optimistic that he will conform to our rules (a copy of which I attach) and make good progress during his time with us. We are also working with his twin brother who also wishes to support Nick in his rehabilitation process. I believe that their family are appreciative of this opportunity and are committed as we are to a successful outcome. Nick has the advantage that the Crisis House is a very small house with only four guests, all of whom receive undivided attention while in residence.

Nick will be expected to obey our House Rules at the Wokingham Crisis Centre. The following are not permitted under any circumstances – abuse of alcohol, abuse of drugs, violence, stealing, abuse of the premises, sexual harassment, religious or racial harassment, smoking, disturbing the peaceful enjoyment of others.

When Danielle visited the crisis centre to meet Pam and other volunteers and to see Nick, she realised he had a lot more freedom there. On her first visit Nick was at Cranstoun, in Reading, so Simon showed her around. The next time Danielle called in, she saw a huge change in both boys. She was positive, although there were still problems:

Nick went through a period where he was 'on the up'. I felt he was doing really well and, at one stage, he seemed more on the up than Simon was. He went through a honeymoon period at the crisis house because it was a change and things were going well for him. But then the pressures came again; sometimes he had a lot of trouble getting from the crisis centre to the appointments at Cranstoun or to my appointments, because he borrowed the house van. It broke down frequently and this began to affect his attendance. He couldn't get to where he should be because of road works or because the van broke down.

He asked for train tickets to get to his meetings and I said we would send a train warrant. However, it was always too late because he didn't know in advance if his van was going to break down. It was an extra pressure to get from Wokingham to Reading. He probably only had about two weeks to go at Cranstoun but he kept putting it back, so it felt to him like he had months to go to get through their programme.

Pam and her team of volunteers supported two other young people at the centre as well as Nick and Simon. One of these was Richard, who was coming to the end of his stay there. The other was a young woman called Alex who had been there a little longer than Simon. The crisis house also operated as a drop-in centre for past residents and for anyone with a mental health problem who wanted to call in and talk.

Pam always made it clear that members of the family, too, were welcome to call in to see her or the boys at any time during the working day. When I met her, I realised straight away what an exceptional woman she is; she has dedicated many years of her life to voluntary work of this sort. I told Tony how hopeful she was for the boys' future and how she felt certain that after their year with her, they would be well enough to move forward. Things certainly appeared to be improving; Nick and Simon looked much healthier and better nourished, and had begun to talk about getting jobs. Nick was still keen to pursue a career as an electrician and Simon showed interest in computers.

As the spring half-term approached in mid-February 2004, Simon had lived at the crisis house for a couple of months and Nick had been there about six weeks. Frances, one of the volunteers, recalled that the boys had settled in extremely well. Of the two brothers, she learnt more about Nick: he was 'cheeky and chirpy', loved to share a joke with the volunteers, and frequently used to sing when he did his washing. To see such visible improvement and to hear encouraging reports about my sons was a huge relief. Tough love seemed to be working. The evidence was there – the boys had taken responsibility for their heroin addiction; they were now on Subutex, they had a weekly giro to live on and a year ahead of them to sort themselves out. The worst was over, surely?

But it was virtually impossible for either of them to break free either from their brotherly bond or their twin addiction. At times they were full of support for each other, but they could also blame each other. And no one in the family or at the crisis centre had any idea that despite their apparent physical recovery, both my sons were still 'giro junkies', shopping for their gear every week using their social security payments. At many of his meetings with Danielle, as he had with Francesca, Nick stressed his intention to manage his giro payment without spending it on drugs. He told Francesca that sometimes he gave the money from his giro to me to look after, but this wasn't true. The consequences of this secretive behaviour were only days away.

Halfway through the school holiday week in February, I went to the crisis house to have a coffee with Pam and ask for news of the boys' progress. I had forgotten that she had her day off on Wednesdays, so I arrived to find the four residents – Nick, Simon, Richard and Alex – in the kitchen having a cup of tea. The atmosphere was upbeat; despite their various problems they all believed that in time they would recover. I learnt that Nick had been on the house computer to look up the local college website to see when he could enrol for an electrician's course. Simon had been searching for courses in computing. It was a happy, informal occasion; there was no mention of drugs. Later on Nick told us that he had his DTTO appointment with Danielle the next day and that he was looking forward to meeting her. Simon mentioned that he had met Danielle a couple of times and said how supportive she was of Nick. Nick said: 'We will both get through this. We know what drugs have done to you and Tony, but we do want to get better and live normal lives. You can see for yourself how well we're doing. Subutex is the best thing that has happened to us for a long while. So don't worry, we're on the bottom rung of the ladder at the moment, but we're going to get to the top – in the end.'

I was deeply moved by what Nick said, as I sensed at the time he truly believed those words. But I couldn't risk getting over-emotional. I knew from past experience that that would be a dangerous road to go down

I had to get home as I had some paperwork to prepare for school the following week. As I was leaving, I asked the boys what they were doing over the next couple of days. They didn't seem to have much on, except for Nick's appointment with Danielle the next day. I mentioned how much I was looking forward to a concert at the Royal Academy of Music in London in a couple of days time. It was Tony's birthday and we were going as guests of Vera Gissing, whom I had befriended after she gave a talk at my school the previous summer. I briefly mentioned that on Saturday Tony and I would be going to a wedding in Old Windsor, an event we were looking forward to very much. As I was leaving the crisis centre, both sons gave me a huge hug, and they waved goodbye as I got into my car. Nick winked at me and called out, 'Love you, Mum, you're the best mum in the world.'

At 3 pm on the next day, Thursday 18 February, Nick met Danielle for his weekly DTTO appointment. Danielle recalled:

> He was rather low that afternoon, there's no doubt about it. I asked him what was wrong and we had a bit of a session together as he was quiet. He said 'Danni, I don't know what's the matter with me, but I feel really low today.'

> I asked him if he thought everything was getting on top of him. I have to be honest with you, that day he was down, but it wasn't out of the ordinary, it wasn't enough to raise alarm bells. Yes, he was fed up trying to battle his drug addiction and it wasn't working, so where was he going to go next? We talked about what he would be doing that night, if he was going to stay in or go out. I didn't think there was a problem, so when he left I wasn't unduly worried. With other clients I've felt the need to ring the doctor, but Nick was expressing frustration about his addiction, rather than desperation that it was just too much. I was due to write a court report for him the following week.

Danielle spent the rest of her meeting with Nick discussing why he felt so frustrated. She encouraged him to take things more slowly and to set himself realistic goals. She had already suggested other types of target setting; she wanted to encourage

Nick to stop injecting, and she felt that one step forward would be to try to alternate between smoking heroin and injecting it. Nick told her that he and Simon had decided not to do drugs any more. She realised it was likely that such a promise would be broken – probably on giro day. But when Nick left Danielle that afternoon, he thanked her and said how much better he felt for getting so much off his chest. She said:

> We had a very good relationship and, as a professional, I had time for him. I treated him with respect because, at heart, he was such a good young man. The biggest shock and sadness for me was that he was a young man with potential. He said so many times 'Danni, I just can't seem to knock these drugs on the head. I try everything but I lapse every time I get my giro. I disappoint people: you, myself, and especially my mum . . .'

Nick made an appointment with Danielle for the following week. But he never kept that appointment.

11
Staring Death in the Face

'I'M SORRY, but your son Nick is dead.'

The woman police officer touched my arm and immediately I left all the memories behind me as the reality of what was happening here and now brought me back to face the harsh truth. Nick was dead. It was 19 February 2004. The officer explained that Simon had found his twin dead at the crisis house. But the circumstances she related didn't coincide with the pictures I had painted in my mind: Nick drifting into unconsciousness after accidentally taking an overdose, Nick having some kind of accident through lack of awareness while under the influence of drugs . . .

He had hanged himself.

I sensed Simon's anguish straight away, realising how frantic he would have been to get hold of me, and I felt guilty that for some months now I had refused to give him my telephone number. The police officer indicated how desperate Simon had been to speak to me. I explained to her that we had been forced to change all our telephone numbers as Simon and Nick had relapsed into serious heroin use and we could no longer bear the strain of their constant pleas and demands for money.

I could clearly visualise Simon's state of mind and his response to his brother's death – how traumatised he must have been when unable to get hold of anyone in the family. His sister was not contactable and his mother had emotionally distanced herself from the nightmare. Simon had tried frantically to contact his father, leaving several distraught messages on his answerphone. But he had got no response.

What a helpless, lonely situation, but one which they had brought upon themselves. Saying yes instead of no to drugs was their choice. Their bond of twinship was incredibly strong. They did everything together, good or bad.

As I picked up the phone to ring Simon, I was haunted by the thought that perhaps I could have prevented all this. I will never forget the conversation I had with him. He told me how he had found his brother hanged in the toilet. 'He's hung himself, Mum, he's hung himself, Mum,' he kept repeating. I listened as he described how he had forced his way into Nick's locked bedroom on that Friday evening because he could get no answer. Nick had been dead for many hours and his body was in an advanced state of rigor mortis. Simon described over and over again, in graphic detail, the condition his brother was in.

This is Simon's version of what happened that night:

On Thursday 18 February Nick and I woke up at our usual time of 2 pm or later. We spent the day watching TV and DVDs. We had no money and not a lot else to do until we bumped into a friend who invited us to go to a mate's party – there were going to be plenty of drugs there. We jumped at the offer and got our stuff together, ready to be picked up by car. Before arriving at the house we got what little money we had together and bought some crack cocaine to take with us as we didn't want to look tight.

Once in the house we spent the night smoking heroin and crack and drinking a large quantity of alcohol. We arrived at about 9 pm and by 5 am we had managed to smoke £600 worth of heroin and crack accompanied by a bottle of vodka, a bottle of brandy and half a bottle of Jack Daniel's. Until then, it had been a great night, everyone laughing and joking. Then Nick got the idea into his head that he wanted to go and bang up some heroin. This wasn't an uncommon thing for either Nick or myself but we had both been trying very hard to stay away from the needles.

Nick proceeded to lie to everyone, saying that he had to leave as he had an appointment at 10 am with his probation officer and if he didn't make it then he would be arrested. I was the only person who knew his real motive – that he just wanted to leave the house, as he couldn't bang up heroin in such a nice house where he had been shown friendship and kindness. This made me angry and frustrated with him because we'd had such a good night. We argued, and Nick ended up punching me around the face and walking out of the house.

I told everyone else the reason for Nick's departure and we ran out of the house to stop him. We chased him down the street, shouting, while the owner of the house was trying desperately to shut us up in case we woke the neighbours. Nick had changed; there was no getting through to him, he was aggressive and violent, he was under the impression that we all hated him and wanted to see him arrested. I think he'd convinced himself of his own made-up story.

Nick stopped the first taxi that came along but got kicked out as he had no money. However, the next car that came past picked him up and took him home. At this point we just left him to it but we were very worried about him as he was so wrecked. About an hour later our friend Annie and I got a taxi back to the house to check on him. We walked through the door to find him fast asleep on the sofa with the handset of the phone off the hook and next to his head.

I walked into his bedroom and found the needle and spoon on the TV. This angered me and I woke him up. Not only had he wrecked the night and made a spectacle of himself but he had banged up as well. Another huge argument started which went on for an hour or so. We were screaming at the top of our lungs and calling each other all the names under the sun.

The argument came to a halt with Nick saying that I didn't love him, that I loved Annie more than him, which was ridiculous. Finally came those dreaded words, 'I'm going to kill myself.' He slammed his bedroom door shut while I shouted back, 'Go on then.' As twin brothers of course we'd had big arguments before. I assumed he wouldn't be so stupid and would just go to sleep once he had calmed down. So I went to bed.

It had been a very late night and I didn't stir until ten the next evening. I opened my eyes and all I could think about for the next hour was Nick and how stupid we'd all been. I decided to get up and go and make up with him. I banged on his door for a few minutes. No response. At first I thought he was just ignoring me but after banging very loudly and shouting his name I really began to get frightened and upset. There was no choice. I had to find out the situation and this meant smashing the door down. Before I did this I went upstairs to get Richard. I couldn't face doing it alone. In fact if I'd been on my own I believe that once I'd realised what had happened to Nick I would have taken my own life to be with my brother. They were big heavy fire doors and we couldn't get his open until we popped a window out with a hammer and reached through to turn the key.

As we entered Nick's room we could see the bed was still made and hadn't been slept in. At this point both of us were starting to panic. I knew something was seriously wrong but I didn't want to believe that my twin brother and lifelong soulmate could possibly be dead. We walked to the toilet door at the end of his room and found it locked. Once again I started banging and shouting his name, with no response. I didn't want to break the door down but I couldn't walk away; it was very upsetting but eventually we plucked up the courage to kick it in.

Nothing could have prepared me for what stared me in the face. Nick was slumped on the floor dead. His body was blue in colour, his face a dead pale blue, his eyes were wide open and bulging out of his face. His tongue was sticking two inches out of his mouth and it was jet black. I ran to him screaming at the top of my lungs, 'No, Nick – you can't be dead, no please, please, someone help me!' I couldn't believe he was dead until I started to cuddle his body. I put my hands around his neck, to find the shoelace pulled tight against his neck and tied to the window. Everything after that is pretty much a blur. I remember little snippets but I was so shocked that only Richard who was with me at the time could possibly understand. It took me nearly ten hours to even start to calm down. In that time I had to relive the night and give statements to the police and then watch my brother's body carried off to the morgue.

Simon's beloved twin brother of twenty-seven years was gone for ever.

I too was heartbroken. Memories of Nick passed through my mind at lightning speed. Nick was dead – yet all my memories, painful as they were, somehow gave me comfort. I knew that Nick would always be in my heart and I felt that he was with God, at peace, free from his addiction.

I was calm yet confused as I listened to Simon. I found it difficult to comprehend, his brother's apparent suicide seemed so out of character. He was seemingly doing well on the recovery programme. Whatever anguish and worry I had gone through, I wasn't prepared for Nick's death to come by hanging. Time after time I had reminded myself that injecting heroin would probably kill both my sons, but this news simply didn't equate with the son I had spoken to only a couple of days ago.

The grief that I felt was and always will be indescribable. If Nick had died as a result of a tragic accident or an illness, it would have perhaps been easier for me to talk about. But this was such a cruel death. When Simon and I eventually spoke about it, he said to me: 'Tony thinks that maybe Nick did what he did because he saw no way out and he thought his death might be a way out for me. I don't know, we'll never know. The only thing I can add is that Nick would never have wanted me to find his body in a state like that. I don't think he would ever have wished something like that on me or you. He loved me so much as his identical twin and he loved you so much as his mum.'

The emotion in Simon's voice on that night encapsulated the shocking reality. He had lost his soulmate, the best friend he ever had. The baby brother, the child, the schoolboy, the teenager, the man he had been closest to all his life was dead. Simon was no longer a twin brother, no longer a twin heroin addict. Many times I had warned both of them: 'It may take the death of one of you to wake the other one up.' Now my frustrated remark had become a reality.

I turned to my husband and pleaded with him, 'Tony, you will now forgive Nick and Simon, won't you?' Tony was simply bewildered.

As soon as I said it I realised again how difficult it must have been for Tony, as a stepfather, to cope with the drug addiction that had almost led to the total breakdown of our married life. I felt enormous guilt that in a continued effort to help my sons, he had lost all his savings, twice remortgaged the house and sacrificed his retirement. Tony had said many times: 'I don't ever regret being with you, but I get angry and regret the way things have turned out. It's very frustrating to watch one's wife get so upset because her adult children have hurt her so much.' How could I now expect him to share my hopes for our future, hope for the mending of family relationships and friendships, hope for our marriage to return to what it had been, hope for a drug-free life for all of us?

Tony and I had been slipping towards marital crisis. Contact with my sons had been destructive to our relationship. Close friends knew how dreadful the situation had become. Tony summed it up very powerfully when he said:

> I felt I was always left to be second best. The boys' addiction came first in your life because you are their mother, but at the same time I was their stepfather and I felt in a catch-22 situation. I felt I was always picking up the pieces of someone else's mess, both financially and emotionally. And in the end, that wears you down to nothing.

I understood how Tony felt, his sense of frustration and anger, sadness and hurt. His patience and tolerance had been stretched to the limit. How could I now expect him to be more compassionate?

Yet my heart reached out to embrace Simon. All my senses urged me to support him the best way I could. So many times since that night, I have thanked God that he was alive.

The female officer had held my hand, commenting on how brave I was. Little did she know that my display of bravery was something I had rehearsed over and over again. I had conditioned myself to believe such a tragedy as this would eventually happen. I had forced myself, trained myself to live it, prepare for it and accept it. Bravery has no alliance with me: it was frustration, helplessness, disappointment, and disbelief as I watched my sons throw away their jobs, their careers, their friends and family, their future. I had indeed mentally prepared myself for this day; it was the only way I could face life.

Tony and I were due to go to a wedding that afternoon. In fact we had spent most of the previous day looking for something to wear. Tony said that he would phone the groom and make our apologies. It was chilling to realise that while we had been shopping for clothes all that day, Nick was dead and none of us knew it. I had tried several times to ring Nick on his mobile as I wanted to tell both the boys about the lovely evening we had spent at the Royal Academy of Music. I had been puzzled and anxious that there was no reply, but never did I dream that such a catastrophe had occurred.

As the police officer held my hand, I tried to be practical. We needed to telephone Marie in London. 'We must tell his sister, we must tell her soon,' I said. 'But do we phone her in the middle of the night? Do we wait, what do we do?' I wanted to be with Simon as soon as possible but first I had to phone my daughter.

Marie realised straight away that something must be desperately wrong, as I would never telephone her at four in the morning unless it was very serious. I forget how I delivered the news – I think it was Tony who took the phone from me and told her gently of her brother's death. We cried together over the phone as I recounted all I knew of what had happened. I felt empty and helpless at not being with my daughter. Her way of coping with her brothers' addiction had been to cut herself off from them until they were clean. However, I realised that, unlike me, she had not been expecting to hear such tragic news. When she and Nick had last met, for the first time in a long time at Christmas 2003, he had appeared to be on the way to recovery.

Still in shock, and as if in a trance, I got dressed. Before Tony and I left to be with Simon, I telephoned my friends Pam and Tom Ward and told them the news. They offered to come with us, so we picked them up on the way. I had become close to both Pam and Tom since joining Crack it!, and I felt I needed to hold on tight to all the support I could get.

We arrived at the crisis house in Wokingham about 5 am. The

shock and disbelief was apparent on the residents' faces, and particularly on that of the director. She explained that she had gone home as usual at about 5.30 pm, believing Nick to be sleeping off his drinking session from the night before. She had spoken to Simon but had no reason to think that something as terrible as this could have taken place.

She turned to me and said gently: 'In my seventeen years of experience here the people who commit suicide are the last people in the world who you think would do so. That was the case with Nick. I would never have envisaged him committing suicide. If I ever go out of that door in the evening and I'm uneasy or worried about anyone I then go back and do something. I've always abided by this rule over the years and it has stood me in good stead. I wasn't worried about Nick at all. He was a cheerful, jolly chap: yes, he had lots of problems, I know that perhaps he had more than his brother, but that wasn't how he came across. He would crack a joke and he was very good at attracting the ladies. Nick could have had a girlfriend for every day of the week – that's how he came across to me.'

Pam reflected on an occasion at the centre when a very well-educated man whose partner had died in a car crash had taken his life, and how someone else who had been unable to make adjustments in his retirement had done the same. She continued: 'I was giving the Subutex tablets to him daily, I didn't know he was also getting heroin. I'm sure it was an accident when his mind was befuddled with drugs and alcohol. I can't believe it was intentional, not when the balance of his mind was right.

'I saw him briefly yesterday afternoon as he had his probation appointment with Danielle. I knocked on his door as I knew he had a lot on and I said, "Come on Nick, you've got probation this afternoon!" He was in a terrific rush but he was fine, his normal self. When the police rang me to say a young man was dead I thought it might have been one of the other residents. I was so shocked when I found out it was dear Nick, I was totally bewildered. Here at the crisis house we accept there's inevitably a risk as we deal with mental health. You accept some patients will die, but not Nick.'

As he heard Pam's words, Simon was utterly bereft. I hugged and held him as he alternately sobbed and wailed. Pam continued: 'I realised they had been to a party and I tried rousing Simon but failed and when I failed with Nick, I gave up. I hadn't a qualm, Simon was snoring his head off, so I went home believing both boys would sleep it off. I was got out of bed at about 11.30 pm by the police, who told me a young man had been found dead at the crisis house and could I organise support for the young people there. I was really shocked when they said it was Nick, I couldn't believe it.

'I was shaking, so I got the driver from my regular taxi firm to drive me back. The crisis team was here. They told me Simon had got up and knocked on Nick's door a couple of times. When it came to 11 pm and there was still no answer, Simon got worried and thought something must be wrong. Richard helped Simon to break the lock to get into the bathroom and he said to Simon, "You realise Nick is dead, don't you?"

'The police doctor came and everyone was sobbing. I said to the woman police officer, "Elizabeth is going to be absolutely devastated," but they're trained well to deal with this kind of thing. When they removed Nick's body, we had to close all the doors as they took him away. It's a nightmare.'

Simon later recalled how he felt when the undertakers came to remove his brother's body, repeating over and over again how he'd heard the wheels of the trolley bang along the corridor and then the sound of the temporary coffin being placed in the hearse. How I loathed the thought of Nick's body being put in a refrigerator, dead and cold, to be cut up by a pathologist. I prayed that he would be dealt with in a dignified and gentle way. I stared into Simon's eyes, wanting to scream to the whole world, 'This is what drugs can do.' I wanted every parent to hear and see this: 'Drugs can kill. They killed my son Nick. Wake up and believe: this is the bitter truth.'

Simon's vivid description of how he discovered his brother rarely leaves me, but I have learnt to live with it. It was a terrible way to die, alone and out of control. No mother in this world would want that to happen to her child. I yearned to have been there to help Simon cope, or to have been there instead of him. It was too much for anyone to bear alone.

Parents of twins will, perhaps, particularly empathise with my feelings. To contemplate the death of one twin is hard enough, but to listen to such a graphic account of the other finding his brother dead was emotional torture. I thanked God that Simon's life had been spared and asked him to give Simon strength to cope with his loss. Above all, I prayed that Simon wouldn't turn to drugs again to escape from the reality of Nick's death.

By now dawn had broken and Simon's father and stepmother arrived. No one knew what to say. I could see the emotion in Lawrence's eyes but all of us were too shocked to be spontaneous with gestures and words. I remained on the sofa, holding on to Simon. There was tea and coffee and some discussion about going to see the body, where the body would be, how to organise the funeral, whom to contact. I felt as if I was partially deaf. I could hear voices but everything was in the background, far off. We sat there for a long time trying to absorb the truth.

Pam and Tom offered to telephone Steve Payne, the minister of our church. I could hardly believe that only the previous Sunday Nick and Simon had been in his church singing, praising the Lord with smiles on their faces. Neither of the boys had hidden their drug history from members of the congregation. I knew that Steve would be shocked and upset but that he and his wife, Linda, would be there to support us in every way they could. I remembered how often Nick had mentioned recently that he liked going to church on Sundays as it lifted him up for the rest of the week. There must be a purpose in all this, I thought to myself.

Steve arrived at the crisis centre not long after Pam and Tom had left. Just having had them there during those few hours was soothing; everything about them was kindness itself, no judgements, just love and help in any way they could offer. I remember that Steve was wearing a red jacket. It had been raining and he was wet through. Yet he walked straight over to us and put his arms round Simon and me, and we all cried together. He wrapped us in prayer and somehow I then felt able to face the day ahead.

Steve offered to join the family to go to see Nick in the morgue and then to help to plan the funeral. But as we set off, we had a telephone call from the coroner advising us not to come: as a result of the hanging, Nick's fragile body was in such a bad state that we weren't allowed to see it. He told us that any-one who wanted to see Nick should visit him later in the week in the chapel of rest at the funeral parlour. At least, I realised, the Nick we would finally say goodbye to would have been prepared for viewing by the embalmer; this stranger would be responsible for making our last sight of Nick bearable. It would be better for Simon, I thought to myself – his last sight of his brother wouldn't be the horrifying image he had seen when he discovered him dead. I prayed that this would eventually give Simon some peace.

The day of Nick's death was without question the worst of my life. Yet I sensed that Nick was at peace; of that I had no doubt whatsoever. There was no panic, no hysteria, just an inner feeling of peace. I realised that what I had to face wasn't going to be easy – a mother never expects to bury her own child. But I felt determined not to let Nick's death be in vain. This testimony is my evidence of that.

12
Forever Twins

IN THE DAYS that followed Nick's death I was in severe shock. I was shattered both physically and emotionally. My head ached and my body was void of any feeling. I seemed to be living in slow motion, waiting for the fragmented parts of my body and mind to solder themselves together. My friend Rosemary recalls:

> You didn't know if Simon was going to survive that night or the next night or the day after. Your biggest fear was not whether Simon would go back to heroin but that he too might kill himself because he had lost his brother. You weren't sleeping at all. I remember wondering what would become of you all. Maybe in some way, it is in God's hands that Nick has gone. I don't think either of them would have lived normal lives, bearing in mind where drugs had taken them.

The day after the tragedy, Tony, Simon and I went to church. I felt completely numb, but I knew that it was important for the three of us to unite and help each other. As we drove into the church car park I saw members of the Crack it! team waiting to support us in any way they could. Yet all through the service I was in a daze, unable to make sense of what was happening to me, to us. I could feel the surge of love and hear the prayers and sympathy of everyone present as Steve Payne announced to the congregation that Nick had died. My eyes were fixed on the seat on which he had sat with Simon only the previous Sunday. It seemed inconceivable that he would never come back. I felt his presence all around me, as if he was reassuring me that he was fine, at peace, free.

For weeks I had great difficulty getting going in the morning. My normal routine as a full-time teacher was to be up by 6.30 am and in school by 8 am. I just couldn't do it any more. My sleep pattern had become very irregular. I found myself getting up in the middle of the night, sometimes wandering into the garden, looking up to the sky. Silently, I would plead, 'Where are you, Nick?' or 'When are you coming back, Nick?' Or I would reproach him and say, 'Why did you have to put us through all this? You were doing so well.' I never stopped telling him how much I loved him; it made me feel at peace in my mind and my heart. Yet there was hardly a night when Simon's vivid description of the scene of his brother's death didn't filter into my subconscious. I was able to find some relief in tears; sometimes I managed to smile, remembering the happy times. And I was fortunate to have Tony's full support. I remembered how desperate and isolated I had felt when both the boys were at their lowest ebb in their addiction. During the middle of the night I was haunted by their father's words two years earlier: 'I have accepted you boys are going to die.' I gradually realised that I would learn to endure the physical loss of Nick, because I believed that he was at peace, away from further harm.

During the five days leading up to our visit to the chapel of rest to say our first goodbye to Nick, our bungalow filled with flowers, and with visitors whose friendship cushioned our pain. Messages of sympathy flooded in from colleagues at work, friends, pupils past and present, governors and members of our church. Even members of the probation service came to visit us after the end of their working day, bringing flowers. I could see that Simon was still unable to comprehend the loss of Nick, but it helped him hugely to talk about his brother to people who had known him well. I was enormously touched to hear that the residents of the probation hostel had clubbed together and bought a rose bush, which they planted in the grounds in Nick's memory.

On the Tuesday after Nick died a letter came from Danielle, his key worker from the DTTO team:

It is with much regret and sadness that I find myself writing to you at this painful time. I have been managing Nick since the end of October 2003 and I was devastated when I had the phone call this morning telling me of his death.

Nick engaged well in my appointments and we developed a good rapport. In the time that I worked with Nick, I found him to be a very pleasant and intelligent young man who had potential in his life. It is such a shame that Nick did not make it to the next step.

My last contact with him was Thursday afternoon last week and although he was struggling with his drug use, which we spent time talking about, he left my appointment much happier and thanked me for listening.

I would like to take this opportunity to wish you and your family comfort and support now and for the future. I hope that it will be acceptable to attend his funeral and pay my respects.

A little while later, Danielle came to see me. She explained that the biggest shock and sadness for her was that Nick had been a young man with the chance of a great future. One of her responsibilities when she saw Nick had been to check regularly to see if he was suicidal. She said: 'On Monday morning when I got the call to say he was dead, I was completely devastated. Of all my clients Nick would have been last on my list to do that. My instant reaction was that it wasn't suicide, this wasn't a suicidal man.'

Francesca, Nick's key worker at the probation hostel, later described to me how Megan, the senior manager, had comforted her when they heard the news that Nick had died earlier that day:

We were both sat on the sofa at the hostel and we were in absolute shock. I haven't seen him for well over a month and it was the last thing I expected. One of my last memories of him was outside of work here. I was coming out of a supermarket and I saw him and he had a great big smile on his face. All the residents who are still at the hostel from the time Nick stayed there just cannot believe it. I am terribly sorry, so terribly sorry, I am sure it wasn't intentional; he wasn't the sort, not Nick.

During this painful time, Simon's friends from both his Berkshire and Bath schooldays came forward to support him. His great school pal Teggie took the day off work on the Monday to be there for him. Many of these young people had dabbled with the drug scene, some more dangerously than others, and I could tell that Nick's shocking death was a real bombshell to them all. I was glad of their reaction. It opened up frank channels of communication between us.

Almost a week had passed before the funeral director advised us that we could say our first goodbye to Nick at the chapel of rest. I had been wondering what was happening to my son's body during that time. Had there been a chance for someone to benefit from organ donation, then surely we would have been approached? I knew from watching TV documentaries and appeals that in such cases speed was of the essence. That another person's life might have been saved would have given me a great deal of comfort. Simon mentioned later that he had been approached about organ donation but he was still too traumatised to think straight. I wish I had known. I would have said yes. And I kept praying that when I saw Nick in his coffin he would not look as Simon had described him. Common sense told me that the embalmer would do his best, but that didn't allay my fears.

Our small family group waited nervously at the chapel of rest on that difficult afternoon. Simon and his friend Richard went outside to smoke a cigarette while the rest of us remained inside, protecting ourselves from the cold February weather. We were unaware that, as the two young men stood outside the funeral parlour, Ricky, the drug dealer who knew both Nick and Simon, was passing by. As he approached Simon and Richard, he looked at them and said, without a trace of compassion, 'Good riddance.'

What chilling hypocrisy from someone who had contributed to the demise of my son, while being only too willing to fill his own pockets with the financial spoils of Nick's addiction. I was relieved that I hadn't heard this dealer make his brutal comment, lest I lash out both physically and verbally. My experience of heroin dealers had made me realise that they don't care a toss about the lives of the addicts and the families they destroy. Yet heroin possesses and corrupts their minds too – drug dealers and drug barons are beyond human understanding. Money becomes their god; the destruction of others' lives and the misery they create is the last thing on their minds. In the world of addiction there are those who profit and those who lose. Nick lost and paid the ultimate price with his life.

As the time edged its way towards 2 pm, we were advised that we could go to see Nick. We agreed that immediate family would go in first: Nick's father, his sister Marie, Simon and myself. There are some moments in life that affect us so deeply that we remember them as if they had only just happened. This was an occasion that will remain forever imprinted on my mind.

Nick looked so calm, so peaceful and so liberated as he lay in his coffin. His hair had been washed and trimmed neatly and his hands and his fingers were carefully linked together across his chest. His hands reminded me of the times when he was a baby and I used to touch them when he was asleep. My heart surged with love for my son. At that moment, I knew that he was with God. His face looked utterly serene. I was full of relief for all our sakes that our last visual memory of Nick was so beautiful and precious.

In the hope that it would be allowed, we had brought one or two personal items with us to place in Nick's coffin. I held a photograph of him and myself taken on the day he had been discharged from the Florence Nightingale Hospital in London after his ten-day detox session. I placed it gently on his chest, near his now silent heart. For the first time, I could be sure that Nick would remain forever drug free. That photograph was of my real son, the drug-free Nick. But now in that quiet chapel of rest I was consumed with sadness as I watched Simon tenderly place his goodbye letter in the coffin next to his twin. It said:

Nick,

I'm so sorry and regret that stupid argument so much. I don't have to tell you how much I love you and how much I miss you because you know it is too much to put into words. I want you to know I forgive you already and I hope you forgive me.

From now on I am going to change and sort my life out. I'm doing this in your memory, as you would still be here now if we had not been so stupid.

I pray and know that you are in a better place now and there's no more suffering and arguing. I would love to be there with you and we could carry on as we always did. Nick, all you need to know is that no matter what, we will always have each other and I believe your soul is with me. I will always try and visit you as often as I can get there. Make sure you stay as happy as you always were, Nick. I am counting the days, months and years, however long it is before I am with you again. Just hold on to our love.

When Tony saw Nick a little later he immediately broke down at the loss of such a young life and he was comforted by Michael, Marie's boyfriend. From that day Tony has always held the belief that Nick's death gave Simon a new life.

In death there is no denying the truth, however hard it is to accept; it's there in the still and silent body of your loved one. Nick's body was like a clock without a mechanism, a car without an engine. He lay gently at rest in the coffin chosen for him by Simon; a body without a soul, because his immortal soul was at peace.

Nick's funeral was due to take place eleven days later, and it would give everyone who knew him the chance to say their own goodbyes. After we left the chapel of rest, we went to Lawrence's house to discuss the funeral arrangements. Lawrence reminded me that he had already mentioned he had a skiing holiday booked for the week in which we hoped the funeral would take place. Time seems to become vague and lose its shape when you are grieving, but I had assumed that Nick's funeral would take place the following week. Now it began to dawn on me that this wasn't the case and that laying Nick to rest would have to be put on hold if Lawrence went ahead with his trip. Tony said: 'Why don't you and Simon and the rest of the family leave it to me to organise the funeral service while Lawrence is away skiing? None of you need the upset to go on any longer than necessary.' But there was no response, we were all in a daze.

Everyone has their own way of dealing with grief. It was difficult explaining to my friends and colleagues that Nick's funeral couldn't take place until 8 March, some eighteen days after he had died, because of a skiing trip. But Lawrence said he would take his laptop with him so that after he came off the slopes, we could email one another about the funeral service. Was this a first? I wondered. But other members of the family held the view that it was Lawrence's way of coping, and I didn't have the emotional energy to challenge the suggestion.

After I arrived home later that day, a friend from school telephoned and told me about an organisation called Compassionate Friends which supports people who are bereaved. Feeling it might help me to be in touch with other mothers who were in a similar situation, she advised me to look up their website. I wasted no time in sitting down to write an email:

My name is Elizabeth. I am the mother of identical twins, or I was. Nicholas died last week on 19th Feb 2004. He and his brother were incredibly close. Simon found his twin brother dead in very gruesome circumstances, as Nick had been dead many hours before Simon found him. Nicholas appears to have hung himself in a drunken drug-fuelled gesture after the boys had been drinking. They had a row but drink and drugs got in the way and clouded their judgement. The coroner feels the final verdict may be 'accidental death' or 'misadventure' but the interim death certificate gave hanging as the cause of death, which is very hard to accept.

Is there anybody who has lost a twin in tragic circumstances that I can communicate my feelings to? I am doing my best to cope and I have great support and a strong faith, but I think it may help me to speak to parents of twins who have been bereaved.

A woman called Julia emailed me the next day:

I am so sorry to hear about your loss. It seems to me that our link is not only suicide but also closeness to the event. I have heard from a number of very kind people who have lost their children in similar circumstances to us and who have been kind enough to reassure me that life at some level continues. You and I are still addressing the terrifying rawness and newness of this pain. My heart goes out to you and your family for having experienced this most terrible of losses. I can't offer you any advice. I can't think how we are to satisfy our instincts as mothers to give comfort to our surviving children. I am trying to imagine Simon's pain – to have lost what must have been part of himself. I am glad that you have strong faith to sustain you, Elizabeth, I am afraid that is something I don't share – how I wish I could.

I have been in contact with the organisation called SOBS (Survivors of Bereavement by Suicide); although I don't at the moment feel I am really surviving, I will email you their address if it will help you. I intend to go to a local meeting in the hope I can find some comfort, support and help to survive this devastating ordeal.

Part of me feels ashamed to gain comfort from the knowledge that we are not alone, Elizabeth, and that other people have experienced this loss. Even as a member of a close family, a loving family, there is an element of this pain, which is entirely and uniquely ours as mothers, isn't there? I hope that we will be able to help each other through these dark days and perhaps share memories of our beloved sons and thoughts that are difficult to share with the members of our families – thoughts that may cause them pain.

Please know that I am thinking of you.

How amazing that from my heartbreak and distress (and in complete contrast to the prospect of organising my son's funeral by the same means), I had via email been offered comfort and emotional support by another mother – someone whom to this day I have never put a face to, but who bonded with me instantly. I was able to talk of my sadness and pain, and I knew she understood. In my first reply I wrote:

How kind of you to open your heart to me so warmly about your own loss; your son sounds to me like he was a great young man. His and Nick's loss is for ever, and is so hard for us mums to fully believe and accept. The stress, tension and anguish at the loss of a loved one, and all those emotions which go with losing a son, have put great pressure on my marriage. My husband is Nick's stepfather and he has suffered many years watching both his stepsons go wild and abuse drink and drugs. How hard it has been for him to continue offering support, but he has stood by me despite all the terrible things that have happened.

You asked after Simon, what can I say? He is utterly devastated and heartbroken. I will never forget as long as I live his pain when he saw his brother in the chapel of rest. As identical twins they were used to having arguments because they were so close, but this one got out of hand because of drink and drugs. He cannot sleep properly at the moment as he is having flashbacks and keeps dreaming about Nick.

I just cannot work out why these things happen to ordinary families, can you?

I believe that Simon will honour his word and turn his life round in memory of his brother. He is determined to put his life in order and to do right by Nick.

Helped by Tony's support and the comforting emails from Julia, I began to turn my thoughts to the funeral service. But I hadn't got far when a card of sympathy from a friend of mine named Mary Brooks landed on the doorstep the next day. I don't know who was the author of the message it bore, but it had a significant impact on me. This is what it said:

The world is full of miracles to those who recognise them
But we have to look the right way
since God will sometimes disguise them.
He shines his light in places where we least expect Him to
and often does the opposite of what we think He'll do
He has a habit of bringing out the best within the worst
The moment we stop worrying and choose to put Him first
And if we do, he'll pull us through and help us find a door
That opens to the very thing that we've been looking for.

I asked myself, how could Nick's death bring out the best within the worst? How could I ever look at Nick's death as a miracle? Had God shone His light on us? I thought about the countless times I had asked God to help Nick break free of his addiction, and how angry and disillusioned I became with God because he did not answer my prayers. I had decided on several occasions God did not exist any more. Yet as I continued to look at the card I began to wonder whether Nick's death was, in some way, a blessing. I felt strengthened, and its message began to shape my thoughts.

I sat in the conservatory of my house, deep in thought, and became very calm. A peace came over me and I was confident from that moment that Nick's funeral service would be a dignified, almost a happy occasion. I felt empowered to use this chance to show that from the terrible tragedy and waste of a young life there was a blessing for all of us.

And so Simon and I began work to put together the most beautiful service in celebration of Nick's twenty-seven years of life. The daily email link with Lawrence proved invaluable, as he was keen to know how we were progressing with the arrangements. Nick's life as a heroin addict had been so chaotic; I decided his farewell service should be a time of peace and quiet, a time to smile as well as cry. I thought about all the different people who might attend: family members, school friends, former teachers, possibly even addict friends; those who had cut Nick out of their lives and those who may not have known about his addiction. I wanted to bring the voice of hope into his service; I hoped that, in spite of this terrible tragedy, the celebration of Nick's life would bring everyone present together.

During the time Lawrence was away skiing, I found the strength to have silent conversations with Nick. I felt I had to come to terms with what death really meant. This was the beginning of my healing process – until then, I had not asked myself what death really meant to me. Is death the irreversible ending of life – of Nick's life? The service of Thanksgiving for the life of my precious son was held on Monday 8 March, some 18 days after he died. It was held at Sindlesham Baptist Church just outside the small market town of Wokingham at 2.00pm. Nick's body was then taken to be cremated at Henley Road Crematorium, Reading. And when the minister gave his address to the congregation of three hundred people at Nick's service, he echoed my feelings.

In life, our experiences are that very often we are blown around; we face many difficulties, many worries. We have many fears. Perhaps there are those here who fear death? Some of us may face many hardships, we face tough decisions and sometimes there is tough opposition. St Paul in his letter to the Romans talks about something that is constant in all of that, that is the love of God that is in Christ Jesus.

The problem today for many of us is that we haven't heard of it. Or perhaps we have heard of it and even that worries us, because we think: 'How do I respond? What in my life does it beckon to do in response to this love?' And if we find ourselves not knowing about it or being frightened about it, we actually rob ourselves of the power that it provides for our life. It provides power to help us in our time of need. If you don't know it, you will not know the power that is there – and I speak as someone who knows it.

I don't know what the effect of the love of God was in Nick's life, or at least the majority of it. Many of you will have known him through difficult times; many of you will be able to testify if it got him through the troubles in his life. I'd known him for six months while he came with Simon and Elizabeth to our church here. It was great to have the boys with us, a real blessing; I want to tell you we loved them to bits.

On the Sunday before he died, Nick was in church with us, he was sitting just behind where Simon is now. It was a communion service and, in communion, we remember Christ's death on the cross. When I offer this meal to the church I say it's OK if at this point in time you don't want to take hold of Jesus Christ. If you don't feel that you've got the faith to grab hold of this, that's OK, just let the bread and wine go past you. But if, today, you want to take hold of Jesus Christ and the love he has for you, then take hold of it, take the bread and take the wine. If it is the first time you have ever done it, that's fine. You don't have to say anything to anyone, no need to do anything, just take Him.

And as I sat at the front where Nick's picture is today, with the boys right in front of me, I looked out at the congregation. I know everyone is supposed to be praying with their eyes shut but I did look. So my last recollection of Nick was of him reaching out and taking hold of the bread and the wine.

Nick was on a journey of discovery, as are all of us in the church. I don't know when he started the journey but I know on that day he continued it, he reached out in faith. Tragically, that journey of discovery got stopped very quickly.

But St Paul says that neither death nor life will be able to separate us from this love. So, if you can be encouraged on this day, then take this, that death cannot separate Nick from the love of God. I guess if he could speak to us he would say take hold of it, find it as the source of hope in your life, when your emotions are in turmoil, take hold of it, discover what a source of strength, power and hope it is, for every situation in your life.

What Steve said helped me and many others to come to terms with the tragedy of Nick's death, even to accept it as a blessing. Sister Joseph, the boys' former infant school teacher, sent us a letter a few days after the funeral:

I thought Nick's funeral was befitting to such a fine young man, too young to die. Your choice of readings, songs and music were very beautiful and Elizabeth's tribute was very moving. I wept throughout the service but I felt once again very honoured being with you all, recalling the days when my twin boys would be in trouble and my heart ached as if I were their mum. Simon, your life has changed but Nick will never be far from you. Remember, Simon, I will always be there for you as long as I live. You are blessed with many friends and Nick would want you to continue your social life. Go out and in the quiet of the night talk to Nick about former times, and you will find comfort.

Simon has indeed been supported by many friends in Reading and Bath. He accepts that they had to walk away from him and Nick after a long period of trying to help them get clean, and he knows that they have been true friends who have otherwise stuck by him through thick and thin:

It has been fun going out and being normal again with them. What they don't realise is how much it's meant to me. I was at the worst place I could have been, I had no self-confidence, no life and I could list the number of my friends on one hand. Then, to make things worse, Nick died and I lost a part of me and the best and closest friend I will ever have. Through these times when I was feeling my lowest Kai, Teggie and Tomsie stuck by me and gave me the confidence I needed to stick with it and learn to live again – because, let's face it, when you're on heroin you are learning to die. I believe that only death will separate the group of friends that I have now.

Ever since I met Carl when I was sixteen years of age and lived in Bath we just clicked. The main thing is that Carl was a true friend through the really rough times too. When he could, he gave me a roof over my head and some cash to buy food or drugs. He didn't judge me, he just felt for me. He had had a few problems with drug use himself, not heroin but enough for him to appreciate that I was in too deep and he would constantly encourage me to give up. Having to sit there and watch me take the stuff must have been unpleasant but he constantly encouraged me to get well. He has visited me regularly since I have been clean and he will be a friend for life.

Nick and I had a unique friendship, one which can never be replaced. Through the toughest times he appreciated that I was there for him and he told me repeatedly that he loved me. At our last meeting, two days before he died, Nick and I were on the computer searching for an electrician's course – and just hours before his death he had gone to the college to collect the application forms. As we parted, we hugged and kissed and he winked at me and said: 'Love you loads, Mum.'

Despite the pain of his death, Nick also gave me a lot of joy; there was much fun and laughter in our lives before the drugs changed him, and these memories are precious. At times I was so proud of him and sometimes utterly ashamed, but I'm now able to let go of the sad memories because the real Nick lives on in Simon.

Simon's dedication to Nick was written at 3 am on 13 March 2004, twenty-three days after his beloved twin brother died:

Forever Twins
To Nick

When life began, there was one split in two
A single egg broke in half, bringing me and you
We began weak and young and grew to be strong with love
And matured naïvely, but that love shone above
Through the good times and the bad times there was always us

Giving love and happiness to all that we loved
I'll never know why you left me that day
And will wonder forever, 'cause it causes that pain
I feel empty now, that emptiness will never leave
Wanting you, loving you, not knowing how to grieve
Give me your strength through these next few years
Because being with you will take away the tears
I cry through the day and all through the night
And feel that nothing will turn on that light
I love you and mourn you until I despair
And know that in heaven it will only repair
Please forgive me as I forgave you
As I know as a single I will always be two

Love Simon

A New Beginning

Five weeks after Nick died, on Saturday 27 March 2004, Simon left Reading station at 7 am on a train bound for Birmingham. I wanted to go with him, or at least drive him there, but I knew this was something that he had to do for himself. Simon told me later about that day:

It was a nerve-racking two hours on the train. It was a nice day for everyone else out there but not for me. On the train I felt nervous, heartbroken and full of sorrow. I was numb with pain. I got to Birmingham University and stood outside breathing heavily and pondering what the next five or six hours were going to be like. I knew it wasn't going to be easy and that's about all.

I walked into the meeting room; I was one of the first to arrive. I think this may have made it a bit easier as there weren't so many staring faces asking me who I was or how my twin died. But it didn't matter whether there

217

were ten people in the room or two; the question was eventually going to be asked.

Telling my story is very hard and upsetting, and it's probably the same for many other 'lone twins' out there, but I didn't find this was the case at my first Lone Twin meeting. I found that the more I spoke to people the easier it became, and the more comfortable I became in the presence of all the strangers.

The first group that I went into was for lone twins who hadn't been to a meeting before. There were about twelve of us; it was very sad. We went round in a circle and told our story from person to person and the feeling of being able to understand each other's pain and grief became evident. By the end of the first group I felt that I wasn't alone and although something tragic had happened, everyone was there for me and we understood each other.

In the afternoon I chose to go into the group for those who had lost their twin suddenly. There were only five of us in this group, so it gave us more time to speak to each other about our experiences. We all managed to get off our chest how we were feeling. It was good to talk about all the times you shared with your twin, the practical jokes you could play on people as an identical twin. In this group I realised I felt completely comfortable and was able to talk about things that I wouldn't talk about with many other people. I could relate to the others because everyone there was a lone twin. I was a bag of nerves at the start of that day but now I felt totally relaxed.

I was glad that only five weeks after the day of dear Nick's death I'd found the courage to go to this meeting. We'd spent twenty-seven years together living in the same houses and we had the same group of friends, hobbies and lifestyle, a lifestyle which, in the end, killed him. Words cannot describe how much I miss him.

For Simon, joining the Lone Twin Network still remains a vital part of his healing process. The organisation was set up in 1989 and offers a network of contacts, supporting anyone whose twin has died at whatever stage in life. It helps twins who have had similar experiences of loss to share their views and feelings and to offer and receive appropriate support. Membership of this unique and continually growing group, coupled with the support of his close friends Teggie, Tomsie and Kai, and his other school friends from Bath, is an invaluable part of Simon's recovery, not only from Nick's death, but also in his resolve never to touch drugs again. When Simon stood by the side of Nick's coffin in the chapel of rest, he promised me that he would turn his life round in memory of his brother. I am enormously proud of him – he has stuck rigidly to his word and honoured his commitment to Nick from that day.

In the early weeks after Nick passed away, Tony had his name engraved in the Memorial Gardens in Woodford Park. By chance, the gardens were built near where Nick and Simon played together as youngsters. It is very comforting to go there, to sit quietly and reflect on the many happy memories I treasure of my sons climbing trees and playing in the park with their friends. When Nick was finally laid to rest on the anniversary of his death at Henley Road Crematorium, this dignified, gentle and peaceful occasion was an opportunity for me to remember the many blessings and joyful days that he brought into our lives as well as the sadness and the difficult times that broke our hearts. As his ashes were placed in the ground, the following words were read by our minister's friend:

> Death is nothing at all; I have only slipped away into the next room.
> I am I, and you are you. Whatever we were to each other – that we still are.
> Call me by my old familiar name, speak to me in the easy way which you always used.
> Put no difference in your tone, wear no air of forced solemnity or sorrow
> Laugh as we always laughed at the little jokes we enjoyed together.
> Pray, smile, think of me; let my name be the household word that it always was
> Let it be spoken without effect, without the trace of a shadow on it.
> Life means all that it ever meant; it is the same as it ever was
> There is unbroken continuity; why should I be out of mind because I am out of sight?
> I am waiting for you, for an interval somewhere very near; just around the corner. All is well.
> (*Henry Scott Holland, 1847–1914, Canon of St Paul's Cathedral*)

On 13 May 2004, ten weeks after Nick died, the coroner gave his verdict. He said that he could not record a verdict of suicide because the vast quantities of drugs and alcohol had impaired Nick's judgement and there was no way of knowing whether he had intended to kill himself. He added that in the absence of a note or proof that Nick wanted to commit suicide, he could only record an open verdict. I felt that such a verdict gave Nick's cruel death a tiny bit of dignity. Somehow the outcome of the inquest gave me peace of mind; I knew from that day that I would survive.

I wrote this on 14 May 2004 and put it on the noticeboard in the staffroom at school:

> Dear Friends,
> The inquest for my son Nick was held yesterday at Windsor Coroner's Court. An open verdict was recorded.
>
> The coroner conducted the inquest with dignity and compassion. Simon, Nick's twin brother, coped very well with the questions about the difficult circumstances of Nick's death.
>
> I very much appreciate all your concerns. Simon and I are well aware of all your support and we gain strength from this.
>
> Making this statement will make you all aware of the final verdict.

As the numbness and shock slowly subsided, I eased my way back into work after the Easter holidays, first part-time and eventually, later in the year, full-time. An invitation to spend a couple of weeks in America in August as guests of my supportive and compassionate friends, Les and Rachel, led me to begin writing this book. I got up in the middle of the night almost six months to the day from Nick's death and began writing.

When I returned to England in late summer, I was invited by Claire Christiansen, then the Substance Misuse Parent and Adult Educator responsible for the National Vocational Qualification, Level Two course in Drugs Awareness, to a meeting in Oxford. Sharafat Ali, then a member of the Bucks Community Substance Misuse Group who was at this meeting, later wrote:

What struck me was the degree to which parents could identify with the first part of Elizabeth's story and how this made everything so accessible. This wasn't another drugs professional citing statistics and facts that we could ignore because 'it couldn't happen to us'. This was a mother speaking and it established how ordinary the family was, to the extent we were left thinking this could have been us.

The Community Substance Misuse Group invited Elizabeth later in the autumn to present her story to the Drug Awareness course. Not only had she developed her material beyond the scope of the original, both Tony and Simon also came to the event and it proved to be very useful for all those involved. It is clear that Elizabeth's story is a unique insight because she decided to keep photos and other items of memorabilia to chart the development of her children from a young age to adulthood. Elizabeth believes in what she is doing and because of her experiences she has a real passion to help other parents. She has impressed me with her courage and I believe that her work will have a lasting impact on the field of drugs education at grassroots level.

Following this meeting, invitations to speak about the impact of drugs on our family came from far and wide, including many Drug Action Teams, the National Treatment Agency, Young People's Drug and Alcohol Services, Community Substance Misuse Groups, the National Probation Service, various Drug Prevention and Education Awareness projects, the Home Office Drug Strategy team, drug and alcohol rehabilitation units, Neighbourhood Watch Forum for Families and Carers conferences and numerous schools and colleges. Our diary fills up every day with future invitations to speak.

One Oxfordshire school where I spoke wrote the following letter to me on 20 December 2004:

> The way you talked about Nick and Simon and their lives in so many ways related to all ours, and the outcome had us all shaken to our roots. The sixth-form students have spoken again and again of the impact on them . . . we are sure that anyone listening to your talk will be affected in, hopefully, a very positive way . . . you have 'been there', so you know what you are talking about.

Later on in the year, it was heart-warming to receive an invitation from my local MP Theresa May, currently the Prime Minister, to be one of the main speakers at the Conservative Women's Organisation Conference in November 2005. I gave an address entitled 'Drugs, the Curse of Our Younger Generation', at the end of which, much to my surprise, I received a standing ovation from the audience of over four hundred women. I had been able to reach out to the many mothers, sisters, aunts and grandmothers present, alerting them to be on their guard against the dangers of addiction and never to allow themselves to fall into the trap of believing that drug abuse would only happen to someone else's family. Later that month I was admitted as a member to the Federation of Drug and Alcohol Professionals and I became a trained volunteer member of the former Crack it! team, which is now a part of DrugFAM.

In March 2006 Tony and I were guest speakers of Chief Superintendent Brian Langston at the launch of Operation Falcon, organised by Thames Valley Police. Operation Falcon was a new multi-agency initiative, swooping down on drug dealers in order to cut drug-related crime on the streets. As it was extremely important to help the police at this event, for the first time Tony and I agreed to local media coverage of our involvement. Tom Hendry at the INS News Agency, Berkshire, read our story in the local paper and encouraged us to accept an invitation to be interviewed by the *Daily Mail*. The interview, published in April 2006, gave us the opportunity to highlight the anguish many families suffer through drug abuse. Within a few hours of the paper going on sale, the Crack it! helpline began to receive calls from as far away as Scotland and Cornwall, while emails poured into the Crack it! website. Parents, grandparents and other family members distraught with anxiety about their children's and grandchildren's use of heroin, cocaine and other drugs telephoned and emailed us:

Can you help me? My youngest daughter aged seventeen is on heroin, she has been begging me for money and stole from her father recently, I have had so much worry over her in the past few years, please help . . .

Sorry to ask for help but we are desperate and we are not getting any younger. Please help if you can as my eldest son in his forties is a heroin addict; we are pensioners and can do no more . . .

Simon, here is a poem about my sister who was murdered. She was a drug user; it helped me when I wrote it down. She left behind a beautiful son. God bless you and your mum . . .

Simon was so touched by one particular letter sent to us as a result of the newspaper article that he wrote to the family personally:

I am contacting you in response to your appeal for help. I am Elizabeth's son and I was addicted to heroin for many years and tragically lost my identical twin to this lifestyle. I feel deeply for your situation. I have only realised since I have been clean from all drugs how much emotional turmoil parents and all the family suffer. I cannot cure the problem in your family although I can tell you what worked for me, but ultimately it will be down to your relative, his determination and self-belief, to get himself off heroin . . .

Simon continued to communicate with this family and gave them as much support and encouragement as he could. They wrote in response to his initial offer of support:

How very kind of you to take the trouble to email us and become involved in our problem of addiction in the family; you are indeed an angel willing to share your sad experiences with my wife and I. We have also had a chance to chat with Tony and Elizabeth and from this we have gained confidence in our continued struggle knowing that there are good people out there, despite their own problems, who are willing to offer assistance. We do gain strength from having you and your family to write to and express our feelings and thoughts, so please accept these words as an expression from two very worried parents, old, powerless but caring people. We do look forward to speaking to you directly.

Much to our delight, an unexpected reunion occurred after the national media coverage. Nick's first true love, Ruth, tracked Simon down after her family read the article and told her about it. She knew that Nick had died some time earlier, but the last time she had seen us was shortly before she ended her relationship with him, and she was fearful that we would want nothing to do with her. Tony, Simon and I were thrilled to hear that she had been well and happy for a number of years, that she had retrained as a fitness instructor and was working in a gym. In one of her first emails she wrote:

I would love to meet up. Seeing the article in the *Daily Mail* was the start of my grieving for Nick. I was removed from the situation because I am now married, it didn't seem real – although I cried when I first heard and I felt sad. It is only now that the full impact of it has hit me. I really need to grieve for him. I am so thankful to him for giving me some of the best times of my life and for loving me the way he did before all the drugs came into our lives. I think that I would like to go and see Nick's grave soon, I feel I could maybe talk to him and say a proper goodbye. I want to tell him how much I loved him and how sorry I am about everything that happened between us. Maybe he will forgive me for some of the stupid things I did in the past. I would love to stay in regular contact with you all. My husband Jim knows everything and he is very supportive. Could you give me some clue how I might find the cemetery and where he is?

Simon immediately replied:

Ruth, I would love to see you. I have read your email to my mother and if you are coming up I must see you and have a good chat about everything, and if you wouldn't mind Mum and Tony would love to see you too. I am so glad that we will finally be able to put the past behind us. You fill my heart with warmth knowing that so much time has passed and you still care. Nick was a loving boyfriend and indeed a loving brother and you touched my heart when you told me you would be hard-pushed to find anyone as close as we were. I am glad that you shared that love. You were such a big part of our lives and I will always remember you. It has taken us a long time to come to terms with the loss of Nick and I will never get over it, but now I live for both of us as a lone twin. I have to keep pinching myself when writing this email as I never thought that we would speak or see each other again. I am so happy that we can finally talk.

The meeting that eventually took place between Ruth, Simon, Tony and me was very special. Ruth had made a private visit to Nick's grave before coming to meet us. We knew that as Nick's first love she would always have a fondness in her heart for their time together. We were able to set things straight and reassure her that although she hadn't finished on the best of terms with him, we knew he would have been as pleased for her recovery as we all were. We wanted her to know that we wished her well for the future, both in her job and her marriage.

A few days later Ruth wrote:

I just wanted to say thank you both so much for Friday, it was great to see you all and thank you for organising it, Simon. Nick was such a loving boyfriend and I am so lucky to have had those years with him. When I think of him I remember those happy years together before drugs and not the time when we were addicts and used together.

You look really great, Simon, and I know Nick would be so proud of you and how you are getting on with your life. I have so much admiration for you, Elizabeth; you have much dignity and courage and I am sure you have saved many mothers from the same agony. You are an inspiration to us all. I so want to keep in touch.

The friendship between Ruth, Simon and myself remains as strong as ever as we all move forword with our lives.

Shortly after Operation Falcon, I accepted an invitation to be a family spokesperson for 'Talk to Frank', the National Drugs Helpline. Perhaps one of the best opportunities given to me as a mother was, in 2006, to speak at the launch of a new drug prevention club in Aylesbury, Buckinghamshire organised by the Drug Action team. This club was a new community-based initiative seeking to provide information and support for people affected by drugs, and an opportunity to meet like-minded people.

Tony and I have received many letters from recovering addicts who have heard our story: one came from a man about the same age as Nick, who was also on a Drugs Treatment and Testing Order programme. It read as follows:

I have been thinking about the things you said on and off all week and I have talked with my mum about it. I have even told her the title of your book, *Mum, Can You Lend Me Twenty Quid?* and what is meant by the title.

Last night, I asked her for twenty quid and she gave me a look and I had to tell her that the money was for the cinema, which thankfully it was. I have never had a heroin habit but I have had a crack cocaine habit. I can relate to all of what you said and so can my mother, although I only told her of my drug problem recently. Now she has had time to look back over my life and knows why I was the way I was, we understand each other much better. I think and feel your book and talks can do nothing but good and open people's eyes to the realities of drug addiction. Most people think that we take drugs out of choice; I know we do at first but it is no easy thing to get off them. People think that addicts don't care about themselves and they just use for something to do. This is not the case – the drugs have made us this way. Your book will open people's eyes to drug addiction and help families that are going through it to cope better. Drugs are not prejudiced in who they choose, they can affect all walks of life. You are very brave to write your book as it must hurt so much but I wish you well with it.

We met this young man at one of our presentations, and at the same occasion we were also introduced to another recovering addict. He later wrote to us:

I am a forty-year-old recovering drug addict. I have been a drug addict since I was seventeen. I tried soft drugs prior to this. I have been through the drug dustbin and I am not proud. All the time I was taking different substances I could only look towards myself, not others around me. I have since given up all class A drugs but I smoke hashish. I know this drug is psychologically damaging. Over the last twenty to twenty-five years, I didn't realise how much pain and anguish I caused my immediate family and friends. When I joined this project the staff gave me a lot of encouragement to talk about my feelings from the past to the present.

After listening to Elizabeth and Tony, I could see the other side of drug taking, see what a family that I didn't know had been through and how they have come out of a very difficult journey. One person in the family with drug problems is enough to handle, but this must have been a total nightmare. I think if Elizabeth and Tony had been around when I was younger I would have thought very differently about taking drugs. Thank you for opening my eyes.

On 23 May 2006, Tony and I were deeply saddened to hear of the sudden death at the age of fifty-one of our friend Les, in whose home in America I had found the peace and quiet to begin my story. The news came from his widow Rachel, who told me: 'My beloved sweetheart was found dead in his bedroom in Germany sometime yesterday. The details are very vague but it sounds like a heart attack. Les should be flown back to Heathrow tonight. Elizabeth, we mustn't lose sight of your book in all of this. More than anything else Les wanted to see you fly with your book and I think I owe it to him to do all I can to help you.'

Les and I had made an agreement that once I had completed the manuscript he would be the first to read it. I therefore invited his nineteen-year-old daughter Becky to read my story on her father's behalf. Becky sent me the following email:

If I had one word to describe your story it would be honest. Everyone can relate to your struggle and that of the boys because, while clearly not everyone has been faced with similar circumstances, everyone is fallible, and the openness with which you relate and assess events make it easy for the reader to engage with your writing. Such a compelling account stems from your honesty, which is why I think it is even more important to see this through. To me your book is not only a tribute to Nick's life but also to Simon's, so much of which is still to come, because you make it clear in the book how much a part of each other the twins were and how easily their fates could have been swapped. You mention that you know in your heart Nick would want his story to be told, particularly in view of the fact that it may help to educate others and save them, or those they care about, from a similar fate. This being the case, you owe it to him, as well as Simon, and most importantly to yourself, to see it through. I can see why my dad was so supportive of what you were trying to achieve and I know how happy he'd be to know that you've achieved it.

In October 2006, Tony and I travelled to Bristol where we were guest speakers at our first Forum for Families Affected by Substance Misuse conference. Esther Harris, an Independent Practitioner and Counselling and Clinical Supervisor who organised the event, said in her introduction:

We are here to provide help to our service users, but an important part of their recovery is having the support of their own families. Families of substance misusers also need to know that we can offer somewhere to go for help, support and advice for themselves. What Elizabeth's story highlights is that she just had nowhere to turn. That's the problem – families do not have any clear guidelines or support to know what to do and how to cope.

One mother who saw my interview with BBC *Points West* advertising the conference contacted me some days later to talk to me about her own son who had died from heroin addiction. I was the first person she had spoken to in the two years following his death. She emailed me the next day:

> It was good to talk to you last night, thank you for sharing your experiences. I am struggling coping with the pain of losing my son and all those years watching him fight addiction while help was so difficult to access.

Having heard from so many parents and addicts since I first started telling our story, I now know that what happened to us happens to many ordinary families all around the world, and that sometimes the ending is tragic. I respect their choice if they don't want to speak about addiction. However, my son's death has given me the strength, the determination and the voice to speak and write about what drugs did to my family and to break the silence that often accompanies addiction.

I wonder what our world of bright young people is coming to when not to take drugs has become abnormal. I do believe that if, as parents, you encourage your children to talk to you, without fear of rejection, about drugs and alcohol, your family can have a drug-free life and that this may prevent them from making choices that they will forever regret. Take time to discuss what has been happening to your children, both at school and with their friends outside school. It is so important to get involved in your children's lives by taking time to be with them, so they feel comfortable that they can talk to you and share things with you.

Tony and I aren't suggesting that anyone who smokes cigarettes will become a heroin addict as Nick and Simon did.

However, we do urge all parents to be on their guard. We know that children and teenagers will take risks without thinking of the consequences. Every family needs accessible educational guidance so they can understand more about drug and alcohol addiction and the impact it could have on them. Tony and I wouldn't want anyone to be in the position we were in of not knowing where to turn to for help because drugs made us feel so isolated and ashamed. Help is out there with DrugFAM, which is why I have included a breakdown of the three strategic aims of the charity and how we work locally, nationally and internationally in the Appendices section at the end of the book.

As I work towards the end of my story, I want to reiterate my thanks to all the professionals who helped Nick and Simon throughout their addiction. I have the highest regard and respect for them and all the good work they do in the world of drug addiction. It was a special day when Simon showed me a letter from his drugs counsellor and substance misuse practitioner which simply said:

> I would like to take this opportunity to say how much I have enjoyed working with you and how proud I am of you for turning your life around despite the terrible things that have happened to you, particularly in the last nine months. I have had a wonderful letter from your mum, and I would be honoured to support you and her book. I wish you every success for the future. Do keep in touch and let me know how you are getting on.

The Nicholas Mills Foundation was founded in 2006 and became the not for profit charity DrugFAM in 2007 which continues to use this story in order to break down the stigma of drug addiction in families. Not only did addiction claim Nick's life, it became our family illness too. It destroyed everything, not least our emotional, marital and financial lives. Tony and I consider ourselves very fortunate that we have come through this together, to become stronger as a couple, but it has changed our lives for ever. We have gone through turmoil, pain and devastation because of what drugs did to my family; but it isn't the experience of Nick's death that now defines our lives, but how we respond to his loss and try to make a difference to other families.

Tony reflects:

> Our ordeal was brought about by a mother's love for her children. I will never condemn Elizabeth for having that love and compassion for Simon and Nick. I admit that I'm not the easiest person to live with but I wish she had told me the truth about the twins' addiction. Heroin brought so much lying and deceit into the lives of an ordinary family and it destroyed trust. At times life was horrendous and there was such a lot I didn't know at the beginning. It wasn't until the financial debts built up that they had to tell me, only because we were getting near to bankruptcy that 'tough love' kicked in. If addiction strikes your family, find some common ground for you and the addict to work on. Don't ever let an addict's debts become your debts, no matter how much you love your child. If you do, you could end up losing your home, your partner and your child.

If Nick hadn't died, maybe I wouldn't have written my story. The legacy he leaves is the knowledge of what drugs could do to you and your family, and for that legacy I am proud to honour him in death. Simon has shown honesty, dignity and courage in cooperating with me to write this story. He is not just my son but my close friend. I am immensely proud of him as he continues to help other parents struggling to cope with their sons' and daughters' addiction.

I am determined that through DrugFAM I will continue to raise awareness of how drugs devastate families and, by doing so, Tony, Simon and I believe that Nick did not die in vain. Nothing gives me greater pleasure these days than to see Tony and Simon developing their friendship, going to the pub together and sharing a joke. It's wonderful to know we can invite Simon into our home because the trust between the three of us has finally been restored.

Simon said:

Nick was in a different place from me in terms of what the drug had done to him. Had he lived, I am sure he would have gone to prison. I wanted to get off drugs but, as a twin, I loved him too much to walk away from him. We always had each other, even at the very worst of times. If Nick had gone to prison, he would have known most of the people in there who were addicts. All the people we were selling drugs to were in and out of prison. It is sad to see nice young people corrupted by drugs, as you are such a different person when you are on heroin. Today I am an honest, decent person with integrity but you could not have said that about me then. There is a massive difference between who I was then and who I am today. That is the tragedy of it and my brother lost his life to it.

I really don't know where I would be if Nick were alive now. All I can say is that the drugs corrupted us. The more drugs you took, the more you needed them. As much as we desperately wanted to get off heroin – we would go through days and days being good and being determined – we constantly failed. To look back on it now, the only thing to snap me out of it was Nick's death. It punched me in the face and knocked me fifteen feet in the air. Nick's death woke me up. It taught me to sort myself out before someone else died or before we ended up killing one of our family with stress. I can't genuinely say that if Nick hadn't died that I would be off heroin. I think it may have been one or the other. Death or drugs – for both of us.

Perhaps Tony, my stepfather, was right; perhaps Nick did what he did because he saw no way out and he thought that his death might be a way out for me. I don't know. We will never know. The only thing that I can reiterate is that Nick would never have wanted me to find his body in the state I did. I don't believe he would ever have wished something like that on me. He loved me and Mum too much.

A Voice for Families

The fondest memory I recall of the late Les Pugh was in May 2006, when he stood outside his elegant home in High Wycombe with his arm wrapped round his youngest daughter, Lucy. As he waved goodbye to me, he said 'Cheerio Elizabeth, see you on the GMTV sofa when your book is finished.' As I drove away I chuckled to myself. 'In your dreams, Les' I thought, and laughed out loud. Les always believed that my book would be published and that I would indeed sit on the former GMTV sofa and bring this story into the living rooms of Great Britain. Little did I realise that his cheerful, encouraging, farewell remark would be the last time that I would see him alive.

It was a bitter-sweet day for myself and indeed more so for his widow, Rachel, and their three lovely daughters when the hard-back version of my book came to fruition on the first anniversary of his death, 23rd May 2007. Thanks to Rachel's kindness and in memory of her dear husband, a very successful book launch party was held on the eve of publication day at their house. Despite the torrential rain in the summer of 2007, the sun shone all that day and wrapped warm rays of sunshine around the 400 guests who came along to support me, Tony and Simon.

I will always remember those last words Les said to me – even more so on publication morning when I sat in the car sent by GMTV to collect Simon and me to begin a succession of interviews on TV, radio and with the press. How sad that the one person from whom I always had such consistent support never saw the book in print or the interviews.

By the time Simon and I had completed two prime-time breakfast interviews on 24th May, the original Nick Mills Foundation website www.nickmillsfoundation.com had been visited hundreds of times. I could never have imagined that morning the extraordinary support Simon, Tony and I would receive for 'going public' with the misery and decay that drug addiction brings to families. Within twenty-four hours, hundreds of emails and personal letters came flooding in. A recovering addict wrote:

> I was a heroin addict for ten years, along with my brother who took his own life. This was as close as death could touch me and I put my heart and soul into getting off drugs and now I am seven years free. I have seen my transformation from death to life. I believe in everything you are doing.

Many parents emailed and left this type of message:

> 'Mum, can you lend me £20?' To every parent of an addict, that is such a strong phrase – with hindsight we all now know what it means. Wish I'd known back then.

The ripple effect that addiction has on all family members, parents, brothers, sisters, grandparents, partners and friends, became more and more evident as I received daily emails and letters like this one from a mother:

> I too have a son who is now on methadone for his heroin addiction, but also cannot stop his crack addiction. I am in so much debt through trying to help him through his addiction; most people wouldn't understand unless, like you, they have been through it themselves. I am sure I have done it all wrong but he is my only son and I did what I thought was right. It does make you feel better to know that you are not alone and I thank you for your honesty.

A young woman told me how her brother died of a heroin overdose eight years ago, aged 28, and how devastating it was for her family. Although she had known about his addiction for years, her brother had only just 'come out' to his mum and dad. She said it was the saddest thing that had ever happened to her, but she could never imagine how it must feel for a parent to lose their child to drugs. Hers was the first of some 30 emails telling me about the death of a son or daughter, brother or sister.

Other families simply left messages like these:

> Your story is my story, our story, and we live in daily fear of that knock on the door you had. Thank you for sharing this story with millions of others.

> We wish you every success in making the public aware of the horrors of drug addiction and what it does to families. Although life has dealt you a cruel blow, you, Simon

and Tony have turned it round to help others. You are an inspiration.

Over the next ten days, the messages continued to increase and have not stopped as news of the book continues to spread both in Britain and overseas. Letters and emails have come from Holland, Portugal, Spain, India, Canada and America. I wanted to go to Nick's grave and read every message to him, but none more so than those that came from his school friends who did not know of his death. One former childhood classmate wrote:

> I remember your sons as cheeky, dear little boys and it was quite a shock to see Simon all grown up on TV. As a mother myself now to three children, I cannot imagine the total despair you must have felt at losing a precious child. Drugs frighten me, they seem to be everywhere. We live in a small village and I am well aware that they are used by the majority of the teenagers and young adults in the village. I shall read your book and pass it on to my sons to read as a tool for life when the time is right. Elizabeth, Nick's death is not in vain, his addiction has taken him away but your story will certainly bring help, much needed help, to the families. You have torn down the walls of secrecy about addiction, now take courage and become a voice for families, for all those in turmoil who need understanding and support.

Another mother wrote echoing the sentiments of hundreds more when she said:

> Elizabeth, I am so scared. My son and my daughter are both addicts, they are dwindling away before my very

eyes. I cannot do anything to help them. And where can we parents go for support? I fear for the future and how it will all end. It is loneliness I struggle with and fear about the reaction of others to the problem I am scared of.

Children and teenagers contacted me about how addiction had affected them:

I am the little sister of two recovering heroin addict brothers. My mum and I read your book and it was just like our life story. We really wish we had heard of you sooner as my mum and I feel so alone with no one to talk to and your book has given us hope to find help. Maybe it will encourage other families not to feel frightened about admitting there is a problem and to seek support. Just knowing you are not alone is such a relief.

Several boarding school pupils emailed me about their lifestyles around the drug culture. This was the theme of their messages time and time again:

Sometimes we feel trapped in our town. Every weekend we binge drink and there are class As flying around everywhere. I have done mushrooms, Es, Charlie - but this is no teenage paradise, it is madness, drugs are in your face every way you turn. We need guidance when we are really young to tell us to avoid them at all costs.

Many teachers expressed their fears to me in these terms:

Some of the pupils in our schools speak so dismissively about drugs, cannabis in particular, with little real thought of the consequences of how drugs take hold of the body and mind, this is a huge attitude battle which we must overcome.

And parents voiced their concerns about schools both from the state and independent sector who they feel may be in denial as to the extent of their pupils' drugs use. I was therefore very pleased to have the opportunity to address the HMC in October 2007. I continue to enjoy a strong working relationship with HMC. The Headmasters' and Headmistresses' Conference (HMC) represents the Heads of some 250 leading independent schools in the United Kingdom and the Republic of Ireland. Following the many emails I had received from pupils and parents in the independent sector, I believed it was right to put the following questions to my audience:

Could it be that one of the significant problems that middle-class youth face in our independent schools is denial that your school could ever have any drug problem or the foolish belief that cannabis is not that serious? As one middle-class parent remarked to me recently, 'Elizabeth, of course we are lucky, we don't have a problem with drugs in our schools in the Royal Borough of Windsor and Eton, because the Queen lives here. This is why we pay our fees.' Does this parental ethos make our pupils feel in some way superior and therefore they feel a false security in their own ability to be in control of their drug taking?

Can you, as head teachers, pretend that there is not a drug problem in your school? There are drug problems in all schools – if not on the premises, certainly within the families and peer groups of your pupils, to whom you have a duty of care. Do you bury your head in the sand? Do you say it won't happen to me, it won't happen in my school? As head teachers, I urge you to be vigilant because drugs, like terrorism, undermine our society. Take the responsibility to encourage your parents, pupils and staff to improve their own knowledge of all the issues involved – drug abuse and addiction education.

I worked in the independent sector for 39 years and it has been a privilege. It has been my observation, however, that a large number of pupils in the senior schools feel that drugs cannot touch them. Sometimes, they are not grounded in family life, and are 'compensated' by having too much money. The drug dealers are very aware of this. As one recovering public school, cocaine addict recently said to me – 'the drug dealers simply charge us twice the street price'.

Since speaking at many schools both in the state and independent sector, I have at times been disappointed to find that the pupils are not consistently informed about the sophisticated grooming techniques used by drug dealers, to help naïve, wealthy or not so wealthy pupils to progress from the 'fun' of recreational drugs to a place of despair and death. All parents are rightly terrified that their children may be targeted and abused by a paedophile. In years past I have questioned why so little is said about the grooming which is done by drug dealers? It is true that schools have made concerted efforts to educate children and parents, but I am convinced that more needs to be done and vigilance must be upheld. I do believe that the entire drugs scene is a threat to all our schoolchildren and that action is required by government, schools and parents. We have a heavy responsibility to educate our pupils not only about drugs but more importantly about the frightening path to addiction they can be groomed into taking.

One of the most important things I want to emphasise is the need for parents not to be complacent and to find out what the policy on drugs is in the schools their children attend. They should ask what the schools do about drug-related incidents. Do they expel, suspend, inform parents, and do have they a written policy? Schools are often notoriously bad at releasing information about drugs in their schools and try to hide it as it may be seen to be 'bad for business'. Parents need to be persistent, ask for parents' drug and addiction education evenings, ask which staff teach drug education, whether they are knowledgeable and up to date with the facts, whether they follow Government guidelines and challenge anything they don't agree with. Drugs are the absolute evil of our society, and addiction is a silent epidemic.

The former, now retired, lead Judge, Justin Phillips, in one of the only two Drug Courts in England at that time wrote to me shortly after publication:

> I found your book heartbreaking. It mirrored so much told me by addicts and their parents. May I invite you to come and see our Drugs Court and have lunch with us one day-we would be delighted if you came and brought Simon and Tony as well.

Tony, Simon and I were privileged to be Justin's guests in early June at Church House Westminster for the London Magistrates Training Day 'A day on drugs'. It was an honour to be his guest speaker and to explain how addiction destroys families and how we have survived, despite Nick's death. I subsequently spent a day in Justin's designated West London drug court during the summer holidays. I was so impressed with the work he is doing to help addicts turn their lives around that I felt sure that had Nick had the opportunity to work with Justin and become one of his successful drug free 'graduates', he would have done him proud.

Later that month, when Scotland Yard had the launch of the Metropolitan Police Drug Strategy for 2007–2010, it was their own initiative to put Nick's picture as he was and what became of him including on the front of their booklet setting out their drug policy for the next three years. We subsequently heard from many of the police stations in London that his pictures were having a huge impact on the young men and women who had been arrested for heroin-related offences.

We as an ordinary family are not unique. Having lost one of my children through drug abuse, I find it impossible to convey to you the anguish of his loss. I felt so helpless watching him and Simon being destroyed by the choices they made after having been cleverly groomed by a heroin dealer. Since Nick's death and particularly since first publication of this book, I have seen too many decent families torn apart by drugs and the trail of destruction it leaves. Drugs not only affect the individual family but also society, as evidenced by gun and knife crime, burglary, and credit card fraud.

Perhaps the most heart-rending are those from bereaved mothers, like myself. One recently bereaved mother put it like this: 'if anyone even doubted the power of drugs over our children's lives, then they only have to walk in our shoes for a day, a week, a year'. If there is one lesson I have learnt from my own complacency and lack of knowledge, it is that drug addiction has no boundaries and all drugs are equal opportunities killers, so we must not normalise them. If, by speaking out this story can prevent addiction happening to more families, then I am proud to honour Nick in death and Simon in life.

Lives Worth Talking About

As I sit at my desk all these years on from my son's death to write this final chapter to update our story, I can say, without any doubt, that through the founding of DrugFAM I have meaning and purpose in my life despite Nicholas no longer being physically part of it. The pain of losing Nick ignited something in me that made me determined to come through the most difficult and painful of experiences, to turn it round and to find recovery for myself and to do something positive to help other families. I believe that Nick would be really proud that out of our family tragedy so much is being achieved. In truth, I did not realise that DrugFAM would be the humble start of positive change for so many families whose lives are derailed by the family illness of addiction.

Let me say first and foremost that there is boundless life, energy, dedication and commitment at DrugFAM. It is not a sad place. It is a lively place thriving on excellent training and supervision, wonderful leadership, genuine friendship and teamwork. All our trustees, staff and volunteers are driven by the same goal which is to reduce stigma and shame so that families and all those affected by someone else's addiction can access our services seven days a week. We want families and friends everywhere and from all backgrounds to know that there is no need for them to feel isolated, alone or helpless when they turn to us for support.

In May 2013, DrugFAM was invited to No 10 Downing Street, to attend an exclusive reception hosted for the charity by Samantha Cameron. The event was held to recognise our achievements in supporting families through the nightmare of drug and alcohol addiction. Mrs Cameron knows only too well the impact of addiction in her own family and was very empathetic and proud of our work, as she said in her speech.

Over 150 guests were invited to walk through the famous black door, and to see for themselves the inside of the official residence and office of the Prime Minister. Guests came from a wide variety of backgrounds and included then Home Secretary and MP for Maidenhead Theresa May, the artist Annie Tempest, the author Clare Francis and the American philanthropist Linda Noe Laine. Amongst the many other guests invited were those who volunteer for the charity and work directly with the affected and bereaved families. In addition to this, there were senior representatives from the police, schools and prisons who came to recognise the work DrugFAM does. Dr Anthony Seldon, then Headmaster of Wellington College, said:

'I am delighted that DrugFAM has been recognised in this way. The tireless work the charity does in supporting the "silent victims" of addiction is exceptional and it has provided a lifeline for many families. By educating children about the dangers of drugs and alcohol, the charity works tirelessly to overcome one of the main issues in society today.'

Nick Leader, then Governor of HMP Peterborough, added his voice in support, saying:

'The work that DrugFAM does has had a profound impact on helping offenders understand the impact of their addiction on others. Elizabeth Burton-Phillips is a mother making a difference, using her own tragic personal experiences in a way that is professional, balanced, engaging and supportive.'

Some four years later in May 2017, DrugFAM were delighted to announce that the charity had been awarded The Queen's Award for Voluntary Service. This is the most prestigious recognition available to voluntary organisations and is the equivalent of an MBE for charities. The award recognises excellence in voluntary activities carried out by groups in the community.

The award was given to honour DrugFAM's outstanding work and commitment to providing a lifeline of support to families, friends and partners. The ceremony and presentation of a glass plaque and certificate signed by the Queen took place in September 2017 at the Mayor's Parlour in High Wycombe. This was presented to us by Lord Lieutenant Sir Henry Aubrey Fletcher, the Queen's representative in Buckinghamshire.

One of many of our DrugFAM family members wrote:

What an amazing achievement for your charity. You have been inspirational in supporting families of those affected by addiction and that includes me. I treat my group like a special family. I can be open and share anything that would maybe shock or upset friends or other members of my real family. My partner is an alcoholic in recovery and you'd think I wouldn't need the support any more but there's always the addiction sitting on your shoulder, the fear of relapse and the changes that recovery brings. As I struggle with learning to trust again, DrugFAM is my little boost every week – an opportunity not just to share, but to listen and learn. I really don't know where I would be without the support I get and the advice I take on board and work hard to adopt in my day-to-day life. I am and will always be eternally grateful to the group. I am so pleased all your hard work has been recognised and rewarded. Thank you for being there for me and everyone else that benefits from DrugFAM. Your Queen's Award for Voluntary Service is truly deserved.

Our CEO, Sarah Bromfield remarked: 'This is an amazing achievement for DrugFAM. Being honoured with this prestigious accolade is particularly special because it recognises the value, dedication, commitment and contribution of our wonderful team of staff, volunteers and trustees. I am so proud, well done to all.'

To celebrate this success, Sarah and I were invited to represent the charity at the Queen's Garden Party on Tuesday 23 May, 2017. This was such a special event for both of us and a rare opportunity to go to Buckingham Palace. DrugFAM thanks sincerely Helena, Fiona, Ali, Neil and Charlotte for the nomination and recommendations for the award

Families are at the heart of everything we do every day, as our friend and ambassador Keith Humphries, Professor of Psychiatry at Stanford University, explains:

'Addiction never truly happens to just one person. Mothers, fathers, brothers, sisters and children are pulled into the pain and destruction that addiction to alcohol and other drugs can cause. Many of the emotions addicted people feel – hopelessness, shame, sadness – are also visited on the hearts of everyone who loves them. As family members understandably focus intently on saving the life of the person they love, they sometimes forget that they too are suffering and need help of their own. That's why the support, compassion, and understanding that DrugFAM provides families is so important.'

It is my privilege to introduce you to some of our wonderful DrugFAM team and volunteers to show what recovery looks like for them and how it can look like on the family journey through addiction. Firstly, we will meet Steve, one of DrugFAM's family support workers, then Karen one of our helpline volunteers. After Karen I will introduce Geoff who is a support group facilitator, and then Dawn our administrator.

Steve describes how the seeds of substance misuse were sown when he was twelve years old with alcohol:

'At fifteen I was really into the subculture of Northern Soul which at the time was heavily influenced by amphetamine use. All this hid my pain of being sexually abused as a child and the shame and inadequacies that came with it. I felt powerless and so alone and I shared with no one.

Inevitably, I got into increasing trouble with the police and my mother sadly took her own life on my first night in prison. I tried to hide my drug use, staying away from home for days. I was granted bail and blocked out the pain of this loss and my part in it. For seventeen years I used and abused everything from alcohol to heroin, amphetamines to acid, nearly dying twice that I can remember.

Recovery began out of the blue with a personal life-changing experience that left me with hope and the courage to begin to unravel and rebuild my life. I found great support in my local church and still do. They had no idea of the work that needed to be done but they were there for me and they listened for the first time to what had been hidden for so long.

Now I am at DrugFAM as a Family Support Worker and I have been drug and crime free for the last twenty-six years, engaging with people in a variety of ways. I listen to those things families keep hidden. Listening is so important, as is giving the individual time and appreciating the risk and trust they are passing to you. Even pain has a value when a choice is made to let something go, entrusting another human being with that emotion. We are often the first people who have really taken the time to listen after many years in great difficulty.

People are given time at DrugFAM, just as I was when I needed it. Time allows trust and gives hope a chance to grow within the individual, developing the courage required to make a change. This is the first job role I have had where I am totally accepted without judgment, where change and recovery is possible. Please do get in touch as we exist to support you. I feel DrugFAM is unique because we don't need to tell people we care because they feel it. It is one of the most genuine, person-centered services that I have come across.'

It is no wonder that we receive such warm and supportive feedback from those Steve supports.

Karen, one of our telephone support workers, explains:

'After many weeks of deliberation, feeling anxious, scared and worried, I decided to take the huge step to call DrugFAM. This was a massive step for me to take. Initially, I found it hard just to talk about my situation without crying. The despair I felt made it seem impossible to talk about my son and his addiction to drugs, and the impact his addiction was having on our family. I felt inadequate as a mother that I could not make my son better. I felt I had betrayed him by discussing him with strangers.

I knew nothing about drugs at all. All I knew was the shame I was feeling and the inability to confide in anyone due to the stigma surrounding addiction. But the decision to call DrugFAM is the best decision I have ever made.

When I got my thoughts together, I felt encouraged to talk and to share the feelings and worries in a very safe environment. I wasn't judged or frowned upon and for the first time I felt I hadn't failed myself as a mother or, indeed, failed my son.

I simply felt assured that there was something I could do, to help me think more clearly in what seemed a life of chaos, uncertainty and desperation. I soon realised there were no quick answers to the complicated disease of addiction, but there was great hope and understanding to be gained, knowledge of how to cope and how to move forward in what seemed an impossible situation.

DrugFAM certainly put "light" back into my life. As a charity, DrugFAM stands strong in support of families affected by the disease of addiction. I wanted to become part of that strength, to increase the awareness of addiction, to take away the shame and to give hope to families out there. I wanted to be a listening ear, and give belief to families that they are not on their own.

With the strength, training and support afforded me by DrugFAM, I now work on the helpline as a volunteer, and have spoken to many wonderful families in this very privileged role. It may be hard to make that first call, but I promise it will be worth it.'

Geoff is a DrugFAM support group facilitator and this is his story of what recovery looks like for him:

'I first heard about DrugFAM from my local doctor. My twin sister had started drinking after the death of our father and she eventually became addicted to any form of alcohol she could get her hands on.

I was quite alarmed at the lack of support as the addiction took hold of her and I found myself being accused of "not sorting her out". There is a stigma attached to addiction in that we should have seen it coming.

After plucking up a great deal of courage I contacted DrugFAM. I attended the Thursday night meeting at High Wycombe. Elizabeth introduced herself and I sat listening to the other group members telling everyone about their experiences of living with someone with an addiction. At last I found people that understood how I was really feeling. When I tried to speak I just burst into tears as I had relief in knowing that, finally, I was not on my own.

By attending weekly meetings I found my own recovery from our family illness. Then I was invited to train to become a support group facilitator. DrugFAM had given me so much support and I was pleased to be able to give something back. It is so rewarding to know that you can offer much needed support. My co-facilitator, Gill, has a fantastic way with people and it's nice to be part of a team that is making a difference as to how loved ones cope with someone else's drug or alcohol misuse.

Over the years, you think you have seen and heard it all, but the stories never cease to amaze me. There is always such courage and strength in the room. DrugFAM has given me the courage to hold my head up high and not be ashamed.'

For many people who contact our charity, Dawn may be the first point of call as she works on the DrugFAM phones during the week. This softly-spoken Irish lady shares her journey with DrugFAM:

'As the mother of a young man who had just turned 20, I was casting about for a way to cope with the chaos of his addiction to drugs and alcohol when I was given the contact details for DrugFAM. I then made the phone call that was to make such a difference to my life.

Rewind eight years to when my son began experimenting with alcohol and cannabis, a time when I believed that this was just a phase he was going through. Sadly, it was not. There followed years of problematic behaviour, both at home and at school. He disengaged from full-time education at the age of sixteen, with the confident assertion that they had nothing left to teach him. The phrase 'ask a teenager while they still know everything' springs to mind.

My son's addiction continued pretty much unabated until the middle of 2015. He had worked his way through a multitude of substances, including ecstasy, ketamine, cocaine, mephedrone and so-called "legal highs", now known as new psychoactive substances. An undiagnosed gastrointestinal disorder saw him lose eight stones in just six months. His father and I were exhausted from visits to hospitals, clinics and consultants and he continued to smoke skunk against medical advice. We watched him destroy himself and we were powerless to stop it. In the middle of 2015 he was, to our great relief, sectioned under the Mental Health Act as he had become psychotic. The years of abuse had taken their toll – he was twenty-one.

In the summer of 2016, he was again admitted to a psychiatric unit, albeit voluntarily on this occasion and I know that this came about as a direct result of boundaries which I put into place, for example I stopped giving him sufficient money to buy drugs. It was one of the hardest weeks of my life before he was admitted, especially when he overdosed three times in as many days and ended up in A&E. It may sound harsh, but after the first admission I told him that

I loved him but that I would not visit him if he overdosed again and I didn't. I could never have imaged being that strong but I can honestly say that through DrugFAM I have gained a strength I never knew I had.

Later that year he was given a formal diagnosis of paranoid schizophrenia. But, far from being upset by it, he told me that it was a relief. He is now supported by a fantastic mental health team and we take it a day at a time. I am sad that his life has taken this direction and that his health has been so badly affected by his decisions around drugs. However, he is a kind, loving, articulate and gentle young man to whom people take an instant liking when they meet him.

I now return to that first phone call to DrugFAM. It is difficult to describe the relief I felt to finally be able to speak to someone who understood what me and my family were going through. With their support I learned to look at my own wants and needs, and began to realise that I could not control my son's addiction, nor could I cure it.

Some months after that initial phone call, I saw that the charity was advertising for an administrator. I applied and the rest, as they say, is history. Fast forward to today and now I am the person on the other end of the phone, supporting families who are overwhelmed and devastated by a loved one's addiction to drugs or alcohol. DrugFAM is making a difference, one call at a time.'

In May 2017 it was a hugely proud moment for Steve, Karen, Geoff and Dawn as they joined two-thousand people from all corners of the UK along with our entire team at the first ever Service of Hope and Celebration for families affected by addiction in the history of Westminster Abbey. The backstory to the service is one of opportunity, vision and commitment.

Five years previously our family story was adapted into a Theatre in Education play which travelled all over the UK to prisons, rehabs, schools and communities. Its reputation as a powerful drama portraying the impact of addiction on families had gathered pace with numerous testimonials to support its true-to-life representation of real lives affected by addiction. I am indebted to all the actors who took part in the numerous performances who gave body and soul to play the most challenging roles and offer a no-holds-barred portrayal of the story.

When we reached our one-hundredth performance, our patron Sir Anthony Seldon wrote:

> 'I have had the privilege of being the educational patron of DrugFAM for many years and in October 2015 I was honoured to attend the one-hundredth celebratory performance of the Theatre in Education play *Mum, Can You Lend Me Twenty Quid* at the Palace of Westminster. The play tells the story of the damage and pain drugs and alcohol can cause to families. I found it to be a profoundly affecting performance and acted with the highest quality and skill of the profession. The occasion was extraordinary and the play was beautifully choreographed from beginning to end. Indeed, I was certainly not the only person attending to have been so affected.'

Word continued to spread about the success of the play and it was soon commissioned by an Irish philanthropist to be performed in Dublin at Christ Church Cathedral in late 2015.

In preparation for the visit of the full cast, I flew to Ireland to meet Sadie Grace from the Irish Family Support Network to plan the performances. During this visit I was taken to look at a unique sculpture and plaque. Sadie explained that on 15 December 2000, a memorial was unveiled by their former president, Mary McAleese, on the junction of Buckingham Street and Sean MacDermott Street in Dublin's North Inner City.

The sculpture *Home* by Leo Higgins is a monument to the memory of all those who died as a direct or indirect result of heroin. The accompanying plaque reads: 'This memorial sculpture commemorates all our loved ones lost to drugs. Unveiled by President Mary McAleese Friday 15 December 2000'.

On the return flight from Dublin to London my vision was born for DrugFAM to organise a major unifying event in the UK which would embrace families affected by addiction. Eighteen months later, with the support of my local MP, the Abbey Events Team and the dedicated leadership and unrelenting hard work of our CEO Sarah and our administrator Dawn, this translated into the first ever national service in Westminster Abbey to highlight the devastating impact of addiction on families. It was given the title 'A Service of Celebration and Hope: Lives Worth Talking About'.

The Very Reverend Dr John Hall, the Dean of Westminster Abbey, said in his welcome address:

'We gather in this ancient church, which has seen many occasions through its long history of sadness and gladness, to recall the bane and blessing of the availability of drugs. We know the blessing of the relief from suffering provided by drug therapy; and we know of the bane of drugs that are abused.

As we remember incidents of the abuse of drugs, and acknowledge the damage and havoc they can wreak, especially in young lives and families, we shall pray for all who have committed themselves to avert drug misuse, to prevent drug addiction and to aid the recovery of those who have become addicted. We shall rededicate ourselves, and all who can join with us, in a commitment to enabling every human being to live with dignity, to be respected, to fulfil their potential.'

Sarah, a family member living with addiction and the first speaker at the service, said:

'Over the years I have been through the various stages of denial, ignorance, enabling, controlling. I struggled to walk away from a lifetime of co-dependency. I felt so isolated, alone and helpless.

You see, not all scars are visible, sometimes you can't see the pain someone is feeling. I thought I hid my pain well. My family and friends could see through me; they just couldn't get near me. I needed to allow myself to be vulnerable and ask for help, but that took too much courage. The stigma and judgement from society also prevented me from reaching out.

Sometimes it is not about having the strength to hold on, but having the strength to let go. Someone said to me: "there comes a time when you have to choose between turning the page and closing the book." I chose to write a new chapter. This chapter is called DrugFAM.

I needed independent support for myself. I needed to be open to taking risks, to change my own behaviour, and be brave enough to ask for help. I no longer wanted to merely survive these experiences; I wanted to thrive again, live my life again, and do so with passion and enthusiasm. I had to re-design a new present. DrugFAM helped me to find the strength to stand alone.

I believe that with every challenge comes opportunity. Picking up the phone and contacting DrugFAM was life-changing. I have moved into a position of strength and determination, and I am so proud to be part of such a wonderful team of staff and volunteers who really make a difference.

We need to move beyond fear and judgement, shame and prejudice. Those affected by someone else's addiction need to be seen and heard. I celebrate the courage, strength and resilience of families, friends and partners affected by someone else's drug or alcohol use. I am no longer defined by the stigma of addiction. We need positive change because we are all lives worth talking about.'

Reverend Graeme Skinner, a bereaved family member whom we supported when he and his wife Philippa lost their son Jim to addiction, spoke after Sarah:

'In another of London's great faith buildings, St Paul's Cathedral, we find the tomb of its architect Sir Christopher Wren. The memorial stone on his tomb simply says: 'Reader, if you seek his monument, look around you'.

Can I invite you now to look around you? But not at the building; look instead at the people, at those behind you and in front of you. Catch the eyes of someone you don't know. Linger for a moment and smile with them.

Many of these people are family members of either those struggling with addiction or of those bereaved by addiction. They are the living and enduring monuments. Just as the solid stones of St Paul's declare something of the life of Wren, so these people in Westminster Abbey today are living stones, representing the lives of those we love who are worth speaking about. This is what DrugFam looks like: families wounded, vulnerable, but still walking and still hoping.

Each of us carries the imprint of those who have shaped who we are. Who I am today has been influenced by my parents, spouse, children, teachers and friends. However, there is one specific and significant person in my life journey that brings me to this point today: our son Jim, who lost his life to heroin almost ten years ago. I like to talk about Jim. I like it even more when someone asks me about him, something about his life not his death. That's a good way to talk to anyone walking with bereavement.

Over time, and by being real to myself, I have begun to weave the disruption that has crashed into my life into the pattern of how I live and who I am. How we respond and react to the rubbish life throws at us, especially the excruciatingly painful feelings that accompany addictions, determine the quality of hope we can lay hold of for ourselves and also hold out to others. This is how and why DrugFAM exists – by offering hope.

We must be sure of one thing: to love is to be vulnerable to pain. In some ways it might be easier to let the stigma and shame around addiction silence us. It goes like this: 'Don't mention their names and you don't get hurt.'

But in DrugFAM, we are choosing love and hope, and to speak their names out loud. We are determined that loss and pain can be held in creative tension with hope and gain. This route is not pain free, trial free or disappointment free; it is the route of vulnerability, which literally means 'easily wounded'. That's us, wounded. But what a difference hope makes.

So we will continue to walk on, even if we are walking with a limp. Today, if you seek hope, look around you.'

There was a moment during Graeme's speech that will stay with me for ever. The Reverend invited everyone in attendance to say the name of one person they know who has either died as a result of drugs or alcohol, or who is struggling with an addiction. It is not enough to just believe that their lives are worth talking about; we must tell their stories aloud. So, when Graeme counted to three, two-thousand voices joined as one to remember and proclaim the lives of their loved ones. It was an amazing moment that still resonates with me because words like drugs, alcohol and addiction attract other negative words like stigma, shame and hopelessness, but we would not be silenced by these words. In our presence at the Abbey that day, and in naming our loved ones out loud, we demonstrated our resolve that there is a life for families after the death of a loved one. For all two-thousand of us present that day, Graeme's invitation to call out the names in Westminster Abbey was one of the most powerful experiences imaginable.

In my own address that day, I explained how this unique, one-of-a-kind event was a moment of opportunity and of realisation.

I shared the difference DrugFAM have made to date by our support for families, friends and partners every day of the year through our helpline. I emphasised how we care, we listen, we give time, we share insights, we educate and we help people see addiction for the disease that it is. We run annual bereavement conferences, we run support groups for those dealing with bereavement and for those living with a loved one in active addiction. A source of particular pride is our pioneering Young People's Bereavement Project for 18–30 year olds.

DrugFAM are committed to using arts activities to engage their audiences, we believe in the power of the arts to achieve our charitable aims in a unique and accessible way. Our new performances and workshop packages are created for families, schools, drug services, those in recovery and professionals. The play shines a light on the effects of addiction on both the addict and their family and has relevance to numerous audiences.

Families are our core and addiction is the disease our loved ones fight. DrugFAM acknowledge the anguish and distress of the day-to-day reality of this family illness.

On that day, we were incredibly proud to enjoy the support of some of the world's leading academics, some of whom travelled from the US to join us in solidarity in Westminster Abbey. The most common message from them to all of us is to treat addiction like the disease that it is, and to stop using the word abuse because it is from this word that the stigma is created for families and for those in addiction. Awareness and positive action combined with positive thinking results in success.

To end what had been a truly remarkable day, I focused on the unity that our Service of Celebration and Hope had provided:

'Here in this national institution we are able to unite in one place to make a major step forward towards breaking down the stigma, shame and prejudice we families are exposed to because of the disease of addiction.

Let us proudly and publicly remember those we have lost to addiction and unite in our common grief and sorrow together.

Let us also acknowledge the strength and courage of those who are still living with active addition in their families.

Through this first ever unifying event you are all people worth caring about and your loved ones' lives are all worth talking about.

As the late actor Robin Williams once said, "I used to think the worst thing in life is to end up all alone. It's not. The worst thing in life is to end up with people who make you feel alone."

Today no one in this abbey is alone.'

In the reality of day-to-day life, none of us are immune from any misfortune or illness. Illness and disease do not discriminate in who they touch and are capable of destroying families, none more so than addiction. At DrugFAM, we are well aware that using disparaging and condemning language about those who suffer with addiction – for example 'alchies', 'smack heads', 'druggies' or 'junkies' – continue to perpetuate stigma and shame for families, as does the accusation of bad parenting. The fear of judgement and prejudice by society means unless there is change we will continue to experience shame, guilt, helplessness and social isolation.

Those of us bereaved by addiction are only too aware that while some deaths are sometimes commemorated publicly, our losses can create volcanic, complex and acute emotions. We families all have scars in our hearts and minds that cannot be seen. All of us affected by addiction are changed forever. Family life is changed forever. Letting go of the life we had planned and accepting the one we have now is our invisible pain.

DrugFAM passionately stands by our shared belief that families affected by substance misuse need care and attention in their own right from specialist support services like ours. Bereavement through addiction is less well understood and acknowledged when compared to other types of family loss, which means that many families who lose a loved one to addiction will experience this devastating loss without the social support that other grieving families receive. Because of the challenging relationships with their loved one when alive, these bereavements have significant and long-lasting effects.

This type of bereavement is made even more traumatic by a premature death as a result of substance use, overdose or suicide, and creates a complicated web of emotions including guilt, anger and sometimes even relief that the chaos is finally over. Combined with the stigma and potentially sensationalised media coverage, this means that the grief suffered by families and friends can be particularly acute and can result in social withdrawal. Sadly, this only perpetuates the distress and can have a significant impact on their psychological and physical wellbeing.

In 2015 DrugFAM became a member of the National Suicide Prevention Alliance (NSPA). Living with the difficulties of a family member in addiction can present the constant threat of suicide by the user as their life becomes unmanageable. Implied suicide is also used as a means to manipulate the family member and therefore leaves families with a very difficult issue to navigate.

DrugFAM's support is invaluable during these periods. Sadly some of our clients may also find themselves at a point of distress where they feel they can no longer cope, sometimes calling us when they are contemplating suicide themselves. They may wish to be with their deceased loved one and need the support of our bereavement service. We believe that offering people a safe place to share their thoughts and feelings with others who have gone through similar experiences can help with grieving, and alleviate any sense of shame and isolation. The excellent training provided by our bereavement counsellor Peter Cartwright gives our team confidence to offer this vital support.

The Universities of Bath and Sterling published the findings of a research project in 2015 that sought to understand and uncover the best ways to respond to adults bereaved through alcohol or drug use. The researchers interviewed 106 bereaved adult family members and conducted eight focus groups with forty practitioners, some of whom were also bereaved. The findings informed a working group of twelve practitioners including Peter.

I was invited to be one of the reviewers of the guidelines in my role at that time as CEO of DrugFAM. The five key messages that came out of this research are supported by DrugFAM as good practice guidelines for those whose work brings them into contact with adults bereaved in this way. Details of this research are available on the DrugFAM website but, to summarise, showing kindness and compassion, using respectful language, treating the bereaved person as an individual, asking the bereaved person what help they want and ensuring that support services co-ordinate their efforts together make up these important guidelines.

Gill, a group facilitator and our DrugFAM dedicated telephone and email befriender, sums up her experiences with us as a volunteer working with the bereaved as well as those with active addiction:

'For some time now I have been supporting a father who lost his only daughter. He openly admitted he desperately wanted to say that his daughter had died from a car crash or from cancer so that people didn't view her differently or judge her.

For sixteen years I was a Samaritan and for three of those I was a Branch Director. I was there when emails were first introduced to our support network. I have to admit I wasn't a fan of the idea: the feeling of pouring out all your emotions to a stranger then pressing that send button felt cold and remote. Where was the closeness and friendly support I hoped to give? But as the system grew I realised it's value, and it was with that in mind I agreed to head up the email and telephone support for DrugFAM for both active addiction and for those who are bereaved.

I have always imagined that to be bereaved is a lonely place unless you have the support that is needed to help you through. Those who contact DrugFAM often live in remote areas, sometimes abroad, or areas where there is little help for the family. Sometimes they are house-bound or unable to find the funds to travel to support groups, and this is where email and telephone support comes in to its own.

So many people who call DrugFAM are isolated and their family network has often broken down because of the strain the addiction has forced upon them. Families are torn apart, marriages ruined, jobs and homes lost, debts accumulated, health put at risk and lives are placed on hold while they have to deal with a terrible situation.

In many cases the people that contact us are grieving along with other family members, so the value in writing or calling a stranger can be immeasurable. The idea of expressing your feelings in a confidential and friendly atmosphere to people who won't judge but understand what it is you're going through can be the first step to acceptance and gaining some understanding of all that has gone on.

Different people seem to need different support after bereavement. Wives and mothers seem to have the guilt about why they didn't see it coming. The men who con-tact us seem to want answers and want to appear in con-trol, being strong for others. Often the young seem to cope well, but I suspect this is only on the surface. All of these people need to talk eventually as bottling the feel-ings up will never help you to move on.

In my role I've come across many callers all desperate to share and off load so by email and phone I try to make sure they feel supported but most of all heard. We can all listen but so often we don't hear and there is a huge difference between the two.

When we began our quarterly bereavement support groups some years back – always on a Sunday afternoon in High Wycombe – I have to say I was surprised at the number of people who attended. Some travelled for hours along the perpetually busy M25. Mothers, fathers, siblings and partners of lost ones came to share their feelings with complete strangers who by the end of the day had become firm friends, all with the same thread running through their lives, all supporting each other as the day wore on sharing memories, photos experiences and eventually email addresses and phone numbers.

There was and still is music, laughter, discussion and, of course, many tears, but the emails of thanks that arrive the following day will remain in my mind for ever. So many have said they will be attending the next event but in the meantime please could they keep in touch by email or telephone? And of course the answer is always yes! We strongly believe that the caller is in charge of the situation and chooses when to end contact with us. There is no time limit on our support.'

Pauline, one of our bereaved mums, said:

'I lost my only son Paul on February 14 2014. He died of an overdose of a combination of prescription and non-prescription drugs. He was 35. Paul had lived a life of drugs for many years, he had battled his demons constantly. When Paul died I knew I could not cope with this on my own and had been told about DrugFAM before my son's untimely death. From then on I knew I would never be alone in my loss. I contacted the charity two weeks after his death and spoke to Elizabeth.

The whole team at DrugFAM immediately befriended me and showed they really understood and cared. I could phone or email them anytime and they would listen. I did this on a regular basis. I went to the DrugFAM Bereavement conference in October 2014 and was so impressed by the welcome, courage and inspiration of everyone attending. I knew I had to go forward too. I also knew my son would want me to. From then on I tried to live my life positively, keeping Paul in my heart always.

I go to all the conferences and attend the quarterly bereavement meetings that DrugFAM arrange. I get so much out of these and consider everyone there to be really caring friends. I live my life fully every day, even though I know that I have suffered a great loss in losing my only son Paul. My daughter and I were talking about our lives one day and we both agreed there was one thing we could do. Paul never lived all of his life so we have to live twice the life for him as he never got the chance. We want to make him proud. This we do and in our way we are honouring and remembering Paul.

I am so grateful to DrugFAM for helping me on my way and guiding me on this journey of hope. DrugFAM have shown me that from the darkest of days there can be a future and hope for all bereaved people that we will see the good days too. I can go forward again. There is life after loss. Thank you, DrugFAM.'

On the tenth anniversary of Nick's death I put it to the board of trustees that we set up The Nicholas Mills Memorial Project to support young people between the ages of 18–30. The aim of the project is to help them to develop ways to process and cope with their loss so they can move forward with their lives, not feel so alone and challenge the stigma which is often associated with bereavement through drugs and alcohol.

Alex, one of the bereaved young people who participated in the project, shares his story:

'Sometimes you don't have to just sit and talk about the issue; time spent with people who understand is just as beneficial. My big brother Jonathan passed away a week after my eighteenth birthday. He was just twenty years old. Grief is a diffcult process to put into words. You're propelled into a terrifying world that includes every available emotion. There's no structure, no rule book and no ending.

Fortunately when you meet someone who has experienced a similar event you don't have to describe these feelings. They just know. I only realised this after my first session as part of the Young Persons Bereavement Project. I had been introduced to DrugFAM by my dad. I was apprehensive when I put my name down to be a part of the project and I still have no idea what made me take the step. It had taken me five or six years to get to that point. But it just felt right. I had never done anything like it before.

The group session I had attended before was with my dad but now I was on my own. I was excited because I had never really been given the opportunity to open up before or the platform to say how I really felt without the fear that I would upset anyone. I still find it amazing how such simple exercises can make people open up and talk about themselves and their experiences without you realising.

The installations we created helped bring back memories and allowed me time to evaluate them in a way I hadn't previously. The installations encouraged me to think about positive memories and share these with others if I felt comfortable. I was so at ease that I shared more about my life and my brother than I have with anyone since his death.

Our time was structured but flexible. This ensured that people could speak without being restricted but also gave a focus to the day. The exercises taught me to look outside the box in terms of support in the future. They showed me that even if I don't like the "sitting in a circle talking about yourself" format, there are many other ways to express how I feel. I think that one of the reasons I was drawn to the workshops was that it would be with a group.

Although this was one of the reasons I was initially apprehensive, in the end it was one of the reasons I would keep going back. If I had been on my own I probably would have felt self-conscious and not participated to the same extent. The people I met were so understanding and empathetic, were willing to listen to everyone and genuinely interested in others.

I'm looking forward to what my relationship with DrugFAM may bring in the future. Rather than just remembering my brother by the sad events around his death, the project gives me the opportunity to talk about him as the kind-hearted, funny character that he is. And for that I will always be grateful. His light will shine for all time.'

Some thirteen years after my son's death on Saturday 5 May 2017, I received a letter from the Cabinet Office. I did not take much notice of the white envelope as it was between my bank statement and some junk mail. A gentleman who described himself as 'ceremonial officer' had penned the following lines to me:

Dear Madam,

The Prime Minster has asked me to inform you, in strict confidence, that having accepted the advice of The Head of the Civil Service and the Main Honours Committee, she proposes to submit your name to the Queen. She is recommending that Her Majesty may be graciously pleased to approve that you be appointed a Member of the Order of the British Empire (MBE) in the Birthday Honours List 2017.

If you accept, your name will be included in the List published in the London Gazette and some national newspapers on Saturday 17 June 2017.

You will be invited to an investiture. These are organized by the Central Chancery of the Orders of Knighthood in St James's Palace. You will receive the invitation about five weeks before the event.

I am, Madam,
Your obedient servant,
Richard Tilbrook

I was asked not to publically disclose the award until after 10.30pm on Friday 16 June – it would be published in the press the next day. It was a tough task keeping it from my family and friends for several weeks, but this is how it read when it was finally published:

Order of the British Empire

Civil Division

Central Chancery of the Orders of Knighthood

St. James's Palace, London SW1

17 June 2017

THE QUEEN has been graciously pleased, on the occasion of the Celebration of Her Majesty's Birthday, to give orders for the following promotions in, and appointments to the Most Excellent Order of the British Empire:

M.B.E.

To be Ordinary Members of the Civil Division of the said Most Excellent Order:

Mrs. Elizabeth BURTON-PHILLIPS

Founder, DrugFAM

For services to people who experience drug addiction and their families.

As soon as it went public my son Simon put this message on social media:

'Let me just say. . . my brother, Nick Mills, took his life addicted to drugs in 2004. Since then he changed me, my mum, our friends and thousands of people's lives. What a legacy he leaves. Nick, your death was not in vain. Your memory lives on. You would be so proud of what has been achieved. So many thousands of people now rely on the support given by the charity created in your name, DrugFAM.

Nick, tonight your mum, Elizabeth Burton-Phillips, became an MBE for everything she has tirelessly achieved in your name and the name of other sufferers of addiction. . . Mum, I love you for everything you have done. You are one in a million and I am so proud of you. I know this is Facebook and it's full of proper rubbish most of the time but this is a true story, real life and LIVES ARE WORTH TALKING ABOUT.
Big up DrugFAM, all the trustees, staff and volunteers – I salute you all. Love you, Mum.'

It is an amazing and fortuitous coincidence that on the same day that this newly updated edition of the book is published, 7 December 2017, I will be at Buckingham Palace receiving my MBE.

Addiction isolates. It cuts off from society the person who experiences it and the families who struggle to help them. The community of fellow sufferers – the people who have 'been there' – is the best remedy for this isolation, and the beginning of healing. If you turn to DrugFAM you can be strengthened, comforted and find understanding for your family.

Some of you reading this book will know us already, but for many you will be getting to know us for the first time. We are here for families seven days a week because our staff and volunteers have walked through the flames of this family illness and now they choose to carry buckets of water for those who are still consumed by its fire.

Many years on since Nick's death, I am personally humbled and inspired by the courage and bravery of those who pick up the phone to us and lean on us in their times of need. Never forget that we, the families, are all lives worth caring about and we are all lives worth talking about.

In the words of Mahatma Ghandi, 'we can all shake the world in a gentle way', and that is what we do at DrugFAM. We see and listen to the pain that is invisible to others.

Recovery from addiction is a reality that tens of millions of people around the world are living today, so never give up hope. We also know that many families facing addiction once seemed on the brink of destruction, but received the help they needed from DrugFAM and as a result are thriving, loving and strong today.

By bringing addiction out of the shadows as we are making clear that the lives of addicted people and their families are lives worth talking about – we are giving countless other families who have been too afraid to reach out the precious assurance that we are here for them.

As our Chief Executive says:

> 'DrugFAM hopes there will come a day when families, friends and partners are no longer shamed by the disease of addiction. We are committed to, and hope all of our partners will continue in helping us to break the silence and stigma. This cannot be achieved alone, it requires a national response.'

I would like to leave the final words to my surviving son Simon, my best friend and an inspirational recovery champion. This is his tribute to his brother, a beautiful poem which he read at the Service of Celebration and Hope at Westminster Abbey on 9 May 2017:

<u>I Walk In Your Shadow But Continue To Glow</u>
I reminisce, think back of the memories of those times
we shared,
All the brotherly love, many moments together,
Time and life ticks by, never could I have known that
you'd ever say goodbye.
A lifetime you've flown, gone, spread your wings,
Both together we had grown and have left many things,
But, after so much time you're still there, I feel you
inside,
You live in my soul and I draw strength and pride.
When a life's chapter ends another begins,
I remember, all around me are friends,
A new family, a wife, children and home,

How I wish you could meet them, and see how they've grown.
I have no fear now in life, not alone when I walk,
Supported by family and friends when I need a talk.
Wherever you are, be happy and know,
I walk in your shadow but continue to glow.

Simon Mills speaking at Westminster Abbey

The Nicholas Mills Foundation trades as the not for profit charity DrugFAM. Support line seven days a week from 9–9pm 0300 888 3853. www.drugFAM.co.uk

Don't be on your own, pick up the phone or email <u>office@drug fam.co.uk</u>, or ring 01494 442777 during office hours.

Registered Charity No: 1123316

www.facebook.com/drugFAM/   @DrugFAM

To donate please go to Just Giving www.justgiving.com/drugFAM

APPENDIX A

RESOURCES

The Government's national drug information service, TALK TO FRANK, supports young people – as well as teachers, parents and other adults – to consider the risks, consequences and harms associated with drugs. The Government ensure that this is updated regularly to reflect changing drug use and the latest available evidence. Further information is available at http://www.talktofrank.com/

Other resources:

- National Suicide Prevention Alliance: http://www.nspa.org.uk/
- The Alliance of Suicide Prevention Charities: http://tasc-uk.org/
- Support after Suicide Partnership: http://supportaftersuicide.org.uk/
- Samaritans: https://www.samaritans.org/

APPENDIX B

INTRODUCTION TO DRUGFAM

DrugFAM was established in 2006 by Elizabeth Burton-Phillips after losing Nick, one of her twin sons, to heroin addiction. As part of her recovery process Elizabeth wrote and published *Mum, Can You Lend Me Twenty Quid*, which has since been translated into five languages and has been adapted into a Theatre in Education stage play.

DrugFAM's primary purpose is to provide a lifeline for families, friends and carers affected by someone else's substance misuse. We aim to ensure that those who turn to us are listened to, understood and supported. We believe passionately that no-one should struggle with the stigma from wider society or be left in isolation, fear and ignorance of local and national support.

The charity has three strategic aims:

1. To support those affected by someone else's drug or alcohol misuse
2. To support anyone who has been bereaved by drugs or alcohol
3. To provide education and raise awareness of the impact of someone's addiction on families, friends, carers and local communities

Supporting family, friends and carers affected by someone else's drug or alcohol misuse

At DrugFAM we understand the difficulties of living with or caring for someone who uses drugs or alcohol and how easily family, friends and carers can find themselves in a position of disempowerment and crisis. We also know how physically and emotionally exhausting this can be, especially when someone seems intent on self-destruction. DrugFAM believes that the families, friends and carers of people who use drugs and alcohol need support in their own right, both to cope with impact of drug and alcohol-using behaviour and with how best to help someone who has lost control of their drinking or drug use.

Our aim is to help families, friends and carers find ways of coping better with their situations, so they can start to regain control of their lives and look after their own well-being.

This is achieved through focusing on the changes which can be made to help improve the situation with the person who uses and, most importantly, for the family member's well-being. During one-to-one sessions families, friends and carers learn how to put boundaries in place, and follow through on the agreed consequences when these are broken; remain consistent; and consider how their own behaviours and actions may impact on the situation. There is also a focus on healthier ways to communicate, which may reduce confrontation with the person who uses. Lastly, consideration is given to how someone can take better care of themselves at such a stressful, difficult and painful time.

Supporting family, friends and carers who have been bereaved by drugs of alcohol

Bereavement through addiction brings up a lot of complex emotions including guilt, anger and sometimes even relief that the chaos is finally over. This combined with the stigma attached to losing someone in this way and the potential negative media coverage means that the grief process can be particularly difficult. This can result in family, friends and carers wanting to withdraw and isolate themselves, thereby perpetuating their distress. We believe offering people a safe place to share their thoughts and feeling with others who have gone through similar experiences can help alleviate this sense of shame and isolation.

At DrugFAM we offer support through:

- The annual Bereaved by Addiction Conference (running since 2009)
- A quarterly bereavement support group
- The Nicholas Mills Memorial Project (18–30 year olds)
- One-to-one support
- 7 day-a-week helpline
- The Bereaved by Addiction handbook

Providing education and raising awareness of the impact of someone's addiction on families, friends, carers and local communities

One of DrugFAM's core purposes is to raise awareness of the effect that someone else's substance misuse has on families, carers and the wider public as a whole. To do this we work closely with schools, prisons and local communities. Many of the staff and volunteers at DrugFAM have personal experience of living with or loving an addict and have lived through the chaos that this often brings. These personal accounts from family members bring the subject to life in a way that reports in the media simply cannot match.

We deliver our message in two main ways:

- Performances of a stage adaptation of *Mum, Can You Lend Me Twenty Quid?*
- Talks in schools, prisons and local communities

The purpose of the talks is to:

- Reduce the stigma of having a substance misuser in the family
- Raise awareness that addiction is a family disease and can happen to anyone regardless of background, race, religion or social class
- Encourage substance misusers to look at the impact of their actions on their families and loved ones

Theatre in Education
In 2012 the Theatre adaptation of *Mum, Can You Lend Me Twenty Quid?* made its debut performance. It has since been performed more than one-hundred times all around the UK and forms the centrepiece of a programme of creative education workshops.

The play raises awareness of the negative impact of drugs and alcohol to young people, youth offenders, adult prisoners, professionals and families. Providing hard-hitting factual information stemming from a personal story, the project aims to reduce the likelihood of young people experimenting with drugs, reduce repeat use by a recognised drug user, improve the skill set of professionals and provide families with hope and much needed information about available support.

Our creative workshops use either the whole play or selected scenes to explore the issues highlighted in the performance with the audience members. Bespoke workshops are suitable for schools, youth offender institutes, adult prisons and industry professionals, and are tailored to suit the needs of each organisation.

Creative arts competition for prisoners
In 2012 DrugFAM ran a pilot Creative Arts Competition at HMP

Peterborough where prisoners were encouraged to portray how drugs or alcohol had impacted those around them through art, poetry, prose or any other creative medium.

Following its success, the competition was rolled out nationally in 2014 and in August of that year an exhibition of the entries was held at the Stephen Friedman Gallery in London where the competition was judged by Sir Antony Seldon, sculptor Annie Tempest, actress Maureen Lipman and Dame Jennie Murray.

The competition will now be run every other year.

"For HMP Peterborough we found the competition helped energise offenders to articulate what was important to them in thinking through the past and, more importantly, the future they wanted to have for themselves and their families.

The work gave a chance for offenders, families and carers to realise and present the way drugs had affected and changed people's lives. It was a way of opening the door for discussions about the future and helped embed a commitment to change.

The pieces provide a legacy and sense of achievement for the prisoners. Through their work with DrugFAM, prisoners have something to reflect on as they continue their varied but overwhelmingly positive response to recovery." – **Nick Leader, Director, HMP Peterborough**

APPENDIX C

Resources for Lone Twins

The Lone Twin Network

The Lone Twin Network (originally called the Lone Twin Register) was set up in May 1989 to offer a network of contacts and support to anyone whose twin has died, at whatever stage of life. The Lone Twin Network (LTN) helps twins who have had similar experiences of loss to share their views and feelings and to offer and receive peer support.

The LTN List (of members) is the means by which lone twins can make contact with one another as soon as they join the network. The list gives information to enable contact between members and there is no obligation for members to participate in ways other than those they have chosen. For example, telephone numbers need not be included in the list.

To become a member, write to Lone Twin Network @, 54, Ventnor Avenue, Hodge Hill, Birmingham B36 8EF, requesting an application form or check the LTN website (www.lonetwin-network.org.uk). Membership is currently open to those over eighteen and there is a joining fee which is currently £10 (as of 2017) and an annual voluntary subscription. We also have a free associate membership for 16 to 18 year olds but they cannot attend meetings.

Members receive the following:

- The confidential LTN List (of members) which is annually updated to enable contact with other members.

- A newsletter twice a year in Spring and Autumn, which contains Network news and members' articles.
- Information about the Lone Twin Network's Annual Meeting which generally alternates between North/South and regional meetings in London, Birmingham, Harrogate and Manchester/Liverpool to which all full members are welcome. We are also working towards meetings in Ireland and Scotland.
- A chance to join the LTN private facebook group

Other resources for lone twins:

Joan Woodward, *The Lone Twin: Understanding Twin Bereavement and Loss*; Revised Second Edition (Free Association Books, 2010)

Twinless Twins Support Group International
Serving in support of twins (and all other multiple births) who suffer from the loss of companionship of their twin through death or estrangement.
11220 St Joe Road, Fort Wayne, IN 46835–9737, USA
www.twinlesstwins.org
contact@twinlesstwins.org
(001) 1 888 205 8962

About the Author

First published in 2007, *Mum, Can You Lend Me Twenty Quid?* has been read by thousands of people in the UK and translated into five languages. Elizabeth has received thousands of letters, telephone calls and emails from families around the world who express their gratitude for sharing her story. Feedback has been overwhelmingly positive:

> 'Reading your book has been an inspiration to me. My son was a crack and heroin addict and is still serving a four year prison sentence for dealing. You have shown me that, as a mother, I am not alone with this problem.'

Since Nick's tragic death, Elizabeth has campaigned continuously to raise awareness of the harm caused to families by drug addiction and to influence policy and practice so that the needs of families are better recognised and met.

Elizabeth founded the charity DrugFAM in 2006, which now helps thousands of people who are affected by someone's drug use, including those who have been bereaved by addiction. The charity is open seven days a week from 9am to 9pm via its helpline (0300 888 3853).

In 2012, *Mum, Can You Lend Me Twenty Quid?* was adapted into a Theatre in Education stage play for schools, police training and prisons, and DrugFAM celebrated its 100th performance in October 2015 at the Palace of Westminster by invitation of the then Home Secretary, Theresa May MP. A podcast and audio CD of the play are also now available as free educational resources for schools, practitioners and the wider community. The play travelled the UK for five years and is currently being redeveloped with additional workshop packages tailored to four key audiences:

- Families – exploring the effect on family relationships
- Schools – exploring actions and consequences
- Prisons/Addicts/Offenders/Rehabs – exploring the decisions of an addict
- Professionals – exploring and understanding the relationship between addict and substance

Elizabeth was co-opted on to the government's Advisory Committee on the Misuse of Drugs New Recovery Committee in 2012, and is currently advisor to a number of organizations. She has contributed to research by the Universities of Bath and Sterling, which have produced new guidelines for professionals working with those bereaved by substance use.

She has delivered numerous lectures and key note speeches in Brussels, Morocco, Jerusalem, Italy, Cyprus, The Shetland Isles, Dublin and all over the UK. Nearer to her home, Elizabeth remains an active support group facilitator and telephone support line helper in her full time role as a volunteer.

Elizabeth was nominated as a *Woman of Achievement* in the *Women of the Year Lunch Awards* from 2009–2012, and her courage and determination to support families continues to be acknowledged around the world. In 2017, she was awarded an MBE in the Queen's Birthday Honours List for 'services to people who experience drug addiction and their families'. This award is given by the Queen to an individual for outstanding service to the community. The MBE is in recognition of her unwavering and tireless contributions to raise awareness of the impact of drug and alcohol addiction on families.